Why Do You Need This New Edition?

Why Do You Need This New Edition of *Writing Logically, Thinking Critically?* Here are six good reasons!

❶ **New selections in Additional Readings** address contemporary topics designed to engage you and challenge your reading and critical thinking skills. All three of these long essays relate to skills and content featured in earlier chapters. For example, the first essay, "The Conservative Case for Gay Marriage" by Ted Olsen, demonstrates the rhetorical strategies of counterargument and refutation emphasized in Chapter 4.

❷ In Chapter 1, the work of **Isaiah Berlin** and **Aristotle** contributes to our discussion of world view and audience.

❸ In Chapter 2, we've expanded the discussion of **visual literacy** and added many new images.

❹ In Chapter 7, Euler diagrams illustrate **a current political issue**.

❺ A new section addresses **evaluating sources** in A Quick Guide.

❻ **New readings, examples, and cartoons** appear throughout the book.

PEARSON

Writing Logically, Thinking Critically

SEVENTH EDITION

Sheila Cooper
Rosemary Patton

PEARSON

Boston   Columbus   Indianapolis   New York   San Francisco   Upper Saddle River
Amsterdam   Cape Town   Dubai   London   Madrid   Milan   Munich   Paris   Montreal   Toronto
Delhi   Mexico City   São Paulo   Sydney   Hong Kong   Seoul   Singapore   Taipei   Tokyo

Senior Sponsoring Editor: Katharine Glynn
Marketing Manager: Sandra McGuire
Senior Supplements Editor: Donna Campion
Production Manager: Ellen MacElree
Project Coordination, Text Design, and Electronic Page Makeup: PreMediaGlobal
Cover Design Manager: Jayne Conte
Cover Designer: Bruce Kenselaar
Cover Art: M.C. Escher's "Symmetry Drawing E85" © 2011 The M.C. Escher Company-Holland.
All rights reserved. www.mcescher.com
Senior Manufacturing Buyer: Roy L. Pickering, Jr.
Printer/Binder: R.R. Donnelley & Sons, Harrisonburg
Cover Printer: R.R. Donnelley & Sons, Harrisonburg

For permission to use copyrighted material, grateful acknowledgment is made to the copyright holders on pp. 234–235, which are hereby made part of this copyright page.

Library of Congress Cataloging-in-Publication Data

Cooper, Sheila, (date)
Patton, Rosemary
    Writing logically, thinking critically / Sheila Cooper, Rosemary Patton. — 7th ed.
       p. cm.
    ISBN-13: 978-0-205-11912-7
    ISBN-10: 0-205-11912-3
       1. English language—Rhetoric. 2. Critical thinking. 3. Academic writing. 4. Logic.
  I. Patton, Rosemary. II. Title.

PE1408.C5485 2011
808'.042—dc23   2011036052

1 2 3 4 5 6 7 8 9 10—DOH—15 14 13 12 11

www.pearsonhighered.com

ISBN 13: 978-0-205-11912-7
ISBN 10:   0-205-11912-3

He who will not reason, is a bigot; he who cannot, is a fool; and he who dares not, is a slave.

—LORD BYRON

A mind that is stretched to a new idea never returns to its original dimension.

—OLIVER WENDELL HOLMES

The vital habits of democracy: the ability to follow an argument, grasp the point of view of another, expand the boundaries of understanding, debate the alternative purposes that might be pursued.

—JOHN DEWEY

BRIEF CONTENTS

DETAILED CONTENTS

CHAPTER 5

CHAPTER 6

CHAPTER 7

CHAPTER 8

GUIDE TO READINGS

PREFACE

"Some things are a matter of opinion; others are not. Education helps you distinguish between the two."

—JON CARROLL

Everywhere in the media today we hear voices raised in support of increasing the critical thinking skills of students. *New York Times* columnist Bob Herbert often wrote about the failure to educate our students, sometimes emphasizing their ignorance of factual information. In a letter to the editor, Nancy Rehm, a high school teacher in Biglerville, Pennsylvania, went further, responding that the biggest deficit lies in students' inability to think critically.

Tony Wagner of the Harvard School of Education and author of *The Global Achievement Gap* would agree with her. He believes that there are three basic skills students need to successfully compete in a knowledge economy (as opposed to a manufacturing economy):

the ability to think critically
the ability to communicate effectively
the ability to collaborate

This book is dedicated to developing and fostering these skills with its emphasis on logical reasoning and written argument. In addition, many of the exercises and writing assignments are designed for students to work on together.

In the seventh edition of *Writing Logically, Thinking Critically*, we have updated essays, examples, and exercises for relevancy. We have expanded visual content to encourage visual literacy, and have added several fresh cartoons, as we believe these images with punch lines reinforce the text. A feature of this text that makes it stand out among others in its field is the inclusion of fiction and poetry. For all readings, we provide a separate list for quick reference.

WHAT'S NEW IN THIS EDITION

- In Chapter 1, "Thinking and Writing—A Critical Connection," we have added British philosopher Isaiah Berlin's categories of hedgehogs and foxes to our discussion of world view and Aristotle's essential triad of logos, ethos, and pathos to our discussion of audience.

- In Chapter 2, "Inference—Critical Thought," we have a new article, "How Facts Backfire," by Joe Keohane. We have greatly expanded our number of images for analysis, emphasizing visual and media literacy.

- In Chapter 3, "The Structure of Argument," we include a new piece, "An Argument Worth Having," by Gerald Graff.

- In Chapter 4, "Written Argument," we've added a new argument, "Elite Colleges, or Colleges for the Elite?", by Richard D. Kahlenberg.

- In Chapter 5, "The Language of Argument—Definition," we have new examples of culture's impact on language and more examples of new words invented to fill a need, as well as a new essay, "Miss G.: A Case of Internet Addiction," by Virginia Heffernan.

- In Chapter 6, "Fallacious Arguments," new examples and cartoons enrich our discussion of fallacious reasoning.

- In Chapter 7, "Deductive and Inductive Argument," we use Euler diagrams to illustrate a current political issue.

- In Chapter 8, "The Language of Argument—Style," we added new examples and reinstated a checklist for revision.

- To A Quick Guide to Integrating Research into Your Own Writing, we have added a section on evaluating sources and a section on bias in the media, hence the new title: A Quick Guide to Evaluating Sources and Integrating Research into Your Own Writing.

- In our closing section, Additional Readings, we continue our emphasis on longer, complex essays with three new examples, each of which relates to earlier chapters. The first, "The Conservative Case for Gay Marriage" by political conservative Ted Olsen, demonstrates the rhetorical strategies we emphasize in Chaper 4: counterargument and refutation. "You Are What You Speak," by Guy Deutscher, focuses on the relationship between language and culture, a topic we touch on in Chapters 2 and 5. In "The Order of Things," Malcolm Gladwell questions the methodology and ideology of *U.S. News & World Report*'s annual "Best Colleges" issue, often relying on reasoning by analogy to make his point. We introduce analogy in Chapter 1 and return to it in Chapter 6. Gladwell's criticism of the magazines's methodology relates to "Thinking Critically About Surveys and Statistics" in Chapter 7. All three essays are well-reasoned and a pleasure to read, and each is followed by questions.

SEQUENCE

We suggest that instructors follow the sequence of chapters in order, with the exception of Chapter 8 (sentence polishing) and the end-of-book materials—A Quick Guide to Evaluating Sources and Integrating Research into Your Own Writing and Additional Readings—which can be referred to throughout the course. Some instructors, however, prefer to create their own order to suit the needs of their particular class. Chapter 8, "The Language of Argument—Style," may serve as a tutorial for individual students.

As before, we assume that *Writing Logically, Thinking Critically* will be most effective in classes where the students have already completed an introductory semester or quarter of composition. But many find the book works well as the foundation in a first-year writing class. Some secondary school instructors have been enthusiastic about its success in their advanced composition classes. Upper-division college students preparing for the LSAT, the qualifying exam for law school, have also found the text useful.

ACKNOWLEDGMENTS

We remain grateful to our students, a few of whom are represented here. Thanks also to those instructors who have used *Writing Logically, Thinking Critically*, some of whom are among those who offered invaluable advice for this revision: Joseph Ervin, Rend Lake College; Amy Hundley, Merced College; Kimberly L. Hutson, Norfolk State University; Ruth Evans Lane, Loyola Marymount University; Cynthia Alleen McDaniel, Southwestern College; Lezlie Christensen Park, Utah State University; and Catherine Rezza, Arizona State University.

Sheila Cooper
Rosemary Patton

CHAPTER 1

Thinking and Writing—
A Critical Connection

It is doubtful whether a man [or woman?] ever brings his faculties to bear with their full force on a subject until he writes upon it.

—CICERO

It would hardly seem debatable that to write well we need to think clearly. And the evidence is strong for concluding that writing about ideas can help to clarify them. Taking this notion a step further, many would argue that the act of writing can create ideas, can lead writers to discover what they think. Language, according to many scholars, can give birth to thought, and written language provides a way to refine our thoughts since, unlike speech, it can be manipulated until it accurately reflects our thinking.

THINKING MADE VISIBLE

Consider writing then as thinking made visible. Writer Isaac Asimov expresses his satisfaction with the link between thinking and writing:

> Thinking is the activity I love best, and writing to me is simply thinking through my fingers.

RICHARD GUINDON. REPRINTED BY PERMISSION OF THE DETROIT FREE PRESS.

Novelist E. M. Forster expresses a similar sentiment:

How can I tell what I think till I see what I've said?

Many writers have groaned over the pain of writing. In his poem, *The Four Quartets*, T. S. Eliot writes of the "intolerable wrestle / With words and meaning." New York writer Fran Lebowitz is more graphic in her complaint: "Writing is torture. It is very hard work. It's not coal mining, but it's work."

After visiting the Galapagos Islands in the 1830s, evolutionist Charles Darwin wrote to his sister from his ship, the *Beagle*, about the special challenge of reasoning on paper, the kind of writing we emphasize in this book.

I am just now beginning to discover the difficulty of expressing one's ideas on paper. As long as it consists solely of description it is pretty easy; but where reasoning comes into play, to make a proper connection, a clearness and a moderate fluency, is to me a difficulty of which I had no idea.

Although writing and thinking may be difficult, mastery and success in both can be well worth the effort. Indeed, clear writing is often essential. If we are not able to articulate a request, a complaint, or an endorsement in precise, forceful language, we may find ourselves settling for less than we deserve. If we can't write a persuasive application, the job or graduate school position may go to someone else.

In a recent *New York Times* piece, long-time professors were asked to give advice to incoming college freshman. Professor Stanley Fish advises students to take a composition course even if it's not required of them:

I have taught many students whose SAT scores exempted them from the writing requirement, but a disheartening number of them couldn't write and an equal number had never been asked to. They managed to get through high school without learning how to write a clean English sentence, and if you can't do that you can't do anything.

Professor Garry Willis also stresses the importance of writing:

Learn to write well. Most incoming college students do not do it and it hampers them in courses and in later life. Read what you write to a friend, and ask the friend to read it back to you. Lack of clarity, coherence or shape will leap out at you.

CRITICAL THINKING

If, as we maintain, there is a strong relationship between thinking clearly and writing well—if one skill strengthens the other—then integrating the two as a course of study makes sense. But what do we mean by "thinking clearly"? For our purposes, we have found it helpful to narrow our focus and concentrate on the phrase **critical thinking**. This term has assumed a central position in both academic and public life and is variously defined today.

In most contexts today, the term **critical** means censorious or faultfinding, but it comes to us from the Greek *kriticos* and Latin *criticus*, meaning able to discern or separate. It is this sense of critical that we have in mind—discerning or discriminating thought characterized by careful analysis and judgment. As student Denise Selleck describes it, "Thinking critically is the ability to understand a concept fully, taking in different sides of an issue or idea while not being swayed by the propaganda or other fraudulent methods used to promote it." She recognizes the importance of an **open mind** and the element of **self-defense** implicit in critical thinking. We must learn to defend ourselves against the false claims, questionable judgments, and confusing or deceptive arguments presented to us in commercials, ads, and political campaigns.

An Open Mind—Examining Your World View

To have an open mind is to listen attentively to the views of others. It is, however, equally important to be aware of where our views come from. Cultures, subgroups within those cultures, and families within these groups tend to share what is called a **world view**, a set of assumptions about the world and the behavior of people in it. We may harbor prejudices about groups that cloud our thinking and restrict fair judgment. Many of these attitudes grow from the contexts of our lives that we take for granted—the opinions of parents and friends, our ethnic and religious backgrounds.

Where does the weakness in Jennifer's defense lie?

When Dominique Strauss-Kahn, head of the International Monetary Fund and a well-known French politician, was arrested for the rape of a maid in a New York City luxury hotel, the hosts of *The View*, a popular talk show, weighed in on the scandal. Barbara Walters, a pioneer in television journalism and a prominent figure in New York society, suggested that the man must suffer from a sexual addiction, something beyond his control; otherwise, why would such an intelligent and prominent man commit such a crime? Elizabeth Hasselbeck, wife of a professional football player and a contestant on the television show Survivor, believed the man did it because he could, that he was a powerful man who thought that he had the right to do what he wanted. Whoopi Goldberg, an African American actress and standup comedienne, believed he did it because he did not consider the maid, an immigrant from Africa, a person. He thought of her as an object to serve his needs. Can you see the world views of these three women reflected in their interpretation of the alleged crime?

In the words of Professor Louis Menand, "Ideas are produced not by individuals, but by groups of individuals—ideas are social . . . ideas do not develop according to some inner logic of their own, but are entirely dependent, like germs, on their human carriers and the environment." Knowledge and ideas are not absolutes but are subject to the time, place, and circumstances in which they are expressed. For instance, up until the twentieth century, women were considered incapable of making rational decisions on political issues and thus were denied the vote. Today, most cultures recognize that such a view was **socially constructed**, not inherently true. Harvard professor Henry Louis Gates Jr. sees history as "a chronicle of formerly acceptable outrages":

> Once upon a time, perfectly decent folk took it for granted that watching two gladiators hack each other to death was just the thing to do on a summer afternoon, that making slaves of Africans was a good deal for all concerned. What were they thinking? You could say that posterity is a hanging judge, except that sooner or later capital punishment, too, will turn up on that chronicle of outrages.

We have an inborn tendency to filter out information that doesn't match our biases. We are inclined to remember news that matches our world view and dismiss facts that contradict it. In his book *True Enough: Learning to Live in a Post-Fact Society*, Farhad Manjoo, a staff writer at Salon.com, emphasizes this point. We resist information "that doesn't mesh with our preconceived beliefs." Manjoo cites two studies to illustrate this point. Students at Dartmouth and Princeton were shown a film clip of a football game between their two teams and asked to note instances of cheating. "Each group, watching the same clip, was convinced that the other side had cheated more." A similar manipulation of facts occurred when Stanford students, one group favoring the death penalty and the other opposing it, "were shown the same two studies: one suggested that executions have a deterrent effect that reduces subsequent murders, and the other [study] doubted that [conclusion]." Each group of students "found the study that supported their position to be well-conducted and persuasive and the other one to be profoundly flawed."

In Chapter 2 we include an article by Joe Keohane, *How Facts Backfire*, in which he describes recent research that suggests "rather than facts driving belief, our beliefs can dictate the facts."

Hedgehogs and Foxes

In a now famous essay, *The Hedgehog and the Fox*, British philosopher Isaiah Berlin (1909–1997) divided thinkers and writers into two categories—hedgehogs and foxes.

The title comes from a fragment of a poem by ancient Greek poet Archilochus: "the fox knows many little things, but the hedgehog knows one big thing." According to Berlin, hedgehogs view the world through a single lens, a dominant idea, while foxes base their view of the world on a wide variety of experiences. Hedgehogs have a focused worldview and strong convictions. Foxes are less rigid and more pragmatic, more aware of complexity and nuance.

Other writers use Berlin's classification scheme for their own purposes. In his book, *Founding Brothers*, historian Joseph Ellis defines George Washington as an "archetypal hedgehog. And the one big thing he knew was that America's future as a nation lay to the West, in its development over the next century of a continental empire." Ellis credits Washington's focus on developing canals to this one big idea.

How would you classify yourself? Are you a hedgehog or a fox?

Questioning our personal world view can be one of the most challenging steps in our growth as critical thinkers. In the following essay, newspaper columnist Jon Carroll points out that our world view, our opinions, can sometimes blind us to the truth.

The Problem with New Data

JON CARROLL

You many have heard that Dr. James Hansen, the man who first popularized the notion that carbon dioxide levels and global warming were inextricably linked, has issued a new report saying that further studies have revealed that in fact other heat-trapping chemicals—methane, chlorofluorocarbons, particulate matter like coal soot, plus other smog-creating chemicals—are probably more responsible for the trend than carbon dioxide. 1

Any advance in scientific understanding is good news. Hansen's report is particularly interesting because it is contrary to his previous position, indicating that he is able to separate his professional ego from his scientific conclusions and change his mind right out in public. 2

This is less usual than it should be. We are all afraid of being wrong, and we will tend to cling to our opinions in the face of mounting evidence to the contrary. In ideal science, all opinions are merely way stations on the road to the truth; in real-world science, though, opinions are the basis of reputation and income, and the difference between the establishment view and the revealed truth is not easy to discern from the outside. 3

And there's another reason why Hansen's conclusions are good news—it's a lot easier to control the production of these new culprits than it is the production of carbon dioxide, which is the unavoidable byproduct of the burning of all fossil fuels, as well as the gas that emerges from our mouths every time we exhale. 4

And yet, Hansen's report was greeted with considerable trepidation. The results might be misinterpreted; big polluters might twist the data; Congress might have a fig leaf to cover its natural inclination to let big corporations do whatever they want. 5

This is what happens when politics and science start to commingle. In politics, 6
opinions—they are called "positions" or "principles"—are the official yardstick of integrity. People who change their minds are considered to be weak, are said to waffle.

Someone who has staked out a tough position on carbon dioxide would be 7
seriously uninterested in data suggesting it's not really the problem. Someone who supported the Kyoto Protocol—which identified carbon dioxide as the principal culprit—would feel the urge to attack Hansen, who would be identified as a "former ally."

Following the facts wherever they lead is always dangerous in the political 8
arena.

In fact, Hansen has not changed his position on global warming at all. He is 9
still of the opinion that it forms a significant threat to the short-term (less than 100 years) ecological health of the planet. But he has a nuanced and evolving view of the causes.

"Nuanced" and "evolving" will, in the political world, buy you a cup of coffee, 10
provided you also have $2.

The urge to hang on tight knows no ideology. The gun lobby reflexively 11
brings up the slippery slope [see Fallacious Arguments, Chapter 6] and the Second Amendment no matter what the issue, making something like trigger locks as controversial as universal confiscation of firearms.

Multiculturalists reflexively support bilingual education, despite new studies 12
suggesting that kids from different cultures learn better when a single language is the classroom standard.

Look into the heart of your opinions: What if early detection of breast cancer 13
had no real effect on mortality rates? What if secondhand smoke turned out to be no health risk at all? What if free condoms for every child lowered disease rates by 50 percent? What if air bags were bad, or good, or whatever is the opposite of what you currently believe they are?

It's the brain lock issue. We want to believe something because it fits with 14
the other things we believe, because the people we know believe it, because the people who believe the other things are loathsome.

Alas, the universe of facts is not a democracy. If it were, I'd vote for fried pork 15
rinds as a health food.

EXERCISE 1A

Examining Your World View

1. Professor Henry Louis Gates Jr. lists gladiators and slavery as two of the "acceptable outrages" that history chronicles. We added denying women the vote. As a class, add to this list.

2. Look closely at these "outrages"—gladiators, slavery, women being denied the vote, and others generated by your responses to question 1 above. In each case, ask which group held this view and what they had to gain from supporting this belief.

3. Gates predicts that one day capital punishment will be viewed as a "formerly acceptable outrage." Here's a chance to "deconstruct" a socially constructed belief, to examine the roots of your own beliefs. As Jon Carroll says, "Look into the heart of your opinions." Write a paragraph stating your position on capital punishment and include the views held by your family, friends, and religion (if you belong to a religious group). Then compare paragraphs with a small group of your classmates. What have you learned about your world view? Are you a hedgehog or a fox? Putting such views into writing or even formulating what you think can be a challenge. There is no right or wrong answer here—just a critical exploration of your thoughts discussed with your peers.

WRITING AS A PROCESS

What is written without effort is in general read without pleasure.

—SAMUEL JOHNSON

Earlier in this chapter we say that writing is thinking made visible, but the process of making our thinking visible is complex, not a matter of simple dictation from our mind to the page. Where do you begin when faced with a writing assignment? Many students turn to the five-paragraph essay format—introduction, three supporting paragraphs, and conclusion—and choose material that will fit easily into this preconceived mold. Writers rely on this formula because they fear that without it they will produce an incoherent essay. They assume that if they follow it, their writing will at least be organized. Even inexperienced writers must learn to let go of this "safety net" because, although it may save them from anxiety and a disorganized essay, it can also determine the content of the essay; if an idea does not fit easily into the mold, the writer must discard it. This rigid structure prevents writers from exploring their topic, from following thoughts that may lead to interesting insights, and from allowing the material, the content, to find the shape that best suits it.

The most common misconception that student writers have is that good writers sit at their desks and produce in one sitting a polished, mechanically correct, cohesive piece of writing. If students are unable to do this, they conclude that they cannot write and approach all writing tasks with dread. As a first step toward improving their writing, students must discard this myth and replace it with a realistic picture of how writers write. Hemingway, in Paris, writing his first collection of short stories, *In Our Time*, spent whole mornings on single paragraphs. While no one expects students, whose goal it is to produce a competent essay, to spend this kind of time on their writing, students, like most writers, must realize that writing is a complicated intellectual act, that it involves many separate tasks, and that the mind is simply not able to handle all of these tasks at once. As writer Henry Miller saw it, "Writing, like life itself, is a voyage of discovery."

What are the distinct tasks involved in the act of writing a paper, of making your thinking visible?

Generating ideas

Conducting research (if necessary)

Focusing a topic

Establishing a thesis

Organizing the essay

Organizing paragraphs

Providing transitions between sentences and paragraphs

Choosing appropriate diction (word choice)

Polishing sentences for fluency

Correcting grammar, usage, spelling, and punctuation

Each of these tasks could, of course, be broken down further. What is the solution to this problem, this mental overload that writing forces on us? The answer is that it must be done in stages.

Writing is a **process** that breaks down into roughly three stages—**creating**, **shaping**, and **correcting**. A common error students make is to focus their energy on what should be the last stage (correcting) at the beginning, when the focus should be on the creative stage of the writing process. The effect of this misplaced attention is to inhibit creative thinking. It is essential that the writer give ample time to the first stage, to generating ideas, to following impulsive thoughts even if they may initially appear unrelated or irrelevant. At this stage a writer must allow himself to experience confusion, to be comfortable with chaos; he must learn to trust the writing process, to realize that out of this chaos a logical train of thought will gradually emerge. Most important of all, writers must learn to suspend all criticism as they explore their topic and their thinking.

Invention Strategies—Generating Ideas

Two concrete methods for beginning this exploration of your topic are brainstorming and freewriting, one or both of which you may already be familiar with.

To **brainstorm**, simply put the topic of the writing assignment at the top of a blank piece of paper or your screen. Then jot down words or phrases that come to mind as you think about this topic—as many words as possible, even if you are not sure they relate directly. After brainstorming, look at your list: circle ideas that you want to develop, draw lines through those that are decidedly unrelated or uninteresting, and draw arrows or make lists of ideas that are connected to one another. At this point you should be able to go to the next stage, organizing your essay either by writing an outline or simply by listing main points that you want to develop into paragraphs.

In **freewriting**, you begin by writing your topic on a blank sheet, but instead of jotting down words and phrases, you write continuously, using sentences. These sentences do not have to be mechanically correct, nor do they have to be connected. The only rule of freewriting is that you may not stop writing; you may not put down your pen or leave the keyboard for a set length of time. After freewriting for five to ten minutes, read over your freewriting, circling ideas that you find interesting or insightful. Now you may do another freewriting on the idea or ideas you have circled, or you may try to formulate a **thesis** or list ideas you want to develop. (For a detailed discussion of your thesis, see Chapter 4.)

These methods have two things in common. They are relatively painless ways to begin the writing process, and they allow you to circumvent your own worst enemy, self-criticism—the voice that says, "That's not right," "That's not what I mean," "This doesn't make sense." Critical evaluation of your writing is necessary but self-defeating if you are critical at the beginning. In addition, freewriting may offer surprising access to ideas you never knew you had.

If your paper requires research, you will want to start reading relevant journals and books and exploring Web sites. You may have started this process when searching for a topic. As you read you will need to take notes either on note cards, in a reading journal, or on a computer where you can store them until you are ready to print them out. No matter the source, be sure to record the data necessary for documentation. We suggest you try to brainstorm and freewrite on writing assignments throughout this text.

The First Draft

After exploring a topic in this way and examining data if you have done research, you will have a sense of what you want to say and will be ready for a first draft.

Successful writer Anne Lamott, in her book *Bird by Bird: Some Instructions on Writing and Life*, discusses the role of first drafts. Her advice grew out of her own experience as a writer and from writing classes she has taught. The title refers to a family story in which her brother, when 10 years old, was overwhelmed by a school report on birds that had been assigned three months earlier and was now due. Their father, a professional writer, put his arm around his almost weeping son and counseled, "Bird by bird, buddy. Just take it bird by bird." Good advice for writing and for life. See if you can start treating your first drafts as what Lamott calls "the child's draft" in the following excerpt from her book.

The Child's Draft

Now, practically even better news than that of short assignments is the idea of shitty first drafts. All good writers write them. This is how they end up with good second drafts and terrific third drafts. People tend to look at successful writers, writers who are getting their books published and maybe even doing well financially, and think that they sit down at their desks every morning feeling like a million dollars, feeling great about who they are and how much talent they have and what a great story they have to tell; that they take in a few deep breaths, push back their sleeves, roll their necks a few times to get all the cricks out, and dive in, typing fully formed passages as fast as a court reporter. But this is just the fantasy of the uninitiated. I know some very great writers, writers you love who write beautifully and have made a great deal of money, and not *one* of them sits down routinely feeling wildly enthusiastic and confident. Not one of them writes elegant first drafts. All right, one of them does, but we do not like her very much. We do not think that she has a rich inner life.

Very few writers really know what they are doing until they've done it. Nor do   2
they go about their business feeling dewy and thrilled. They do not type a few stiff warm-up sentences and then find themselves bounding along like huskies across the snow. One writer I know tells me that he sits down every morning and says to himself nicely, "It's not like you don't have a choice, because you do—you can either type or kill yourself." We all often feel like we are pulling teeth, even those writers whose prose ends up being the most natural and fluid. The right words and sentences just do not come pouring out like ticker tape most of the time. . . .

For me and most of the other writers I know, writing is not rapturous. In fact,   3
the only way I can get anything written at all is to write really, really shitty first drafts.

The first draft is the child's draft, where you let it all pour out and then let it   4
romp all over the place, knowing that no one is going to see it and that you can shape it later. You just let this childlike part of you channel whatever voices and visions come through and onto the page. If one of the characters wants to say, "Well, so what, Mr. Poopy Pants?," you let her. No one is going to see it. If the kid wants to get into really sentimental, weepy, emotional territory, you let him. Just get it all down on paper, because there may be something great in those six crazy pages that you would never have gotten to by more rational, grown-up means. There may be something in the very last line of the very last paragraph on page six that you just love, that is so beautiful or wild that you now know what you're supposed to be writing about, more or less, or in what direction you might go—but there was no way to get to this without first getting through the first five and a half pages.

The Time to Be Critical

In agreement with Anne Lamott, teacher and writer Donald Murray, in an essay on revision titled "The Maker's Eye," points out a key difference between student writers and professional writers:

> When students complete a first draft, they consider the job of writing done—and their teachers too often agree. When professional writers complete a first draft, they usually feel that they are at the start of the writing process. When a draft is completed, the job of writing can begin.

The time to be critical arrives when you have a complete draft. Now is the time to read with a critical mind, trusting your instinct that if a word, a sentence, or a passage seems unclear or awkward to you, your reader will most likely stumble over the same word, sentence, or passage. You are ready to reshape your first draft, adding and deleting ideas, refining your thesis, polishing sentences for fluency, and finally writing another draft. Sometimes the writing of the first draft will tell you when you need to do a little more research, expand your explanation of a point, or check some of your facts to be sure of your evidence.

Finally, you will be ready to proofread for small errors and to read your essay aloud to yourself or to a friend. Always be ready to write another draft if it becomes necessary.

Every stage in the writing process is important. To slight one is to limit the success of the final product. There are exceptions, of course. Some writers are able to compress some of these steps, to generate and organize ideas in their minds before ever putting pen to paper. But for most of us, successful writing results from an extended writing process that is continually recursive.

As Donald Murray notes in his essay on revision, "Most readers underestimate the amount of rewriting it usually takes to produce spontaneous reading." But we can take heart from novelist Kurt Vonnegut: "This is what I find most encouraging about the writing trades: They allow mediocre people who are patient and industrious to revise their stupidity, to edit themselves into something like intelligence."

A caution: The danger in the way we have described the writing process is that we make it seem as though it progresses in three neat steps, that it proceeds in a linear fashion from prewriting to writing to rewriting and correction. In fact, this process is messy. You may be editing the final draft when you decide to add a completely new paragraph, an idea that didn't exist in any of the previous drafts. Nevertheless, if you realize that writing involves many separate tasks, that it is chaotic and unpredictable, you will not be defeated before you begin by criticizing yourself for having to do what all writers do—struggle to find your way, to express your thoughts so that you and your reader understand them.

AUDIENCE AND PURPOSE

A major distinction between writing outside the classroom and writing for a class lies in the audience to whom we write, what novelist and essayist Virginia Woolf referred to as "the face beneath the page." Job-related writing tasks, for example, include a designated audience and a real purpose. An employee may write to another company proposing a cooperative venture or to a superior requesting a raise. Readers of a newspaper often express their opinions in persuasive letters to the editor. But in a class, students are asked to write papers for the teacher to critique and grade, usually with no specified purpose beyond successfully completing an assignment. Teachers cannot remove themselves from the role of ultimate audience, but for most of the major writing assignments in this text we have suggested an additional audience to lend some authenticity to each project and to guide you in your writing choices.

Although different academic disciplines require variations in format, all good writing of an explanatory or persuasive nature is built on a balance between three essential elements: **knowledge of the subject or argument**, an identified **audience**, and a clearly defined **purpose**. The task of thinking through an argument, its audience, and purpose introduces a significant critical thinking component to an assignment. Only when you take a conscious rhetorical stance toward your writing can you have an appropriate voice and give power to what you write. The goal for you, therefore, is to **define your subject or argument, identify your audience, and determine your purpose** in writing to this particular audience. (For more on the relationship between writer and audience, see the section on Rogerian Strategy in Chapter 4.)

Consideration of one's audience is not a recent concept. Over two thousand years ago Aristotle, known as the father of logic, spoke of an essential triad in argument: *logos*, *ethos*, and *pathos*.

> *Logos:* the use of reason to persuade an audience. (Much more on this in the chapters ahead.)
>
> *Ethos:* the use of one's own character and credibility to persuade an audience.
>
> *Pathos:* the use of emotional appeals to persuade an audience. Empathy with the audience's concerns would be included in these emotional appeals. (More on this in Chapter 4.)

Aristotle saw the essential bond between writer and reader that leads to meaningful communication. To write convincingly, you must present yourself as a reasonable, sympathetic person at the same time you convey respect for your readers. Aristotle suggests that effective persuasive writing depends not only on a well-informed writer but also on a writer who is acutely aware of her audience and well-disposed toward them. The same holds true for public speaking.

E-Mail and Text Messaging

The informality encouraged by e-mail and text messaging requires us to carefully consider our audience. Language flies through cyberspace, and text messages are transcribed in a whole new shorthand. Impressions are made quickly. "2moro" for "tomorrow" is fine in a text message to a friend but not in an e-mail to an instructor or a potential employer. When speaking with others, we each vary our language depending on whom we are speaking to—slang with our friends, even a profanity or two, more formal language when speaking to a boss or teacher. And each family has many words or expressions that they use only with each other. We make these shifts in language without much thought but when writing, we need to become consciously aware of the particular audience we are addressing and then adopt the appropriate language. Getting it right in an e-mail matters in the academic and business worlds, where persuasive writing remains important.

A recent *New York Times* article, which addressed the concerns of many corporations, stressed the high cost to American companies of poorly written e-mails. A university professor, who now heads an online business writing school, quoted an example of a request he received:

> i need help I am writing a essay on writing I work for this company and my boss wants me to help improve the workers writing skills

No punctuation, no attention to the sentence. How far is this employee going? How can he help others?

Writer Brent Staples claims that the information age "requires more high-quality writing from more categories of employees than ever before."

EXERCISE 1B

Thinking About Your Audience

Write an e-mail introducing yourself to your instructor. You will need to include information useful to your instructor, such as why you are taking this class, what writing or logic courses you have already completed, what you expect to gain from the class, and anything else bearing on your participation during the semester or quarter. If your instructor wants you to be in direct contact by e-mail, send this assignment over the Internet; if not, turn in a printout.

WRITING ASSIGNMENT 1

Considering Your Audience and Purpose

Choose any public issue that disturbs you—be it small or large, campus, community, or cosmic—and write *two* short papers (one to two pages *each*), expressing your concern. Before you start this assignment, look back in this chapter to the suggestions under "Writing as a Process" and follow the stages outlined there.

1. In the first version, direct your writing to someone connected to, perhaps responsible for, the problem you are concerned about. Your purpose here is to communicate your concern or displeasure and possibly persuade the person responsible to take appropriate action.

2. In the second version, address an individual who is in no way connected to the problem you are disturbed about. Your purpose here is to explain the situation and to inform your reader of something he may know nothing about and is not necessarily in a position to change. This means you must include more background detail than was necessary in your first paper.

Label the two papers at the top (*1*) and (*2*) and clearly identify each audience.

REASON, INTUITION, IMAGINATION, AND METAPHOR

The heart has its reasons which reason knows nothing of.

—BLAISE PASCAL

While good critical thinking depends on reason and embraces scientific methods, it can also include intuition, imagination, and creativity as well as logic. Our theory of critical thinking welcomes originality, encourages personal opinion, embraces creative thinking, and considers paradox and ambiguity to be central to thinking and writing well. Playwright Tony Kushner learned from his Columbia University Shakespeare professor that "everything in Shakespeare was paradoxical and contradictory." From this Kushner began "to understand something about life, . . . that two opposites can exist simultaneously." He embraced the notion that theatre should present contradictions and thus encourage active critical thought.

The French philosopher Blaise Pascal, quoted above, declared that there were two extravagances: "to exclude reason and to admit only reason." Contemporary biologist Richard Dawkins, supporting this view, claims that scientists must also be poets and thinks that poets are well served by a knowledge of science. Poet John Ciardi joked about reason and the natural world:

> *Who could believe an ant in theory?*
> *A giraffe in blueprint?*
> *Ten thousand doctors of what's possible*
> *Could reason half the jungle out of being.*

Sometimes a **metaphor—a figure of speech that helps us understand one thing in terms of another**—can carry, through images and associations, an understanding beyond what explicit reasoning can convey. Seeing comparisons, exploring relationships, is fundamental to successful critical thinking.

In their book *Metaphors We Live By*, linguists George Lakoff and Mark Johnson point out how deeply dependent on implicit metaphor we are when we think and speak, citing the relationship between the way we use the term *argument* and the metaphors of war associated with it. Here are a few of their examples:

He *attacked* every weak point in my argument.

He *shot down* all of my arguments.

His criticisms were *right on target*.

Advertising frequently relies on metaphor to deliver its message. Look at the ad below and note all the words that support the war metaphor. The advertising industry knows the power of such metaphors, and the medical profession casts many of its approaches to disease in the same language. Strong metaphors create images often more powerful than simple presentation of facts.

CANCER.

IT'S A WAR.

THAT'S WHY WE'RE DEVELOPING

316 NEW WEAPONS.

America's pharmaceutical companies are developing 316 new medicines to fight cancer—the second leading cause of death in the United States. Gene therapies, "magic bullet" antibodies, and light-activated medicines are all new weapons in the high-tech, high-stakes war against cancer. Pharmaceutical company researchers have already discovered medicines that are allowing more and more cancer survivors to say, "I won the battle." We hope one day we can all say, "We won the war."

America's Pharmaceutical Companies

Leading the way in the search for cures

www.searchforcures.org

In the following poem, Richard Wilbur uses metaphor to describe his daughter's struggle to produce a story.

THE WRITER

In her room at the prow of the house
Where light breaks, and the windows are tossed with linden,
My daughter is writing a story.

I pause in the stairwell, hearing
From her shut door a commotion of typewriter-keys
Like a chain hauled over a gunwale.

Young as she is, the stuff
Of her life is a great cargo, and some of it heavy:
I wish her a lucky passage.

But now it is she who pauses,
As if to reject my thought and its easy figure.
A stillness greatens, in which

The whole house seems to be thinking,
And then she is at it again with a bunched clamor
Of strokes, and again is silent.

I remember the dazed starling
Which was trapped in that very room, two years ago;
How we stole in, lifted a sash

And retreated, not to affright it;
And how for a helpless hour, through the crack of the door,
We watched the sleek, wild, dark

And iridescent creature
Batter against the brilliance, drop like a glove
To the hard floor, or the desk-top,

And wait then, humped and bloody,
For the wits to try it again; and how our spirits
Rose when, suddenly sure,

It lifted off from a chair-back,
Beating a smooth course for the right window
And clearing the sill of the world.

It is always a matter, my darling,
Of life or death, as I had forgotten. I wish
What I wished you before, but harder.

EXERCISE 1C

Understanding Figurative Language

1. Consider this poem for a few minutes. To what two things does Wilbur compare the writing process? What do these images say about his view of the writing process?

2. Identify and explain a metaphor that describes your own writing process. Begin this exercise by brainstorming or freewriting to help discover this metaphor.

"I was on the cutting edge. I pushed the envelope. I did the heavy lifting. I was the rainmaker. Then I ran out of metaphors."

Reasoning by Analogy

Analogy, like metaphor, is a comparison of two or more things. But an analogy is explicit, not implicit and suggestive as a metaphor is. When we reason by analogy, we compare two or more things, noting the characteristics they share and suggesting that since they share these characteristics, they probably share other characteristics as well. For example, those opposed to the Iraq and Afghanistan wars compare them to the war in Vietnam. Since the war in Vietnam failed, the wars in Iraq and Afghanistan will fail.

In a recent newspaper editorial, Elisabeth Ostrow begins her argument against football by comparing it to smoking:

> My father tells me that when he was a boy, people didn't know that smoking was bad for you. Really? For those to whom it is not intuitively obvious that inhaling smoke into your lungs (which you use for breathing) is harmful to your health, we now have a wealth of scientific evidence that smoking causes heart disease and cancer. So now we try to keep cigarettes out of the hands of kids. My father also played football when he was a boy, and claims people didn't know that smashing your head into other people or the ground was bad for you either. Again, I wonder, really?
>
> Could anyone have ever believed that banging your skull (which is where you keep your brain, which you use for thinking) was a good idea? Regardless, for those to whom it is not intuitively obvious that head banging is really bad for your brain, we now have a wealth of scientific evidence that it is.

Do you find the analogy effective? For more examples of the use of analogies in written argument, see "The Order of Things" by Malcolm Gladwell in Additional Readings.

EXERCISE 1D

Understanding Analogy

Make your own short argument by analogy in much the same way cartoonist David Horsey does in his cartoon above (no drawing required). (You may want to skip ahead to *False Analogy* in Chapter 6 to see how yours holds up.)

SUMMARY

This book emphasizes the relationship between thinking clearly and writing well and stresses the importance of expressing ourselves persuasively while thinking critically about what we read, view, and hear. As we think critically, we need to understand the world view of others and recognize our own world view.

When writing, we need to think about the **audience** and the **purpose** for which we are writing. For an essay to be successful, we need to follow a sequential **writing process** that avoids formulaic structure and doesn't rush directly to a finished draft. While our main concern is with analytical thinking and argument, we also embrace creative thought and the imagination.

KEY TERMS

Analogy   reasoning by analogy, we compare two or more things, noting the characteristics they share and suggesting that since they share these characteristics, they probably share other characteristics as well.

Brainstorming   unrestrained, spontaneous generation of ideas.

Critical thinking   discerning or discriminating thought characterized by fairness, open-mindedness.

Ethos   the use of one's own character and credibility to persuade an audience.

Freewriting   unrestrained, spontaneous, continuous generation of complete sentences for a set length of time.

Logos   the use of reason to persuade an audience.

Metaphor   figure of speech that imaginatively implies a comparison between one object and another.

Pathos   the use of emotional appeals to persuade an audience and to have empathy for the audience's concerns.

World view   a set of assumptions about the world and the behavior of people in it.

CHAPTER 2

Inference—Critical Thought

Question

What do you infer from this cartoon?

"Try rolling on the ground! Roll around on the ground!"

Answer

Santa Claus is on fire! How do we know this? First of all, we see two elves, as indicated by their peaked hats, shouting down the smoking chimney of a snow-covered roof. The Elves, the snow, the chimney can suggest only one individual: Santa Claus. The smoke and the elves' frantic suggestion indicate that Santa is in trouble. We do not see him on fire, but on the basis of the **evidence**, we make an **inference**.

WHAT IS AN INFERENCE?

An inference is a conclusion about the unknown made on the basis of the known. We see a car beside us on the freeway with several new and old dents; we infer that the driver must be a bad one. A close friend hasn't called in several weeks and doesn't return our calls when we leave messages; we infer that she is angry with us. Much of our thinking, whether about casual observations or personal relationships, involves making inferences. Indeed, entire careers are based on the ability to make logical inferences. In *Snow Falling on Cedars*, a novel by David Guterson, a coroner describes his job:

> It's my job to infer. Look, if a night watchman is struck over the head with a crowbar during the course of a robbery, the wounds you're going to see in his head will look like they were made with a crowbar. If they were made by a ball-peen hammer you can see that, too—a ball-peen leaves behind a crescent-shaped injury, a crowbar leaves, well, linear wounds with V-shaped ends. You get hit with a pistol butt, that's one thing; somebody hits you with a bottle, that's another. You fall off a motorcycle at 40 miles an hour and hit your head on gravel, the gravel will leave behind patterned abrasions that don't look like anything else. So yes, I infer from the deceased's wound that something narrow and flat caused his injury. To infer—it's what coroners do.

Such reasoning is the basis for the popular television series *CSI: Crime Scene Investigation*, in which a team of investigators use cutting-edge scientific tools to examine the evidence, make logical inferences, and catch the killer. Critical thinking has always been an essential part of a good mystery.

How Reliable Is an Inference?

The reliability of inferences covers an enormous range. Some inferences are credible, but inferences based on minimal evidence or on evidence that may support many different interpretations should be treated with skepticism. In fact, the strength of an inference can be tested by the number of different explanations we can draw from the same set of facts. The greater the number of possible interpretations, the less reliable the inference.

In the cartoon, given the elves, the snowy roof, the smoking chimney, and the caption, we can arrive at one inference only: Santa Claus must have landed in a burning fireplace. But the inferences drawn in the other two cases above are less reliable. The driver of the dented car may not be the owner: she may have borrowed the car from a friend, or she may own the car but have recently bought it "as is." Our friend may not have called us for a number of reasons: a heavy work schedule, three term papers, a family crisis. She may not have received our messages. These alternate explanations weaken the reliability of the original inferences. Clearly, the more evidence we have to support our inferences and the fewer interpretations possible, the more we can trust their accuracy.

THE LANGUAGE OF INFERENCE

The verbs *infer* and *imply* are often confused, but they can be readily distinguished:

    to imply: to suggest, indicate indirectly, hint; what a writer, speaker, action, or object conveys.

    to infer: to arrive at a conclusion by reasoning from facts or evidence; what a reader, listener, or observer determines or concludes.

    A writer, speaker, action, or object implies something, and readers, listeners, or observers infer what that something is. A final distinction: only *people* (and animals) **can make inferences**; *anything* can **imply meaning**.

EXERCISE 2A

Interpreting a Cartoon

Quickly determine the message the following cartoon implies. What inferences do you draw from the evidence given? After writing a short response, compare your interpretation with those of others in the class. Are they the same?

© JEFF DANZIGER.

EXERCISE 2B

Thinking Critically About Your Own Thinking

Write a paragraph or two about a recent inference you've made. Include what evidence the inference was based on. Discuss with other students whether the inference was logical given the evidence that led to it and whether others might have made a different inference from the same data.

WHAT IS A FACT?

You're neither right nor wrong because others agree with you. You're right because your facts and reasoning are right.
—INVESTOR AND COLUMBIA PROFESSOR BEN GRAHAM TO CEO WARREN BUFFETT

We make inferences based on our own observations or on the observations of others as they are presented to us through speech or print. These observations often consist of **facts—information that can be verified**. The snowy chimney is smoking. We see dents in the car. You have not spoken to your friend in several weeks. "A crowbar leaves linear wounds with V-shaped ends." Our own observations attest to the truth of these claims. But often we are dependent on others' observations about people, places, and events that we cannot directly observe. Take, for example, the claim that in Boston, on September 11, 2001, Mohamed Atta boarded a flight that flew into the World Trade Center. Few of us observed this action firsthand, but those who did reported it, and we trust the veracity of their reports. Books, newspapers, magazines, television programs, and the Internet are filled with reports—facts—giving us information about the world that we are unable to gain from direct observation. If we doubt the truth of these claims, we usually can turn to other sources to verify or discredit them. As the late United States senator Daniel Patrick Moynihan stated, "Everyone is entitled to his own opinion, but not his own facts."

Reliability of Facts in a Changing World

In a recent *New Yorker* magazine, writer John McPhee discussed the critical roll played by **fact checkers**, particularly in the past. A few publications still do rigorous fact checking, but the tradition of meticulous checking in journalism for precise factual accuracy is fading. Information now moves globally at dizzying speed on the Internet. Online news in the blogosphere and rapid-fire talk radio are replacing print newspapers and magazines. Fact-correcting <u>after</u> publication, often by readers of uncertain credentials, is replacing responsible <u>prepublication</u> fact-checking. What is published or broadcast as fact is often unverified opinion, frequently unreliable. Much of the news delivered through the Internet comes from citizen journalists in contrast to professionals. Bias also exists among professionals, and facts can be manipulated and interpreted in various ways, but consumers of news need to be wary of information whose factual sources can't be verified. For more on this subject, see "A Quick Guide."

In an article analyzing a number of studies relating facts and beliefs, writer Joe Keohane alerts us to the mental difficulty we have in digesting facts that contradict our strongly held beliefs. He cautions that we need to keep open minds when presented with facts contrary to those we previously held dear. Flamboyant writer and journalist Christopher Hitchens, known for frequently changing his position on political issues, quoted British economist John Maynard Keynes: "When the facts change then my opinion changes." A good policy to follow.

How Facts Backfire
Researchers discover a surprising threat to democracy: our brains
BY JOE KEOHANE

July 11, 2010

1   It's one of the great assumptions underlying modern democracy that an informed citizenry is preferable to an uninformed one. "Whenever the people are well-informed, they can be trusted with their own government," Thomas Jefferson wrote in 1789. This notion, carried down through the years, underlies everything from humble political pamphlets to presidential debates to the very notion of a free press. Mankind may be crooked timber, as [philosopher] Kant put it, uniquely susceptible to ignorance and misinformation, but it's an article of faith that knowledge is the best remedy. If people are furnished with the facts, they will be clearer thinkers and better citizens. If they are ignorant, facts will enlighten them. If they are mistaken, facts will set them straight.

2   In the end, truth will out. Won't it?

3   Maybe not. Recently, a few political scientists have begun to discover a human tendency deeply discouraging to anyone with faith in the power of information. It's this: Facts don't necessarily have the power to change our minds. In fact, quite the opposite. In a series of studies in 2005 and 2006, researchers at the University of Michigan found that when misinformed people, particularly political partisans, were exposed to corrected facts in news stories, they rarely changed their minds. In fact, they often became even more strongly set in their beliefs. Facts, they found, were not curing misinformation. Like an underpowered antibiotic, facts could actually make misinformation even *stronger*.

4   This bodes ill for a democracy, because most voters—the people making decisions about how the country runs—aren't blank slates. They already have beliefs, and a set of facts lodged in their minds. The problem is that sometimes the things they think they know are objectively, provably false. And in the presence of the correct information, such people react very, very differently than the merely uninformed. Instead of changing their minds to reflect the correct information, they can entrench themselves even deeper.

5   "The general idea is that it's absolutely threatening to admit you're wrong," says political scientist Brendan Nyhan, the lead researcher on the Michigan study. The phenomenon—known as "backfire"—is "a natural defense mechanism to avoid that cognitive dissonance."

Most of us like to believe that our opinions have been formed over time by   6
careful, rational consideration of <u>facts</u> and ideas, and that the decisions based on
those opinions, therefore, have the ring of soundness and intelligence. In reality,
we often base our opinions on our *beliefs*, which can have an uneasy relationship
with facts. And rather than <u>facts driving beliefs</u>, our <u>beliefs can dictate the facts</u> we
choose to accept. They can cause us to twist facts so they fit better with our preconceived notions. Worst of all, they can lead us to uncritically accept bad information
just because it reinforces our beliefs. This reinforcement makes us more confident
we're right, and even less likely to listen to any new information. . . .

This effect is only heightened by the information glut, which offers—   7
alongside an unprecedented amount of good information—endless rumors,
misinformation, and questionable variations on the truth. In other words, it's
never been easier for people to be wrong, and at the same time feel more certain
that they're right.

What's going on? How can we have things so wrong, and be so sure that   8
we're right? Part of the answer lies in the way our brains are wired. Generally, people tend to seek consistency. There is a substantial body of psychological research
showing that people tend to interpret information with an eye toward reinforcing
their preexisting views. If we believe something about the world, we are more likely
to passively accept as truth any information that confirms our beliefs, and actively
dismiss information that doesn't. This is known as "motivated reasoning." Whether
or not the consistent information is accurate, we might accept it as <u>fact</u>, as confirmation of our beliefs. This makes us more confident in said beliefs, and even less
likely to entertain <u>facts</u> that contradict them.

In an ideal world, citizens would be able to maintain constant vigilance, moni-   9
toring both the information they receive and the way their brains are processing it.
But keeping atop the news takes time and effort. And relentless self-questioning, as
centuries of philosophers have shown, can be exhausting. Our brains are designed
to create cognitive shortcuts—inference, intuition, and so forth—to avoid precisely
that sort of discomfort while coping with the rush of information we receive on
a daily basis. Without those shortcuts, few things would ever get done. Unfortunately, with them, we're easily suckered by political falsehoods.

Nyhan ultimately recommends a supply-side approach. Instead of focusing on   10
citizens and consumers of misinformation, he suggests looking at the sources. If
you increase the "reputational costs" of peddling bad info, he suggests, you might
discourage people from doing it so often. "So if you go on 'Meet the Press' and
you get hammered for saying something misleading," he says, "you'd think twice
before you go and do it again."

Unfortunately, this shame-based solution may be as implausible as it is sen-   11
sible. Fast-talking political pundits have ascended to the realm of highly lucrative
popular entertainment, while professional fact-checking operations languish in the
dungeons of wonkery. Getting a politician or pundit to argue straight-faced that
George W. Bush ordered 9/11, or that Barack Obama is the culmination of a five-
decade plot by the government of Kenya to destroy the United States—that's easy.
Getting him to register shame? That isn't.

Questions for Discussion

1. How does Keohane describe the relationship between facts and our beliefs? What does he mean by "motivated reasoning"? What is surprising about his findings?

2. Identify a belief of your own which you've held for some time and provide the facts that support this belief. Can you think of facts that might lead you to a different belief on the same issue?

WHAT IS A JUDGMENT?

When we infer that Santa Claus is on fire, we laugh but are unlikely to express approval or disapproval. On the other hand, when we infer that the woman in the car in front of us is a poor driver, we express disapproval of her driving skills; we make a **judgment**, in this case a statement of disapproval. Or, when we infer from a friend's volunteer work with the homeless that she is an admirable person, we express our approval; that is, make a favorable judgment. **A judgment is also an inference, but although many inferences are free of positive or negative connotation, such as "I think it's going to rain," a judgment always expresses the writer's or speaker's approval or disapproval.**

Certain judgments are taken for granted, become part of a culture's shared belief system, and are unlikely to be challenged under most circumstances. Most of us would accept the following statements: "Taking the property of others is wrong" or "People who physically abuse children should be punished." But many judgments are not universally accepted without considerable well-reasoned support or may be rejected regardless of additional support and cogent reasoning. Frequently, a judgment is further complicated by potentially ambiguous language and even punctuation. Take, for example, the highly controversial wording of the Second Amendment to the Constitution

Amendment II

A well-regulated militia, being necessary to the security of a free State, the right of the people to keep and bear arms, shall not be infringed.

Those in favor of gun control interpret this to mean that only "a well-regulated militia," not every individual, is guaranteed the right to bear arms. "Well-regulated" implies an official militia, not a private one free of government regulations. But those against gun control believe that the Second Amendment guarantees "the people," meaning all individuals, the right to bear arms. This interpretation of the Second Amendment led the majority of the United States Supreme Court to a June 2010 decision striking down most features of gun control legislation in the District of Columbia. Gun rights supporters hailed the

decision, the first conclusive interpretation of the amendment since its passage in 1791. "I consider this the opening salvo in a step-by-step process of providing relief for law-abiding Americans everywhere that have been deprived of this freedom," said Wayne LaPierre, executive vice president of the National Rifle Association. Senator Dianne Feinstein, D-Calif., a leading gun control advocate in Congress, criticized the ruling. "I believe the people of this great country will be less safe because of it," she said. Two opposing judgments of the same Supreme Court decision.

What judgment would cartoonist Charles Schulz have made about the recent Supreme Court decision?

EXERCISE 2D

Distinguishing Between Facts, Inferences, and Judgments

Determine whether the following statements are facts, inferences, or judgments and explain your reasoning. Note that some may include more than one, and some may be open to interpretation.

> *Example:* I heard on the morning news that the city subway system has ground to a halt this morning; many students will arrive late for class.
>
> "I heard on the morning news that the city subway system has ground to a halt this morning." [*Fact:* I did hear it and the information can be verified.]
>
> "Many students will arrive late for class." [*Inference:* This is a conclusion drawn from the information about the breakdown of the subway.]

1. The war in Afghanistan is the longest war in U. S. history.
2. Material on the Internet should not be censored by government or any other organization.
3. For sale: lovely three-bedroom house in forest setting, easy commute, a bargain at $475,000.
4. Forty-one percent of Californians who die are cremated—almost twice the national average of 21 percent.
5. Artist Winslow Homer didn't begin to paint seriously until 1862.

6. Eric has a drinking problem.

7. Critic Ben Brantley called the latest production of Shakespeare's *As You Like It* "exhilarating."

8. After I took those vitamin pills recommended by the coach, I scored a touchdown. Those pills sure did the trick.

EXERCISE 2E

Drawing Logical Inferences

A. Read these "traffic facts" taken from Tom Vanderbilt's *Traffic: Why We Drive the Way We Do (and What It Says About Us)*. What *do* these facts about how we drive say about us?

Traffic Facts
TOM VANDERBILT

1. "Children at Play" signs don't reduce accidents.
2. Drivers honk less on weekends. Men honk more than women, and both men and women honk more at women than at men.
3. New cars crash more frequently than older cars.
4. Half of all fatalities occur at a speed of less than 35 mph.
5. 1 in 5 urban crashes occur when one of the drivers is searching for parking.
6. Saturday at 1 p.m. has heavier traffic than weekday rush hours.
7. Driving aggressively burns up more gas, increases crash risk and saves one minute on a 27-mile trip.
8. Solo motorists drive more aggressively.
9. FasTrak® lanes have been shown to increase crash rates.
10. Fifty percent of American schoolchildren walked or biked to school in 1969. Today it's 16 percent.
11. Drivers seated at higher eye heights tend to drive faster. Studies show that SUV and pickup drivers speed more than the average driver.
12. Car insurance premiums are tied not only to driving records but also to credit scores. The greater the credit risk, researchers find, the more likely someone is to be involved in a crash.
13. Although more fatalities occur from 2 to 3 a.m. on weekends than any other hour, 70 percent of all crashes occur in daylight on dry roads.

B. What inference can you draw from this fact taken from *Dry Manhattan* by Michael A. Lerner?

There were 15,000 saloons in New York when Prohibition started; within a few years, there were 32,000.

EXERCISE 2F

Solving Riddles, Reading Poetry

Use your inferential skills to solve these riddles by English poet John Cotton:

   1.
Insubstantial I can fill lives,
Cathedrals, worlds.
I can haunt islands,
Raise passions
Or calm the madness of kings.
I've even fed the affectionate.
I can't be touched or seen,
But I can be noted.

   2.
We are a crystal zoo,
Wielders of fortunes,
The top of our professions.
Like hard silver nails
Hammered into the dark
We make charts for mariners.

   3.
I reveal your secrets.
I am your morning enemy,
Though I give reassurance of presence.
I can be magic,
or the judge in beauty contests.
Count Dracula has no use for me.
When you leave
I am left to my own reflections.

   4.
My tensions and pressures
Are precise if transitory.
Iridescent, I can float
And catch small rainbows.
Beauties luxuriate in me.
I can inhabit ovens
Or sparkle in bottles.
I am filled with that
Which surrounds me.

   5.
Containing nothing
I can bind people forever,

Or just hold a finger.
Without end or beginning
I go on to appear in fields,
Ensnare enemies,
Or in another guise
Carry in the air
Messages from tower to tower.

6.
Silent I invade cities,
Blur edges, confuse travelers,
My thumb smudging the light.
I drift from rivers
To loiter in the early morning fields,
Until Constable Sun
Moves me on.
—JOHN COTTON, *THE TOTLEIGH RIDDLES, TIMES LITERARY SUPPLEMENT*

Now apply the same skills to these two poems by Sylvia Plath (1933–1963). What does each describe?

I am silver and exact. I have no preconceptions.
Whatever I see I swallow immediately
Just as it is, unmisted by love or dislike.
I am not cruel, only truthful—
The eye of a little god, four-cornered.
Most of the time I meditate on the opposite wall.
It is pink, with speckles. I have looked at it so long
I think it is a part of my heart. But it flickers.
Faces and darkness separate us over and over.
Now I am a lake. A woman bends over me,
Searching my reaches for what she really is.
Then she turns to those liars, the candles or the moon.
I see her back, and reflect it faithfully.
She rewards me with tears and an agitation of hands.
I am important to her. She comes and goes.
Each morning it is her face that replaces the darkness.
In me she has drowned a young girl, and in me an old woman
Rises toward her day after day, like a terrible fish.

I'm a riddle in nine syllables,
An elephant, a ponderous house,
A melon strolling on two tendrils.
O red fruit, ivory, fine timbers.
This loaf's big with its yeasty rising.
Money's new-minted in this fat purse.
I'm a means, a stage, a cow in calf.

I've eaten a bag of green apples,
Boarded the train there's no getting off.

Turn your inference skills to this more serious poem by Philip Levine. What question did the boy have? What answer does the man find?

ON ME!

In the next room his brothers are asleep,
the two still in school. They just can't wait
to grow up and be men, to make money.
Last night at dinner they sat across from him,
their brother, a man, but a man with nothing,
without money or the prospect of money.
He never pays, never tosses a bill
down on the bar so he can say, "On me!"
At four in the morning when he can't sleep,
he rehearses the stale phrase to himself
with a delicate motion of the wrist
that lets the bill float down. He can't pace
for fear of waking his mom who sleeps
alone downstairs in the old storage room
off the kitchen. When he was a kid, twelve
or fourteen, like his brothers, he never knew
why boys no older than he did the things
they did, the robberies, gang fights, ODs,
rapes, he never understood his father's wordless
rages that would explode in punches
and kicks, bottles, plates, glasses hurled
across the kitchen. The next morning would be
so quiet that from his room upstairs
he'd hear the broom-straws scratching the floor
as his mother swept up the debris and hear
her humming to herself. Now it's so clear,
so obvious he wonders why it took
so long for him to get it and to come of age.

ACHIEVING A BALANCE BETWEEN INFERENCE AND FACTS

We need to distinguish inferences, facts, and judgments from one another to evaluate as fairly as possible the events in our world. Whether these events are personal or global, we need to be able to distinguish between facts, verifiable information that we can rely on, and inferences and judgments, which may or may not be reliable.

We also need to evaluate the reliability of our own inferences. Are there other interpretations of the facts? Have we considered all other possible interpretations? Do we need more information before drawing a conclusion? These are useful thinking skills that we need to practice, but how do these skills relate to writing? To answer that question, read the following paragraph and distinguish between statements of fact and inference.

> A white player's life in the National Basketball Association is a reverse-image experience all but unique in American culture. Although fewer than 13 percent of United States citizens are African-American, about 80 percent of the N.B.A.'s players are. Of the 357 players on N.B.A. rosters, 290 were African-American, including several of mixed descent. Every one of the league's 20 leading scorers was black, and all but 2 of its leading rebounders. Not one N.B.A. team has as many whites as blacks.
>
> —ADAPTED FROM "THE LONELINESS OF BEING WHITE" BY BRUCE SCHOENFELD

This paragraph contains one inference while the remaining statements are factual, capable of verification. Notice that the facts support and convince us of the inference.

INFERENCE	FACTS
A white player's life in the National Basketball Association is a reverse-image experience all but unique in American culture.	Although fewer than 13 percent of United States citizens are African-American, about 80 percent of the N.B.A.'s players are.
	Of the 357 players on N.B.A. rosters, 290 were African-American, including several of mixed descent.
	Every one of the league's 20 leading scorers was black, and all but 2 of its 20 leading rebounders.
	Not one N.B.A. team has as many whites as blacks.

Facts Only

> Now, what I want is Facts. Teach these boys and girls nothing but Facts. Facts alone are wanted in life. Plant nothing else, and root out everything else. You can only form the minds of reasoning animals upon Facts: nothing else will ever be of any service to them. This is the principle on which I bring up my own children, and this is the principle on which I bring up these children. Stick to Facts, sir!

So says Thomas Gradgrind in Charles Dickens's novel *Hard Times*, an indictment against Victorian industrial society. Dickens knew that facts alone do not make for a good education nor for good writing and thus gave that speech to an unsympathetic character. Expository writing frequently consists of a blend of inference and fact, with the one supporting the other. If you were to write a paper consisting only of facts, it would be of no interest to the reader because reading facts that lead nowhere, that fail to support a conclusion, is like reading the telephone book. Jeff Jarvis, a reviewer for the *New York Times Book Review*, comments on the dangers of this kind of writing:

> Objectivity, in some quarters, means just the facts, ma'am—names, dates, and quotations dumped from a notebook onto the page. But facts alone, without

perspective, do not tell a story. Facts alone, without a conclusion to hold them together, seem unglued. Facts alone force writers to use awkward transitions, unbending formats or simple chronologies to fend off disorganization.

A facts-only approach can also have serious consequences in our schools' textbooks. A recent report on public education cites such facts-only textbooks as one of the causes of students' lack of interest and poor achievement.

Elementary school children are stuck with insipid books that "belabor what is obvious" even to first graders. At the high school level, history—or "social studies"—texts are crammed with facts but omit human motivations or any sense of what events really meant.

Keep the danger of a facts-only approach in mind when you are assigned a research paper. Do not assume that teachers are looking exclusively for well-documented facts; they also want to see what you make of the data, what inferences you draw, what criticisms and recommendations you offer. Do not fall into the trap of one eager young college freshman, Charles Renfrew, who, proud of his photographic memory, expected high praise from his philosophy professor for a paper on French philosopher Descartes. He suffered disappointment but learned a lasting lesson when he read the comment "Too much Descartes, not enough Renfrew." A photographic memory for factual information is an asset, but your own inferences and judgments fully explained are also important. Don't leave your readers asking "so what?" when they finish your paper. Tell them.

Inferences Only

Is it possible to err in another direction as well? Yes. A paper consisting only of inferences and judgments would irritate readers as they search for the basis of our claims, the facts to support our opinions and beliefs. In his biography of William Shakespeare, *Will in the World*, noted scholar Stephen Greenblatt annoyed some Shakespeare authorities and other readers by stretching a sketchy collection of facts to reconstruct the life of the great playwright about whom little is known. Greenblatt tells a good story, but are his inferences supported by the facts?

For example, in trying to create a childhood love of the theatre for Shakespeare, Greenblatt cites the surviving record of another man of Shakespeare's time, Willis, who, at a young age, went with his father to the theatre in Gloucester, where the boy stood "between his [father's] legs." Greenblatt then assumes that when Shakespeare's father, the mayor of Stratford, 30 miles from Gloucester, hired players he would have taken his five-year-old son. "When the bailiff [or mayor] walked into the hall, everyone would have greeted him. . . . His son, intelligent, quick, and sensitive, would have stood between his father's legs. For the first time in his life William Shakespeare watched a play." But are the facts sufficient to support his inference? Oxford professor Richard Jenkyns ridicules Greenblatt's reasoning: "Some people have birthmarks, and so Shakespeare may have had one."

EXERCISE 2G

Distinguishing Facts

In this excerpt taken from a newspaper article, carefully distinguish those statements that are factual from those that are not. (Note that the sentences are numbered.)

> On Wednesday, March 9, a Los Angeles court dismissed charges against two physicians who allowed a terminally ill patient to die.[1] For generations organized medicine has focused on saving lives, no matter what the price in emotional trauma, physical pain, or economic cost, because we are a death denying society.[2] But keeping people alive in the face of a painful death should not be inevitable, as Drs. White and Rosenbaum maintained when they shut off artificial life-support for their brain damaged patient at the urging of his family.[3] Although doctors and nurses should remain bound by some rules of law and ethics, they should be able to treat their patients in the most humane way possible as long as they have the informed consent of the patient or of his/her family if the patient can't give it.[4] Thus doctors should not be penalized for allowing a terminally ill patient's life to end mercifully, especially if the patient is clearly "brain dead."[5] The definition of "brain dead" remains a controversial issue but not one which should halt humane medical decisions.[6]

Overall, do you consider this article to be based on fact or judgment?

In what section of the newspaper would you expect to find this article?

WRITING ASSIGNMENT 2

Reconstructing the Lost Tribe

*"When we first started seeing each other, we would
always use the same word for snow."*

The cartoon above refers to the fact that Eskimos have many words for snow, their vocabulary reflecting their environment. Similarly, the Hmong of Laos have many words for mountains—their shapes, slopes, and elevations—to describe their environment. As anthropologist Clyde Kluckhohn points out, "Every language is a special way of looking at the world and interpreting experience. Concealed in the structure of language are a whole set of unconscious assumptions about the world and the life in it." Simply put, a language reflects its culture. Refer to "You Are What You Speak" by Guy Deutscher in Additional Readings for a detailed discussion of the relationship between language and culture. For this assignment, feel free to refer to and quote from the article if you think it appropriate.

Imagine that a previously unknown civilization has been discovered and that linguistic anthropologists, after observing the civilization for a while, have delineated the following characteristics about the society's language:

Three words for *terrain*, designating "absolutely flat," "rolling," and "slightly hilly."

No word for *ocean*.

Dozens of terms for grains, including eight for wheat alone.

Several words for *children*, some of which translate as "wise, small one," "innocent leader," and "little stargazer."

Seven terms to describe the stages of life up to puberty; only one term to describe life from puberty to death.

The word for *sex* translates as "to plant a wise one."

Terms for *woman* are synonymous with "wife and mother."

Terms for *man* are synonymous with "husband and father."

Twenty words for *book*.

No words for violent conflict or war.

Nine words for *artist*.

Terms for *praise* translate as "peacemaker" and "conciliator."

Words designating *cow*, *pig*, *calf*, and *sheep* but no terms for *beef*, *pork*, *veal*, *leather*, or *mutton*.

Several words for precipitation, most translating as "rain," only one meaning "snow."

Several words for *leader*, but all are plural.

Four words meaning *theater*.

The Topic

Write an essay in which you characterize the society that uses this language. (Consider giving a name to this tribe to help focus your sentences.)

As you analyze the language, you will be reconstructing a culture. Obviously, because the data are limited, you will have to make a few educated guesses and qualify conclusions carefully. ("Perhaps," "possibly," "one might conclude," "the evidence suggests," and similar hedges will be useful.)

The Approach

Examine and group the data; look for patterns.

Draw inferences, depending only on the data given.

Be sure to use all the data.

Cite evidence to support these inferences—be sure to base all your conclusions on the linguistic evidence provided. Do not draw inferences that you don't support with specific examples. Explain your line of reasoning—how and why the data lead to the inferences you have made.

The Structure

The **opening section** of any essay must provide readers with the necessary **background information**. In this case: What information do you have? How have you come by this information? What are you going to attempt to do with this information?

Each **supporting paragraph** should deal with one distinct aspect of the civilization. Arrange the paragraphs so you can move smoothly from one paragraph to the next.

Some possibilities for the **conclusion** of the essay: What general conclusion(s) can you come to about this society based on the more specific conclusions you have presented in the supporting paragraphs? Is there any overall point you want to make about this society?

OR

What do you find admirable about this society? Do you have any criticisms of the society?

OR

Do you have any questions about the society?

Of course, the conclusion can deal with more than one of these possibilities.

Audience and Purpose

You have a wide range of possibilities here; we leave the choice to you. Your paper may assume the form of a report, scholarly or simply informative, directed to any audience you choose. It may be a letter to a personal friend or fictional colleague. It may be a traditional essay for an audience unfamiliar with the assignment, explaining what the language tells us about the people who use or used it. **What is crucial for success is that you, as the reporter-writer, assume that *you have not seen this tribe and have no firsthand evidence of it. You will also assume that your*** *reader does not have a copy of this assignment; it is up to you to cite all the specific evidence (the terms given in the list) to justify your inferences.*

READING CRITICALLY

Distinguishing between facts, inferences, and judgments and evaluating their reliability allow us to analyze information, to read critically as writers, as consumers, as voters. Whether it is an article we find on the Internet, a pitch from an auto salesperson, or a speech by a political candidate, we need to be able to separate facts from judgments and to ask that the judgments offered be supported by the facts. If we read or listen without these distinctions in mind, we are susceptible to false claims and invalid arguments, often with serious consequences for us as individuals and for society as a whole. (To practice these skills, see Additional Readings.)

MAKING INFERENCES—WRITING ABOUT FICTION

These **critical reading** skills also prove helpful when reading and writing about fiction. Many students are intimidated by assignments that require them to write about a poem, play, short story, or novel. What can they say about a piece of literature? Isn't there a right answer known to the author and the teacher but not to students?

Fiction is **implicit**; it does not explain **explicitly**. Writers of fiction—through character, plot, setting, theme, point of view, symbolism, irony, and imagery—imply meaning. Fiction is oblique. The work implies meaning; you, the reader, infer what that meaning is. As you can see, interpreting literature requires **critical thinking**; it asks you to make inferences about the meaning of the work and to support these inferences with details from it as you have done with cartoons, statistics, texts, and poems earlier in this chapter.

Reading is the making of meaning, and the meaning we make depends on who we are. Our sex, age, ethnicity, culture, and experience (our world view), all create the context for our reading. Given the multiple interpretations possible, there is not a single right answer but only well-supported inferences that add up to a logical interpretation.

A final point: your critical essay is not a continuation of class discussion but a formal piece of writing that can stand on its own apart from the class. To accomplish this, you may think of your audience as one who is not familiar with the work you are writing about. This does not require you to retell every detail of the piece, but it ensures that you include the relevant details, the facts, on which your inferences are based rather than assume your reader knows them.

The next two assignments will give you an opportunity to practice the skills of **reading closely** and **thinking critically** while making and supporting inferences about literature.

WRITING ASSIGNMENT 3

Making Inferences About Fiction

Read "The Story of an Hour" by Kate Chopin and, in a short essay, answer the following question: Does Louise die "of joy" as her doctors suggest or do you have a different interpretation? Support your answer, your inference, with facts from the story.

The Story of an Hour

KATE CHOPIN

Knowing that Mrs. Mallard was afflicted with a heart trouble, great care was taken   1
to break to her as gently as possible the news of her husband's death.

It was her sister Josephine who told her, in broken sentences; veiled hints that   2
revealed in half concealing. Her husband's friend Richards was there, too, near her.
It was he who had been in the newspaper office when intelligence of the railroad
disaster was received, with Brently Mallard's name leading the list of "killed." He
had only taken the time to assure himself of its truth by a second telegram, and
had hastened to forestall any less careful, less tender friend in bearing the sad
message.

She did not hear the story as many other women have heard the same, with a   3
paralyzed inability to accept its significance. She wept at once, with sudden, wild
abandonment, in her sister's arms. When the storm of grief had spent itself she
went away to her room alone. She would have no one follow her.

There stood, facing the open window, a comfortable, roomy armchair. Into   4
this she sank, pressed down by a physical exhaustion that haunted her body and
seemed to reach her soul.

She could see in the open square before her house the tops of trees that were   5
all aquiver with the new spring life. The delicious breath of rain was in the air. In
the street below a peddler was crying his wares. The notes of a distant song which
some one was singing reached her faintly, and countless sparrows were twittering
in the eaves.

There were patches of blue sky showing here and there through the clouds   6
that had met and piled one above the other in the west facing her window.

She sat with her head thrown back upon the cushion of the chair, quite mo-   7
tionless, except when a sob came up into her throat and shook her, as a child who
has cried herself to sleep continues to sob in its dreams.

She was young, with a fair, calm face, whose lines bespoke repression and even   8
a certain strength. But now there was a dull stare in her eyes, whose gaze was fixed
away off yonder on one of those patches of blue sky. It was not a glance of reflection, but rather indicated a suspension of intelligent thought.

There was something coming to her and she was waiting for it, fearfully. What   9
was it? She did not know; it was too subtle and elusive to name. But she felt it,
creeping out of the sky, reaching toward her through the sounds, the scents, the
color that filled the air.

Now her bosom rose and fell tumultuously. She was beginning to recognize   10
this thing that was approaching to possess her, and she was striving to beat it back
with her will—as powerless as her two white slender hands would have been.

When she abandoned herself a little whispered word escaped her slightly   11
parted lips. She said it over and over under her breath, "free, free, free!" The vacant
stare and the look of terror that had followed it went from her eyes. They stayed
keen and bright. Her pulses beat fast, and the coursing blood warmed and relaxed
every inch of her body.

She did not stop to ask if it were or were not a monstrous joy that held her.   12
A clear and exalted perception enabled her to dismiss the suggestion as trivial.

She knew that she would weep again when she saw the kind, tender hands   13
folded in death; the face that had never looked save with love upon her, fixed and
gray and dead. But she saw beyond that bitter moment a long procession of years
to come that would belong to her absolutely. And she opened and spread her arms
out to them in welcome.

There would be no one to live for her during those coming years; she would   14
live for herself. There would be no powerful will bending hers in that blind per-
sistence with which men and women believe they have a right to impose a
private will upon a fellow-creature. A kind intention or a cruel intention made
the act seem no less a crime as she looked upon it in that brief moment of
illumination.

And yet she loved him—sometimes. Often she had not. What did it matter!   15
What could love, the unsolved mystery, count for in face of this possession of self-
assertion which she suddenly recognized as the strongest impulse of her being!

"Free! Body and soul free!" she kept whispering.

Josephine was kneeling before the closed door with her lips to the keyhole, im-   16
ploring for admission. "Louise, open the door! I beg; open the door—you will make
yourself ill. What are you doing, Louise? For heaven's sake open the door."

"Go away. I am not making myself ill." No; she was drinking in a very elixer of   17
life through that open window.

Her fancy was running riot along those days ahead of her. Spring days, and   18
summer days, and all sorts of days that would be her own. She breathed a quick
prayer that life might be long. It was only yesterday she had thought with a shud-
der that life might be long.

She rose at length and opened the door to her sister's importunities. There was   19
a feverish triumph in her eyes, and she carried herself unwittingly like a goddess
of Victory. She clasped her sister's waist, and together they descended the stairs.
Richards stood waiting for them at the bottom.

Some one was opening the front door with a latchkey. It was Brently Mallard   20
who entered, a little travel-stained, composedly carrying his gripsack and umbrella.
He had been far from the scene of the accident, and did not even know there had
been one. He stood amazed at Josephine's piercing cry; at Richards' quick motion
to screen him from the view of his wife.

But Richards was too late.   21

When the doctors came they said she had died of heart disease—of joy that kills.   22

WRITING ASSIGNMENT 4

Interpreting Fiction

Read the short story "Hostess," by Donald Mangum, and write an essay based on the inferences you make about the hostess, the narrator of the story. Include the facts on which these inferences are based and an explanation of why you made such inferences.

Audience

Someone who has not read the story.

Purpose

To read closely and characterize the hostess—what kind of woman is she?

Hostess

DONALD MANGUM

My husband was promoted to crew chief, and with the raise we moved into a 1
double-wide, just up the drive. Half the park came to the house-warming. Well,
Meg drank herself to tears and holed up on the toilet, poor thing. "Meg? Hon?"
I said from the hall. "You going to live?" She groaned something. It was seeing
R.L. with that tramp down in 18 that made her do this to herself. Now there was
a whole line of beer drinkers doing the rain dance out in the hall, this being a
single-bath unit. I was the hostess, and I had to do something. "Sweetheart," I said,
knocking. "I'm going to put you a bowl on the floor in the utility room." The rest
of the trailer was carpeted.

Dale, my husband, was in the kitchen with an egg in his hand, squeezing it for 2
all he was worth. Veins stuck out everywhere on his arm. Paul and Eric were laughing. "What's going on in here?" I said.

Dale stopped squeezing and breathed. "I got to admit," he said, "I never 3
knew that about eggs." I could have kicked him when he handed Paul five dollars.
I found the bowl I was after, plus a blanket, and took care of Meg.

Then Hank and Boyce almost got into a fight over a remark Hank made about 4
somebody named Linda. They had already squared off outside when it came out
that Hank was talking about a Linda *Stillman*, when Boyce thought he meant a
Linda *Faye*. Well, by that time everybody was ready for something, so the guys
agreed to arm-wrestle. Hank won, but only because Boyce started laughing when
Kathy Sueanne sat in Jason's supper and Jason got madder than Kathy Sueanne did
because there wasn't any more potato salad left.

You won't believe who showed up then. R.L.! Said he was looking for Meg. 5
"You think she wants to see you, R.L.?" I said. "After what you did to her with that
trash Elaine?" So he said he'd only kissed Elaine a couple of times. "Or not even
that," he said. "She was the one kissed *me*."

"You know what you can kiss," I said. He stood there looking like some dog 6
you'd just hauled off and kicked for no good reason. "Well, come on," I said,

taking him by the shirt. I led him to the utility room to show him the condition he'd driven his darling to. I'm here to say, when R.L. saw that precious thing curled up in front of the hot-water heater he sank to his knees in shame. I just closed the door.

Back in the den, there was this Australian kangaroo giving birth on the televi- 7 sion. The little baby kangaroo, which looked sort of like an anchovy with legs, had just made it out of its mama and was crawling around looking for her pouch. The man on the show said it had about ten minutes to get in there and find a teat or it would die. He said a lot of them don't make it. I got so wrought up watching that trembly little fellow that I started cheering him on. So did everyone else. Well, to everyone's relief, the little thing made it. Then Gus wanted to know why everyone over there always called each other Mike. Nobody had any idea.

Eric ate a whole bunch of dried cat food before figuring out what it was and 8 that somebody had put it in the party dish as a joke. He tried to act like it didn't bother him, but he didn't stay too long after that. Melinda went out to her car for cigarettes, and a yellow jacket stung her behind the knee, so when she came in howling, Rod slapped this wad of chewing tobacco on the spot to draw out the poison, which made her howl even louder, till I washed it off and applied meat tenderizer and let her go lie in the guest bed for a while.

That's when something strange happened. The phone started ringing, and 9 I ran back to get it in Dale's and my bedroom, which was the closest to quiet in the trailer. I answered and just got this hollow sound at first, like you get with a bad connection over long-distance.

There was a mumble, then a woman's voice said, "She's gone." I didn't recog- 10 nize the voice, but I was sure what "gone" meant by the way she said it. It meant someone had died. Then she said—and she almost screamed it—"Someone should have been here. Why weren't you and Clarence here?"

Now, I don't know a soul in this world named Clarence, and this was clearly a 11 case of the wrong number. "Ma'am," I said as gently as I knew how.

"You'll have to talk louder," she said. "I can hardly hear you."   12

I curled my hand around my lips and the mouthpiece and said, "Ma'am, you 13 have dialed the wrong number."

"Oh, God, I'm sorry," she said. "Oh dear God." And here is the strange thing. 14 The woman did not hang up. She just kept saying, "Dear God" and crying.

I sat there listening to that woman and to all the happy noise coming from 15 everywhere in the trailer and through the window from outside, and when she finally brought it down to a sniffle I said, "Honey, who was it that passed away?"

"My sister," she said. "My sister, Beatrice." And it was like saying the name 16 started her to sobbing again.

"And none of your people are there?" I said.   17

"Just me," she said.   18

"Sweetheart, you listen to me," I said, trying to close the window for more 19 quiet. Sweet Christ, I thought. Dear sweet Christ in Heaven. "Are you listening, angel? You should not be alone right now. You understand what I'm telling you?" I said, "Now, I am right here."

MAKING INFERENCES—ANALYZING IMAGES

In the same way that we make inferences about what we read, we make inferences about what we see. Look at Dorothea Lang's famous photograph, "Migrant Mother." With this one photo, Lang captured the desperation of thousands who were forced off the land and into poverty by the Dustbowl and the Depression in the 1930s. Indeed, certain images have become a part of our national consciousness; a single iconic image can signify an entire historical event.

EXERCISE 2H

Analyzing Two Historic Images

For the following two images, identify the historic context and explain why you think each has remained so powerful.

LIBRARY OF CONGRESS, PRINTS & PHOTOGRAPHS DIVISION, [LC-USF34-009058-C].

A Iwo Jima   **B** "Falling Man" NY

Persuading with Visual Images

We live in a world of intense visual stimulation. The Internet, television, print media, billboards—we are surrounded by images designed to persuade, telling us what to buy, what to think, how to vote. Thus it is important that we train ourselves in media literacy—to interpret visual images in much the same way that we develop our skills in making inferences as we read printed texts.

In the cartoons you looked at earlier in this chapter, we discussed the ways in which the illustrator led you to make inferences, to reach a conclusion that was implied by the picture. Images on Facebook and YouTube frequently replace written communication. In a similar way, a news photo on the front page of a newspaper may suggest a particular way to interpret an event or view a political figure. Photos of war scenes often carry an antiwar message or promote one side in the conflict over another. An unflattering photo of a political candidate may be chosen to discourage voters.

You may remember a photo of former President Bush published by many newspapers in which he is shown peering from the window of Air Force One as it flies over New Orleans four days after that city had been struck by Hurricane Katrina. Bush was criticized for his late and detached reaction to the crisis, and this photo greatly contributed to that criticism.

During the Vietnam War, pictures of coffins being unloaded at US air bases fueled the war's unpopularity. For several years, no such pictures were shown of the soldiers who died in Iraq as politicians recognized that mistake. Publication of photos of wounded or dead soldiers is a particularly sensitive issue.

Examining Ads

Knowing the value of visual images, advertisers rely on them in magazines, billboards, television, and the Internet. Studying these ads to determine their underlying suggestive messages can be fun as well as instructive. In advertising, the visual image provides the evidence leading to an inference that usually carries a judgment: a product is better than others of its kind. The judgment is sometimes obvious, sometimes implicit.

When you see an image of a luxury car speeding up a steep mountain road surrounded by gorgeous scenery, it doesn't take you long to realize that the auto company is suggesting you should buy their model because it is powerful and beautiful and will take you to dramatic places at a thrilling speed. Most of us drive cars. Most of us would willingly be transported to such a world.

When a beer commercial excites your interest with glamorous models having fun and scarcely mentions the brand, the argument is more subtly suggestive. Some ads are so subtle that you are left wondering what the product is or exactly how the image relates to the product. The hope here is usually that the inference is subliminal, below the viewer's conscious reasoning, the argument indirect. But with careful analysis, you can evaluate the visual clues and infer the message.

A number of companies refused our requests to use their ads in this text. Can you figure out why? We appreciate those who cooperated and wonder why others wouldn't rejoice over multiple copies of free advertising.

In the ad that follows, note how the product name, Pirelli (tires made in Italy), is reduced to a small corner. It is the image that carries the message. Even if you don't recognize Rio de Janeiro, or Brazil's famous soccer player, Ronaldo, standing in for the statue of Christ the Redeemer, which presides on the mountaintop above the city, you can see a figure of tremendous power filling the foreground, towering over an impressive landscape. With arms outspread, he suggests control of this landscape, a godlike figure dominating the world, as reassuring as he is powerful. The picture catches a reader's attention even before he has a chance to read the caption. Were you able to see the picture in color, you would recognize a mystical light emanating from the figure, the whole scene bathed in a warm reddish glow. The image is one of inspiration—inspiring both power and control, underscoring the combination of power and control any driver would want in a tire.

EXERCISE 21

Making Inferences About Visual Images in the Media

1. Using the analysis of the Pirelli ad above as your model, select one of the ads that follow, the first for Paul Mitchell hair products, the second for the Norton Commando 750 Roadster, and the third for Guess Clothing. In full color, the Norton Roadster ad leaps off the page. The bike has yellow highlights on the seat; the young woman is wearing a body-suit of brilliant blue, her long hair seductively gold. Analyze all the features of the ad, and in a few paragraphs fully explain exactly how the advertisers are using the visual image to make their argument and sell their product. List all the features of the ad that contribute to your conclusions, explicit and implicit details. Do you find the ad effective? Why or why not?

The copy on the left side of this ad urges readers to "Create change and build a better future. Join the John Paul Mitchell Systems family of hairdressers worldwide to fight hunger and poverty, safeguard our planet's water, and give hope to children in need." On the right side we are told that "Each of us can make a difference. Only in salons and Paul Mitchell schools. www.paulmitchell.com" Also note that the man in the ad is Paul Mitchell.

2. Find a magazine or Internet ad that persuades with visual images and write an analysis of it. (A possible source: www.advertisingarchives.co.uk/) Attach the ad or a copy of it to your response. You may have a chance in class to try out your choice on classmates and see if they reach the same conclusion you do. If they don't, what does it say about the effectiveness of the ad?

3. Select a news photo that implies a judgment of an event or a prominent political or sports figure. Write a paragraph in which you discuss the editor's choice of photo. What is he implying with this choice?

Vivid Warnings

In 2010, the Surgeon General decided to go beyond the textual warnings on cigarette packs and replace them with powerful images depicting the damage of smoking. You can check to see if these have started appearing. Similarly, campaigns against drinking and driving and athletes' use of steroids have turned to striking visual warnings. The idea is that a picture can speak louder than words alone.

EXERCISE 2J

Behavior-Changing Images

Examine these images and then write an evaluation of how effective they will be in deterring people from driving under the influence and using steroids. In other words, do you think such advertising campaigns will result in changes in behavior?

The "It's Only Another Beer" Black and Tan

8 oz. pilsner lager
8 oz. stout lager
1 frosty mug
1 icy road
1 pick-up truck
1 10-hour day
1 tired worker
A few rounds with the guys

Mix ingredients.
Add 1 totalled vehicle.

Never underestimate 'just a few.'
Buzzed driving is drunk driving.

AdCouncil.org   U.S. Department of Transportation

Drunk Driving

Buzzed Driving

Buzzed driving is drunk driving.

IMAGES COURTESY OF THE AD COUNCIL, THE U.S. DEPARTMENT OF TRANSPORTATION AND THE NATIONAL HIGHWAY TRAFFIC SAFETY ADMINISTRATION.

When you take steroids, there's no hiding it. Eventually everyone will see you for what you really are. A fake. A fraud. An asterisk.

Ad Council   DontBeAnAsterisk.com   USA

EXERCISE 2K

Analyzing a Film

Using strategies similar to those you've applied to fiction and visual images, view the John Sayles film *Limbo*. The conclusion of the movie is open to interpretation; members of the audience are left to decide for themselves if the three individuals stranded on the island are rescued or murdered. What do you think? Write a short paper explaining your answer, citing as evidence specific details from the movie.

Visual Images and the Law

As our world has steadily veered toward visual images in all areas of media, it is not surprising that the use of images without permission or financial remuneration has grown.

When football star Sam Keller found his college image on an Electronic Arts video game, he sued. Although his name never appeared, the game shows him actively playing, with his jersey number and his exact physical appearance easily recognizable. The case boils down to who owns the images of public figures, a clash between personal ownership and First Amendment rights. As *New York Times* writer Katie Thomas said,

> The case is drawing attention because it gets to the heart of a highly contested legal question: when should a person's right to control his image trump the free speech rights of others to use it?

EXERCISE 2L

Exploring a Legal Case

Can you think of other examples of a celebrity's image being used, for profit, without the express permission of that celebrity? Write a paragraph or two stating your position on this controversy, using the example of football star Sam Keller above as well as any other examples you (or other students in the class) have come up with.

SUMMARY

In order to interpret the world around us and write effectively about it, we need to be able to distinguish **facts**, **inferences**, and **judgments** from one another and to evaluate the reliability of our inferences. In written exposition and argument, it is important to achieve a balance between fact and inference and to support our inferences with facts and reasoning.

In the interpretation of literature, readers need to draw inferences from what the writer implies. In a world increasingly filled with visual images, we need to interpret both explicit and implicit messages in many venues.

KEY TERMS

Explicit   clearly stated or explained, distinctly expressed.

Facts   information that can be verified.

Implicit   suggested or hinted at, not directly expressed.

Inference   a conclusion about something we don't know based on what we do know.

Judgment   an inference that expresses either approval or disapproval.

CHAPTER 3

The Structure of Argument

You always hurt the one you love!

In logic, an argument is not a fight but a rational piece of discourse, written or spoken, that attempts to persuade the reader or listener to believe something. For instance, we can attempt to persuade others that an individual's carbon footprint contributes to global warming or that a vote for a particular candidate will ensure a better society. Though many arguments are concerned with political issues, arguments are not limited to such topics. We can argue about books, movies, athletic teams, and cars, as well as about abstractions found in philosophy and politics. Whenever we want to convince someone else of the "rightness" of our position by offering reasons for that position, we are presenting an argument.

What is the difference between an argument and an opinion? When we offer our own views on an issue, we are expressing an **opinion**. We all have them. But we should recognize the difference between voicing an opinion and developing an argument. Someone might insist that using animals for medical research is wrong; a research physician might respond that this attitude is misguided. Both are expressing opinions. If they both stick to their guns but refuse to elaborate on their positions, then each may simply dismiss the opponent's statement as "mere opinion," as nothing more than an emotional reaction. If, on the other hand, they start to offer reasons in support of their opinions, then they have moved the discussion to an argument. The critic might add that animals suffer pain in much the same way that humans do, and thus experiments inflict cruel suffering on animals. The physician might respond that modern techniques have greatly reduced animal suffering and that such experiments are necessary for medical breakthroughs. They are now offering support for their opinions. Don't dismiss your opinions. Just be prepared to defend them with good reasoning. Think of opinions as starting points for arguments.

PREMISES AND CONCLUSIONS

The structure of all arguments, no matter what the subject, consists of two components: premises and conclusions. The **conclusion** is the key assertion that the other assertions support. These other assertions are the **premises**, reasons that support the conclusion. For example:

> Because gambling casinos pay a significant amount of taxes, Indian tribes should be allowed to build as many as they want on their land.

In this example, the conclusion—that Indian tribes should be allowed to build as many [gambling casinos] as they want on their land—is supported by one premise: gambling casinos pay a significant amount of taxes.

For a group of assertions to be an argument, the passage must contain both these elements—**a conclusion and at least one premise**.

Now look at the same argument with an additional premise added:

> Because gambling casinos pay a significant amount of taxes and provide employment for unskilled workers, Indian tribes should be allowed to build as many as they want on their land.

Which argument do you think is stronger?

Now look at the following letter to the editor of a news magazine:

> I was horrified to read "Corporate Mind Control" and learn that some companies are training employees in New Age thinking, which is a blend of the occult, Eastern religions, and a smattering of Christianity. What they're dealing with is dangerous—Krone Training will be disastrous to the company and the employee.

This writer thinks that she has written an argument against Krone Training, but her letter consists of a conclusion only, which is in essence that Krone Training is not a good idea. Because she fails to include any premises in support of her conclusion, she fails to present an argument and fails to convince anyone who did not already share her belief that Krone Training is "dangerous" and "disastrous." A conclusion repeated in different words may look like an argument but shouldn't deceive a careful reader. (See the fallacy of Begging the Question in Chapter 6.) Can you formulate a premise that would transform the letter into an argument?

DISTINGUISHING BETWEEN PREMISES AND CONCLUSIONS

In order to evaluate the strength of an argument, we need to understand its structure, to distinguish between its premises and conclusion. **Joining words**—conjunctions and transitional words and phrases—indicate logical relationships between ideas and therefore often help us to make this distinction. Notice the radical change in meaning that results from the reversal of two clauses joined by the conjunction "because":

> I didn't drink because I had problems. I had problems because I drank.

The use of joining words in argument is especially important because they indicate which assertions are being offered as premises and which are offered as conclusions. For example:

> Instead of building another bridge across the bay to alleviate traffic congestion, we should develop a ferry system *because* such a system would decrease air pollution as well as traffic congestion.

> A ferry system would decrease air pollution as well as traffic congestion, *so* we should develop a ferry system rather than build another bridge.

In the first example, "because" indicates a premise, a reason in support of the conclusion that creating a ferry system makes more sense than building a bridge. In the second example, "so" indicates the conclusion. Both statements present essentially the same argument; the difference between the two sentences is rhetorical—a matter of style, not substance.

"Because" and "since" frequently introduce premises.

"So," "therefore," "thus," "hence," and "consequently" often introduce conclusions.

conclusion because *premise*

premise therefore *conclusion*

Note: "and" often connects premises.

Joining words are essential for conveying a logical sequence of thought. If logical connections are missing, the reader cannot follow the line of reasoning and either stops reading or supplies his own connections, which may not be the ones intended.

EXERCISE 3A

Joining Sentences for Logic and Fluency

Make this disjointed argument cohesive and logical by joining sentences with appropriate joining words. You don't need to change the sequence of sentences.

> Obstetricians perform too many Cesareans. They can schedule deliveries for their own convenience. They can avoid sleepless nights and canceled parties. They resort to Cesareans in any difficult delivery to protect themselves against malpractice suits. Cesareans involve larger fees and hospital bills than normal deliveries. Cesarean patients spend about twice as many days in the hospital as other mothers. The National Institutes of Health confirmed that doctors were performing many unnecessary Cesarean sections. They suggested ways to reduce their use. The recommendation was widely publicized. The obstetricians apparently failed to take note. In the 1980s, the operation was performed in 16.5 percent of U.S. births. In the 1990s, 24.7 percent of the births were Cesareans. The Caesarean rate has risen 48 percent since 1996. It reached a level of 31.8 percent in 2007. A 2008 report found that fully one-third of babies born in Massachusetts in 2006 were delivered by Caesarean sections.

STANDARD FORM

With the help of joining words and transitional phrases, we can analyze the structure of an argument and then put it into **standard form**. An argument in standard form is an argument reduced to its essence: its premises and conclusion. In other words, it is an outline of the argument. In the previous argument on Indian gambling casinos, each premise is indicated by the "because" that introduces it, the conclusion then following from these two premises. In standard form, the argument looks like this:

Premise 1 Gambling casinos pay a significant amount of taxes.

Premise 2 Gambling casinos provide employment for unskilled workers.

∴ Indian tribes should be allowed to build as many casinos as they want on their land.

Note: ∴ is a symbol in logic meaning "therefore."

Read this argument about college grading policies by Clifford Adelman, a senior research analyst with the Department of Education.

> If there are 50 ways to leave your lover, there are almost as many ways to walk away from a college course without penalty. What are prospective employers to make of the following "grades" that I have seen on transcripts: W, WP, WI, WX, WM, WW, K, L, Q, X and Z. What does "Z" mean? "The student 'zeed out,'" one

registrar told me. At another institution, I was told that it stood for "zapped." Despite the zap, I was informed, there was no penalty.

But there is a penalty. The time students lose by withdrawing is time they must recoup. All they have done is increase the cost of school to themselves, their families and, if at a public institution, to taxpayers.

This increasing volume of withdrawals and repeats does not bode well for students' future behavior in the workplace, where repeating tasks is costly. Many employers agree that work habits and time-management skills are as important as the knowledge new employees bring. It wouldn't take much for schools to change their grading policies so that students would have to finish what they start.

Though this argument is three paragraphs long, in standard form it can be reduced to four sentences:

Premise 1 The time students lose by withdrawing is time they must recoup.

Premise 2 They increase the cost of school to themselves, their families, and, if at a public institution, to taxpayers.

Premise 3 Work habits and time-management skills are as important as the knowledge new employees bring to the workplace.

∴ **Schools should change their grading policies so that students would have to finish what they start.**

The first paragraph provides the reader with necessary background information because the writer can't assume that his readers will know the specifics of current college grading policies. The second paragraph contains two of his three premises, while the final paragraph contains his third premise (and development of that premise) and his conclusion.

The conclusion of this argument—that schools should change their grading policy—is an inference, a judgment. Indeed, all conclusions are inferences. If they were facts, we would not need to supply premises to support them; we would simply verify them by checking the source. In this argument, the first two premises are factual and the third is an inference; one that, on the basis of experience, most of us would be inclined to accept.

Examine the following argument:

Baseball fans have long argued that the city should build a downtown baseball stadium. If the city doesn't build a new stadium, the team may leave, and a major city deserves a major league team. Furthermore, downtown's weather is superior to the weather at the present site, and public transportation to downtown would make the park more accessible.

In this example, four separate premises are offered for the conclusion.

Premise 1 If the city doesn't build a new stadium, the team may leave.

Premise 2 A major city deserves a major league team.

Premise 3 Downtown's weather is superior to the weather of the present site.

Premise 4 Public transportation to downtown would make the park more accessible.

∴ **The city should build a downtown baseball stadium.**

EXERCISE 3B

Reducing Simple Arguments to Standard Form

Put each of the following arguments into standard form by first underlining the joining words and transitional phrases, then identifying the conclusion, and finally identifying the premises. List the premises, numbering each separate statement, and write the conclusion using the symbol ∴. Leave out the joining words and phrases, because standard form identifies premises and conclusions, but write each premise and the conclusion as a complete sentence.

> *Example:* All politicians make promises they can't keep, <u>and</u> Jerry is nothing if not a politician. He will, <u>therefore</u>, make promises he can't keep.
>
> 1. All politicians make promises they can't keep.
> 2. Jerry is a politician.
> ∴ He will make promises he can't keep.

1. Because fast food restaurants contribute to the obesity epidemic in this country, they should be required to post the calorie count for their food on the menu.

2. Because donors to presidential campaigns wield too much influence over their candidates and because political ads on television are too costly, presidential campaigns for the major candidates should be financed by the government.

3. The student union building is ugly and uncomfortable. The preponderance of cement makes the building appear cold and gray both inside and out. Many of the rooms lack windows, so that one is left staring at the cement wall. The chairs are generally cheap and uncomfortable, while the poor lighting makes studying difficult, and the terrible acoustics make conversation almost impossible.

4. Abortion raises important moral questions, for abortion involves both a woman's right to privacy and the question of when life begins, and anything that involves personal rights and the onset of life raises serious moral questions.

5. Many biologists and physicians argue that life does not begin at conception. And the Supreme Court ruled in 1973 that to restrict a woman's right to have an abortion violates her right to privacy. These two facts lead us to believe that abortion should remain a woman's choice.

6. Capital punishment is not justified, since with capital punishment, an innocent person might be executed, and no practice that might kill innocent people is justified.

7. Because some killers are beyond rehabilitation, society should have the right to execute those convicted of first-degree murder. More uniform implementation of the death penalty may serve as a deterrent, and victims' families are entitled to retribution. Furthermore, the costs of maintaining a prisoner for life are too great, and no state guarantees that life imprisonment means no parole.

8. In his celebrated work *On Liberty*, a defense of freedom of speech, John Stuart Mill argues that "power can be rightfully exercised over any member of a civilized community" only to "prevent harm to others." Because he maintains that no opinion, no matter how disagreeable, can inflict harm, it follows that we don't have the right to suppress opinion.

9. Every major airport should install and use full body scans for all passengers. These scans reveal weapons and bombs hidden by clothing. The privacy of the individual must take a back seat to making air travel safe for everyone, and the images are ghost-like, not explicit. Also, anyone can demand a full body patdown in place of the full body scan.

10. The Pope should allow priests to marry. Currently in the United States there is one priest for every 1,400 Catholics, and the average age of this one priest is 60. The Church needs more priests, and surely more young men would join the priesthood if celibacy were not required. And a majority of American Catholics are in favor of allowing priests to marry. In fact, before the 11th century, priests and popes did marry.

WRITING ASSIGNMENT 5

Creating a Political Handout

The following handout urges Californians to vote "No" on Proposition 174. This proposition (like other school voucher initiatives) would require the state to give parents vouchers to apply to their children's tuition if they choose private schools over public. This issue is debated at the national level as well. As you will recognize, the content of this handout is essentially an argument in standard form: premises in support of a conclusion. Each premise is then developed and supported by a sentence or two.

After evaluating the effectiveness of this handout, create one of your own in support of or in opposition to a current political issue, on campus or off. Pay special attention to the format and visual appeal of your document. Your computer program may allow you to add graphics to your design.

Five *Good* Reasons to Oppose the Vouchers Initiative

It provides no accountability.

- Though they would receive taxpayer dollars, the private and religious schools would be wholly unaccountable to the taxpayers—or to anyone other than their owners. Anyone who could recruit just 25 youngsters could open a "school." It would not need to be accredited, to hire credentialed teachers, or to meet the curriculum, health, and safety standards governing the public schools.

It undermines "neighborhood" schools, making large tax hikes likely.

- The initiative would strip our public schools of 10 percent of their funding—even if not one student transferred to a private or religious school—to give vouchers to students currently in nonpublic schools. Either the public schools would be devastated—or hefty tax increases would be needed . . . not to improve education in the public schools, but to pay for subsidizing private, religious, and cult schools.

It permits discrimination.

- Private and religious schools could refuse admission to youngsters because of their religion, gender, IQ, family income or ability to pay, disability, or any of dozens of other factors. In fact, they wouldn't even have to state a reason for rejecting a child.

It transfers taxpayer money to the rich.

- Rich parents already paying $10,000 to $15,000 or more in private school tuition would now gain $2,600 from the vouchers—a form of "Robin Hood in reverse."

It abandons public school students.

- The children left behind, in the public schools, would sit in classrooms that were even more crowded—and that had even less money, per student, for textbooks, science equipment, and other materials and supplies.

Vote No on Prop. 174
California Teachers Association/NEA • 1705 Murchison Drive • Burlingame, CA 94010

AMBIGUOUS ARGUMENT STRUCTURE

Sometimes the precise direction of an argument seems ambiguous; what is offered as a conclusion and what is meant as a supporting premise can be unclear. In such cases, it is important to look for what is most reasonable to believe, to give **the benefit of the doubt**. Try each assertion as the conclusion and see if the premises provide logical support for it, beginning with what seems most likely to be the intended conclusion.

Closely allied with the benefit of the doubt is the ancient principle known as **Occam's razor**. Named for William of Occam, a 14th-century European philosopher, this principle advocates economy in argument. As William of Occam put it, "What can be done with fewer assumptions is done in vain with more." In other words, the simplest line of reasoning is usually the best. Newspaper columnist Jon Carroll invoked Occam's razor when commenting on a sensational murder trial: "I am not a juror; I am not required to maintain the presumption of innocence. I used Occam's razor, a tool that has served me well before. The simplest explanation is usually the true one; if a wife is killed, look to the husband."

Medicine, too, follows this principle, as Dr. Lisa Sanders tells us in *Diagnosis*, a *New York Times Magazine* column:

> . . . you should strive to come up with the simplest possible explanation for the phenomena you observe. In medicine, that means we try to find a single diagnosis to explain all that we see in a patient. Occam's razor, it's called—the art of shaving the diagnosis to the simplest most elegant solution.

EXERCISE 3C

Reducing an Editorial to Standard Form

Put the argument presented in the following editorial into standard form.

Solves Surplus Problem

To The Editor:

At last, someone else—Elizabeth Joseph (Op-Ed, May 23)—has put into words what I have been silently thinking for some time: Polygamy makes good sense.

Ms. Joseph writes from the perspective of a wife. I write from the perspective of a divorced working mother. How much more advantageous it would be for me to be part of a household such as Ms. Joseph describes, rather than to be juggling my many roles alone.

If polygamy were legal, the problem—and I see it as a problem—of the surplus of extra women would disappear rapidly. No matter how many polemics there may be in favor of the free and single life-style, a divorced woman can feel extra in today's society, more so if she has children, which can isolate her from a full social life. How much easier to share the burdens—and the jobs.

When more women can rediscover the joys of sisterhood and co-wifehood (which are as old as the Bible), and overcome residual jealousy as a response to this type of situation, I think our society will have advanced considerably.

Frieda Brodsky
Brooklyn, New York

HIDDEN ASSUMPTIONS IN ARGUMENT

Many real-life arguments come to us incomplete, depending on **hidden assumptions**, unstated premises and conclusions. Sometimes a missing premise or conclusion is so obvious that we don't even recognize that it is unstated.

Ken is lazy, and lazy people don't last long around here. [Missing conclusion: Ken won't last long around here.]
Since I've sworn to put up with my tired Honda until I can afford a BMW, I must resign myself to the old wreck for a while longer. [Missing premise: I can't afford a BMW now.]
The senator is a Republican, so he is opposed to gun control. [Missing premise: Republicans are opposed to gun control.]

Filling in the omitted assumptions here would seem unnecessarily pedantic or even insulting to our intelligence.

Literature, by its nature elliptical, depends on the reader to make plausible assumptions:

Yon Cassius has a lean and hungry look; such men are dangerous.

—SHAKESPEARE, *JULIUS CAESAR*

Shakespeare assumes his audience will automatically make the connection—Cassius is a dangerous man. But not all missing assumptions are as obvious or as acceptable. At the heart of critical thinking lies the ability to discern what a writer or speaker leaves **implicit**—unsaid—between the lines of what he has made **explicit**—what he has clearly stated.

Dear Abby's readers took her to task for a response she made to a man who complained that because he shared an apartment with a man, people thought he was gay. She called this rumor an "ugly accusation." The implicit assumption here is that homosexuality is ugly, an assumption many of her readers—both gay and straight—objected to. One reader asked, "If someone thought this man was Jewish, Catholic or African American—would you call that an 'ugly accusation'?" Dear Abby apologized.

During the 2008 presidential race, when a McCain supporter yelled that she didn't trust Obama because "he's an Arab," Senator McCain corrected the woman: "No, ma'am. He's a decent family man, citizen." What is the hidden assumption here? In fairness to the Senator, we assume this was a misstatement rather than his belief.

A new kind of therapy called philosophical counseling is based on the belief that many personal problems stem from faulty logic, from irrational assumptions. One practitioner of this therapy, Elliot D. Cohen, gives as an example of such faulty reasoning the assumption that one should demand perfection from oneself and others. He teaches his clients critical thinking skills so that they can identify and correct such damaging assumptions.

Law professor Patricia J. Williams, in *The Alchemy of Race and Rights*, examines the implicit assumptions that led to the death of a young black man in New York. In this incident, three young black men left their stalled car in Queens and walked to Howard Beach looking for help, where they were surrounded by eight white teenagers who taunted them with racial epithets and chased them for approximately three miles, beating them severely along the way. One of the black men died, struck by a car as he tried to flee across a highway; another suffered permanent blindness in one eye.

During the course of the resultant trial, the community of Howard Beach supported the white teenagers, asking, "What were they [the three black teenagers] doing here in the first place?" Examining this question, Williams finds six underlying assumptions:

Everyone who lives here is white.

No black could live here.

No one here has a black friend.

No white would employ a black here.

No black is permitted to shop here.

No black is ever up to any good.

These assumptions reveal the racism that led the white teenagers to behave as they did and the community to defend their brutality.

Dangers of Hidden Assumptions

Examine this seemingly straightforward argument:

John is Lisa's father, so clearly he is obligated to support her.

What's missing here? The premise that all fathers are obligated to support their daughters (or their children) is omitted. But would everyone find this premise acceptable under all conditions? Probably not. What about the age factor? Is Lisa over 21? What about special circumstances: Lisa's mother has ample means while John is penniless and terminally ill? Or Lisa was legally adopted by another family, John being her birth father?

The danger with such incomplete arguments lies in more than one direction. A writer may leave his readers to supply their own assumptions, which may or may not coincide with those of the writer. If the issue is controversial, the risks of distorting an argument increase. Or, writers may deliberately conceal assumptions to hide an unsound, often misleading argument. Watch for these in advertising and politics. If you are on the alert for such deceptions, you are better able to evaluate what you read and hear and thus protect your own interests.

Some politicians are in favor of privatizing Social Security. They argue that individuals should have the right to invest their own retirement savings. But this argument is based on the following unstated assumptions—that everyone has the necessary knowledge to invest successfully in the stock market and that the stock market will perform well for each individual when he or she reaches retirement age. How realistic are these assumptions?

Hidden Assumptions and Standard Form

To help sort out the stated and unstated assertions in an argument, it can be illuminating to write out the argument in standard form. This means including the important hidden assumptions so the complete argument is before you and putting brackets around these assumptions to distinguish them from stated premises and conclusions.

Examples:

1. Harold is a politician, so he's looking out for himself.
   a. [All politicians look out for themselves.]
   b. Harold is a politician.
   ∴ Harold is looking out for himself.

2. Products made from natural ingredients promote good health, so you should buy brand X breads.
   a. Products made from natural ingredients promote good health.
   b. [Brand X breads are made from natural ingredients.]
   ∴ You should buy brand X breads.

3. Products made from natural ingredients promote good health, and brand X breads are made from natural ingredients.
   a. Products made from natural ingredients promote good health.
   b. Brand X breads are made from natural ingredients.
   ∴ [You should buy brand X breads.]

EXERCISE 3D

Identifying Hidden Assumptions

A. The following arguments are missing either a premise or a conclusion. Put them into standard form, adding the implicit premise or conclusion; then place brackets around the missing assumptions you have inserted. A word to the wise: as with all argument analysis, **find the conclusion first and then look for what is offered in its support**.

1. Maggie is a musician, so she won't understand the business end of the partnership.

2. Those who exercise regularly increase their chances of living into old age, so we can expect to see Anna around for a very long time.

3. I never see Sophie without a book; she must be highly intelligent.

4. Those who buy stock on margin lose their money eventually. Yet that is what Sam is doing.

5. That is not a star because it gives steady light.

6. The Western industrialized nations will resolve the energy crisis if they mobilize all the technological resources at their disposal. If financial incentives are sufficiently high, then the mobilization of resources will occur. The skyrocketing cost of energy—as a result of increased oil prices—has produced just such sufficiently high financial incentives. The conclusion is clear.

7. "Most professional athletes don't have a college degree and so have no idea how to handle the big salaries suddenly dumped in their laps." (Harry Edwards, college professor and financial consultant for professional athletes)

8. Having become so central a part of our culture, reality television shows cannot be without their redeeming features.

9. **CONVICTED:** U.S. Petty Officer 3/c Mitchell T. Garraway, Jr., of premeditated murder in the stabbing of a superior officer. The military court must now decide his sentence; its options include the death penalty. The last execution carried out by the Navy took place in 1849. (*Newsweek*)

10. From a letter to the *Sacramento Bee* after an article reporting that a nursing mother had been evicted from a downtown department store cafeteria:

    It was inhumane to deny this woman the right to nurse her baby in the cafeteria because she was simply performing a natural bodily function.

    Where will this argument take you once you supply the suppressed assumption?

B. Look closely at the following two cartoons from the *New Yorker* magazine archives. What do they suggest about relationships between men and women in the workplace in the 1950s? What hidden assumptions are they based on?

1998 12 07 144 RTA .HG Months

"Three more months and he reaches mandatory retirement age, thank God."

"Notice, class, how Angela circles, always keeping the desk between them. . ."

Now look at the following recent cartoon. What unstated assumptions about relationships between men and women are suggested here?

A SUCCESSFUL WEDDING PARTY
RETURNS FROM THE HUNT

Hidden Assumptions and Audience Awareness

Politicians and advertisers may deliberately suppress assumptions in order to manipulate the public. We will assume that we, as careful writers, do not share this goal and would not deliberately leave important assumptions unstated. At the same time, we don't want to bore our readers by spelling out unnecessary details. How do we determine what material to include, what to leave out?

George Lakoff and Mark Johnson, in their book *Metaphors We Live By*, point out that meaning is often dependent on context. They offer the following sentence as an example:

We need new sources of energy.

This assertion means one thing to a group of oil executives and quite another to an environmental group. The executives may assume the writer is referring to more offshore drilling, whereas the environmentalists may think the writer is referring to greater development of solar or other alternate sources of energy.

As writers, we must consider our audience carefully and understand the purpose for which we are writing. We make choices about which assumptions must be made explicit according to our knowledge of the reader. Are we writing for an audience predisposed to agree with us or for one that is opposed to our point of view? Are we writing for readers who are knowledgeable about the subject or ignorant? The answers to these questions help us to determine what material to include and what to omit.

EXERCISE 3E

Responding to an Opinion Piece

Choose an opinion piece from one of the following: salon.com, slate.com, huffington-post.com, nytimes.com, politico.com, wsj.com, dailybeast.com, or a similar website you are familiar with which presents controversial topics. Reduce it to standard form, supplying any hidden assumptions you may find (put brackets around these), and then write a brief (a paragraph or two) response expressing your reaction to the piece.

SUMMARIES

Standard form is a simplified method of outlining and thus summarizing arguments. Another way to explore an argument and reveal the important premises leading to a conclusion is to write out a **summary**.

Educator Mike Rose sees summarizing as an essential writing skill: "I [can't] imagine a more crucial skill than summarizing; we can't manage information, make crisp connections, or rebut arguments without it. The great syntheses and refutations are built on it."

Professor Gerald Graff of the University of Illinois claims that **summarizing** is an important feature of successful students' strategies.

An Argument Worth Having
BY GERALD GRAFF

Freshmen are often overwhelmed by the intellectual challenge of college—so many   1
subjects to be covered, so many facts, methods and philosophical isms to sort out,
so many big words to assimilate. As if that weren't enough, what your different
instructors tell you may be flatly contradictory.

Students understandably cope with this cognitive dissonance by giving each of   2
their teachers in turn whatever he or she seems to want. Students learn to be free-
market capitalists in one course and socialists in the next, universalists in the morning
and relativists after lunch. This tactic has got many a student through college, but the
trouble is that, even when each course is excellent in itself, jumping through a series
of hoops doesn't add up to a real socialization into the ways of an intellectual culture.

What the most successful college students do, in my experience, is cut through   3
the clutter of jargons, methods and ideological differences to locate the common

practices of argument and analysis hidden behind it all. Contrary to the cliché that no "one size fits all" educational recipe is possible, successful academics of all fields and intellectual persuasion make some key moves that you can emulate:

1. Recognize that knowing a lot of stuff won't do you much good unless you can do something with what you know by **turning it into an argument**.
2. Pay close attention to what others are saying and writing and then **summarize** their arguments and assumptions in a recognizable way. Work especially on summarizing the views that go most against your own.
3. As you **summarize**, look not only for the thesis of an argument, but for who or what provoked it—the points of controversy.
4. Use these **summaries** to motivate what you say and to indicate why it needs saying. Don't be afraid to give your own opinion, especially if you can back it up with reasons and evidence, but don't disagree with anything without **carefully summarizing** it first.

It's too often a secret that only a minority of high achievers figure out, but the better you get at entering the conversation by summarizing or putting in your own oar, the more you'll get out of your college education.

Summaries come in many lengths, from one sentence to several pages, depending on the purpose of the summary and the length of the piece to be summarized. Note, for example, the brief summaries at the conclusion of each chapter in this text.

A good summary is both **complete** and **concise**. To meet these conflicting goals, you must convey the essence of the whole piece without copying whole passages verbatim or emphasizing inappropriate features of the argument. Background information, detailed premise support, and narrative illustrations are usually omitted from summaries. Paraphrases of ideas, rather than direct quotations, are preferred (except for a critically important phrase or two). A summary should also be **objective**, excluding inferences and opinions. These are reserved for argument analysis.

Strategies for Writing a Summary

1. Read the piece you are to summarize carefully to determine the writer's main point or conclusion. Write this conclusion **in your own words**.
2. Write a sentence expressing the most important point(s) in each paragraph **in your own words**.
3. Write a first draft by combining the conclusion with your one-sentence summaries of each paragraph, **making sure the beginning of the summary includes the title and author of the piece**.
4. Edit your draft by eliminating repetition and any details that are not **essential** to the writer's argument. If you decide to include a significant sentence or phrase from the original, use quotation marks.
5. Check this edited draft against the piece being summarized to make sure you haven't overlooked an important idea or included an opinion of your own.
6. Revise for coherence by combining sentences and inserting transitional phrases where necessary. Edit for conciseness by eliminating all "deadwood" (unnecessary words) from your sentences. Check grammar and spelling.

An Example of a Summary

Following the steps outlined above, we have summarized "Could It Be That Video Games Are Good for Kids?" an editorial included in Chapter 4, page 88.

> Steven Johnson in his editorial "Could It Be That Video Games Are Good for Kids?" argues that children are not negatively affected by playing video games. In fact, he believes high school football encourages more violent thoughts and behavior than video games. As for explicit sexual content, Johnson recommends appropriate ratings.
>
> He contends that children have always played games and most children are not giving up reading the classics to do so. He also maintains that video games are much more challenging than traditional board games. Video games "force kids to learn complex rule systems, master challenging new interfaces, follow dozens of shifting variables in real time and prioritize between multiple objectives," all skills that will prove useful in the workplace. Johnson also points out that teenagers are watching fewer televised sporting events and that playing video games is more demanding than passively watching television.
>
> Violent games are plentiful, but kids today are less violent than in the past, according to Duke University's Child Well-Being Index—a fact that suggests that these games act as a safety valve. And SAT scores are improving as well. Johnson does concede that children don't get exercise when playing video games and that the rising obesity among children is a serious problem.

In this summary, the 16 paragraphs of the original have been reduced to three paragraphs that reflect the **essence** of the original. If summarizing for note-taking purposes only, you may want to limit yourself to steps 1 and 2 of the summary strategies listed above.

> Summaries should be objective, concise, complete, and coherent, and written in your own words.

WRITING ASSIGNMENT 6

Summarizing an Article

Read the following essay by high school senior Nathan Yan carefully, and write a summary of the article. You may want to compare summaries with classmates.

AP Courses—Mounting Burden, Declining Benefit

NATHAN YAN

For many high school juniors and seniors, this school year has been the year of   1
the AP, a nonstop rush of drills, flash cards and night-before cramming. In every
advanced placement class, students devote an immense effort to studying for these
tests; they buy prep books, stay excessive hours after school and spend a dispro-
portionate amount of time on AP over their regular classes.

As one of many AP students, I've experienced the madness myself. Perhaps it is   2
part of our natures, as "top tier" students dedicated to success, but at its core, the
work ethic of the majority of AP students represents an unhealthy obsession with
the AP test.

The AP tests are nationwide standardized tests administered by the private   3
College Board Association. Successfully passing an AP test will count toward college
credit and, depending on the college or university, may grant exemptions from
certain general education courses. For many high schools it represents the highest
class level for students taking a particular course.

While preparing for AP tests is not so much of a problem, the issue for almost   4
any AP student is that their focus on passing the test takes precedence over the
subject matter of the course. Students spend days and days practicing how to manage their time on the essay prompts, and learning the grading process that AP scor-
ers use, and listening endlessly to the useless "guessing is good if you can eliminate
one answer choice" rubbish. Interest in understanding the actual subject takes a
backseat, and worst of all, confined by the College Board defined AP curriculum,
teachers are stripped of the power to direct the AP crazed students toward actual
subject comprehension. School administrators, with their "pass the AP" mandate,
are about as inclined to teach the subjects as students are to learn it.

All of the time wasted and knowledge lost in studying for the AP test aside, if   5
a student actually needed night time and weekend study sessions, third party prep
books and a specialized class *just to pass a test*, one must wonder if passing the AP
exam really means anything. Those who have immersed themselves in this AP trap of
test drills and endless study are fooling themselves into a false sense of security that a
score of 3 or 4 or 5 on some AP test means that they're "smart," that they can get into
a University of California campus, that they're ready for the University of California.

As for teachers, have they blindly accepted this "pass the AP" mantra as simply   6
part of the job description? Any teacher who has ever taught an AP class knows
every hour wasted on explaining how AP graders score essays is an hour that could
have been used to educate students on something of real substance. Every AP
teacher knows that the AP syllabus, mandating what must be taught, restricts the
teachers' freedom in what the class can learn. Despite this, teachers seem willing to
approach the standard AP formula as simply another quirk in the education system
that must somehow be accommodated.

As students, we shouldn't buy into this "failing AP equals Apocalypse" para-   7
noia, this "Oh my God, this AP seems so hard and if I fail I've got no future, I've
got to do everything humanly possible to prepare for it!" This is what puts us into
a black-or-white, "will this help me on the AP or not?" perspective that distracts
us from real education. We don't need AP prep books or daily after-school study
sessions, and if any students still feel they do, they need to reassess their ability to
handle an AP course.

Teachers, similarly, need to realize that they don't need to gear their classes   8
to training for a test; teaching it like any other non-AP class, they will discover that
those students who understand the material will be able to pass it, and others will
not, simply because they're either lazy or unable to grasp the subject. Both teachers and the administration need to realize that a student will never fail an AP test for
a lack of test preparation.

Maybe the best solution, then, is to completely drop the college credits and the AP test itself, thereby eliminating all the competitive pressure and failure anxieties of today's AP courses. We would return classroom autonomy to the teachers, and, with a de-emphasis on competition and achieving a good score "on paper," the administration, teachers and, most especially, the students can get back to an environment where we're more concerned with learning about a subject, rather than learning how to pass a test on the subject. 9

ARGUMENT AND EXPLANATION—DISTINCTIONS

As you elaborate support for premises in written argument, you often rely on explanation—of terminology, of background, of your reasoning—but you must not lose sight of your purpose, which is to persuade your reader of the wisdom of your position.

In **argument**, you present reasons for your conclusion in order to convince someone of your point of view.

In **explanation**, on the other hand, you are clarifying what has happened, why something has happened, who someone is, giving a context to your argument. Look at these examples:

Don't go to that market because it's closed for renovation.

Don't go to that market because the prices are higher than anywhere else and the checkout lines are slow.

In the first example, we are given an explanation of why the market is closed. In the second, we are given two reasons, two premises, for not shopping at that market— it's too expensive and the checkers are slow. This is an argument.

This distinction between explanation and argument may play a crucial role in your understanding of specific writing assignments and save you wasted effort on a false start. Is the instructor asking for an explanation, information on a particular subject, or is he asking you to write an argument, to take and support a position? The following exercise should help to clarify further this important distinction.

EXERCISE 3F

Distinguishing Arguments from Explanations

The following two pieces both address evolution, the first written by a journalist, Elizabeth Bumiller, the second by a professor and former veterinarian, Lisa Fullam. One presents an argument while the other offers an explanation. Read them both carefully and decide which is which. Keep in mind that the writer of an argument **takes a position** and attempts to persuade the reader of the rightness of that position. Explain your answer with references to specific passages in both pieces. (Note that paragraphs are numbered for easy reference.) You may want to discuss your answer with other students in your class.

You'll note that both pieces were written when George Bush was still president, but the issue is very much alive today, with some states ruling that high school biology texts must contain both evolution and intelligent design.

Bush Remarks Roil Debate over Teaching of Evolution
ELIZABETH BUMILLER

A sharp debate between scientists and religious conservatives escalated Tuesday 1
over comments by [former] President Bush that the theory of intelligent design should be taught with evolution in the nation's public schools.

In an interview at the White House on Monday with a group of Texas newspa- 2
per reporters, Mr. Bush appeared to endorse the push by many of his conservative Christian supporters to give intelligent design equal treatment with the theory of evolution. Recalling his days as Texas governor, Mr. Bush said in the interview, according to a transcript, "I felt like both sides ought to be properly taught." Asked again by a reporter whether he believed that both sides in the debate between evolution and intelligent design should be taught in the schools, Mr. Bush replied that he did, "so people can understand what the debate is about." . . .

On Tuesday, the president's conservative Christian supporters and the leading 3
institute advancing intelligent design embraced Mr. Bush's comments while scientists and advocates of the separation of church and state disparaged them. At the White House, where intelligent design has been discussed in a weekly bible study group, Mr. Bush's science adviser, John H. Marburger 3rd, sought to play down the president's remarks as common sense and old news. . . .

Intelligent design, advanced by a group of academics and intellectuals and 4
some biblical creationists, disputes the idea that natural selection—the force Charles Darwin suggested drove evolution—fully explains the complexity of life. Instead, intelligent design proponents say that life is so intricate that only a powerful guiding force, or intelligent designer, could have created it.

Intelligent design does not identify the designer, but critics say the theory is a 5
thinly disguised argument for God and the divine creation of the universe. Invigorated by a recent push by conservatives, the theory has been gaining support in school districts in 20 states with Kansas in the lead. . . .

Of God and the Case for Unintelligent Design
LISA FULLAM

As the theory of intelligent design again hits the news with [former] President 1
Bush's encouragement this week that the theory be taught in schools alongside evolution, I have one question: What about unintelligent design?

Take rabbit digestion, for example. As herbivores, rabbits need help from bac- 2
teria to break down the cell walls of the plants they eat, so, cleverly enough, they have a large section of intestine where such bacterial fermentation takes place.

The catch is, it's at the far end of the small intestine, beyond where efficient absorption of nutrients can happen. A sensible system—as we see in ruminant animals like cattle and deer—ferments before the small intestine, maximizing nutrient absorption. Rabbits, having to make do with an unintelligent system, instead eat some of their own feces after one trip through, sending half-digested food back through the small intestine for re-digestion.

Horses are similarly badly put together: They ferment their food in a large, blind-ended cecum after the small intestine. Unlike rabbits, they don't recycle their feces—they're just inefficient. Moreover, those big sections of hind gut are a frequent location for gut blockages and twists that, absent prompt veterinary intervention, lead to slow and excruciating death for the poor horse. The psalmist writes: "God takes no delight in horses' power." Clearly, if God works in creation according to the simplistic schemes of the intelligent design folks, God not only doesn't delight in horses, but seems positively to have it in for them. 3

Furthermore, why wouldn't an intelligent designer make it possible for animals to digest their natural food without playing host to huge populations of bacteria in the first place: Couldn't mammals have been equipped with their own enzymes to do the job? 4

But that's not all: Consider mammalian testicles. In order to function optimally, they need to be slightly cooler than the rest of the body and so are carried outside the body wall in the scrotum. Why would one carry one's whole genetic potential in such a vulnerable position? Clearly it's not a gonad problem in general—ovaries work just fine at body temperature and are snuggled safely within the pelvic girdle for protection. But for testicles, nope—the scrotum is jerry-rigged to allow for a warm-blooded animal to keep his testicles cool. Surely an intelligent designer could have figured out a way for testicles to work at body temperature, as ovaries do. 5

Here's another: Do you know anyone beyond the age of 20 or so who has not had a backache? Let's face it: The human body is that of a quadruped tipped up on end to walk on only two legs. The delicate and beautiful cantilever curve of the human spine compensates (but not enough) for the odd stresses that result from our unusual posture. Perhaps the God of intelligent design has a special place in his plan for chiropractors? And what about the knee? Between the secure ball-and-socket of the hip and the omnidirectional versatility of the ankle is a simple hinge joint, held together only by ligaments (including the anterior cruciate ligament) whose names are known to athletes and sports fans because they're so easily and frequently injured. Again, unintelligent design. 6

The real problem with intelligent design is that it fails to account for the obvious anatomical and physiological making-do that is evident of so much of the natural world. Evolutionarily minded folks see this as the result of genetic limitations and adaptations accumulated in specialization for certain environments, while the intelligent design folks are left with a designer who clearly cannot have been paying close attention. 7

While there are extremely precise and fine-tuned mechanisms in nature, there is also lots of evidence of organisms just cobbled together. For instance, take marsupials, who give birth to what in other animals are analogous to fetuses, then have to carry them around in what amounts to an exterior uterus until the offspring are ready to face the world. 8

As a theist who sees natural evolution not as a theory but as well-established   9
observation, I take comfort in the catch-as-catch-can of the natural world. I have
every confidence that an all-loving creator walks in and with the natural world as
it struggles to fruition, cheering on our evolutionary triumphs (let's hear it for the
opposable thumb!) and standing in solidarity with the evolutionary misfits and misfires, like rabbit guts and horses generally.

Isn't this how God walks in and with us in our individual lives as well, cheering   10
us on, emboldening us and consoling us in our often misguided attempts to live
well and do right, and standing in compassion and solidarity with us when we fail,
and loving us into trying again? And isn't this a more compelling vision of God,
and truer to the biblical God who comes again and again to offer salvation to err-
ing humankind, than that of a designer who can't quite seem to get things right?

SUMMARY

In logic, the word **argument** has a special meaning, referring to rational discourse composed of **premises** and a **conclusion** rather than to a fight. It is useful to be able to recognize premises and conclusions in order to fully understand
what an argument is proposing. Expressing arguments in **standard form** is a
helpful strategy for understanding arguments.

Arguments are frequently presented with some of the premises or the conclusion implied rather than stated. Sometimes such **hidden assumptions** are
obvious, but in other instances they can be misleading and need to be made
explicit. Recognizing hidden assumptions in argument is an important part of
critical thinking.

Writing a **summary** is a good way to explore an argument and reveal the
important premises leading to a conclusion.

The distinction between **argument** and **explanation** may play a role in
your understanding of specific writing assignments. In argument, you present
reasons for your conclusion in order to convince someone of your point of view.
In explanation, you are clarifying what and why something has happened.

KEY TERMS

Argument   a rational piece of discourse, written or spoken, which attempts to persuade the reader or listener to believe something; composed of at least one premise
in support of a conclusion.

Conclusion   the key assertion in an argument, the statement that the other assertions support; the point one hopes to make when presenting an argument.

Explanation   an attempt to clarify why something has happened or why you hold a given opinion.

Hidden assumptions   missing, unstated premises and conclusions in arguments; assertions that are necessary to recognize in order to fully understand an argument.

Joining words   words or phrases that indicate, or signal, the logical relationship between assertions in an argument. "Therefore" and its synonyms signal a conclusion; "because" and its synonyms signal a premise.

Occam's razor   a principle of argument that advocates economy, maintaining that the simplest line of reasoning is usually the best.

Opinion   a provisional judgment or belief, requiring proof or support; a first step in developing an argument.

Premise   a reason that supports the conclusion in an argument.

Standard form   an argument reduced to its essence, its principal premises and conclusion listed in simple outline form, with premises numbered and conclusion stated at the end.

CHAPTER 4

Written Argument

I told him he ought not simply to state what he thinks true, but to give arguments for it, but he said arguments would feel as if he was dirtying a flower with muddy hands. . . . I told him I hadn't the heart to say anything against that, and that he had better acquire a servant to state the arguments.

—BERTRAND RUSSELL

In Chapter 3, we focused on the structure of argument, distinguishing between premises and conclusions and reducing arguments to these two basic components. But how do we flesh out these bare bones to create a complete **written argument**?

FOCUSING YOUR TOPIC

A first critical step is to **focus** and refine the topic. At one time or another, we have all been part of heated political discussions between friends or family members. Dad states that taxes are too high. Cousin Susan points out that corporations do not pay their fair share, while Grandfather shouts that the government funds too many social programs and underfunds social security. These discussions are often discursive and unsatisfying because they are not focused on one clear and precise **question at issue**. Bloggers often think they're presenting an argument, but they are simply offering a one-sided, unfocused rant when they fail to focus on a single question at issue.

For an argument to be successful, one person does not necessarily have to defeat another; one point of view does not have to be proven superior to another. An argument can also be considered successful if it opens a line of communication between people and allows them to consider—with respect—points of view other than their own. But if an argument is to establish such a worthwhile exchange, it must focus first on a single issue and then on a particular question at issue.

The Issue

An **issue** is any topic of concern and controversy. Not all topics are issues, since many topics are not controversial. Pet care, for instance, is a topic but not an issue; it has no **argumentative edge**. Laboratory testing of animals, on the other hand, is an issue. In the hypothetical family discussion above, three issues are raised: taxes, government-funded social programs, and social security. No wonder such a discussion is fragmented and deteriorates into people shouting unsupported claims at one another.

Where and how do you find appropriate topics for an argument? In your work or personal life you might need to write an argument that has a real-world purpose. Why is product X superior to all other brands? Why are you the most qualified applicant for the job? For your classes, you are often assigned topics, but sometimes in a writing class you are asked to select a topic of interest to you. Newspapers, news broadcasts, and websites can suggest issues, as can blogs and podcasts. Don't be afraid of exploring new areas. In a freshman history class some years ago, one of us was handed the unknown name *Leon Trotsky*. That required paper led to a whole new world of knowledge: Russia, the Soviet Union, the Russian Revolution, and communism. Your writing assignments can be a way of opening new worlds.

The Question at Issue

Whether you choose your own issue or are assigned one, the next step is to select one question at issue—a particular aspect of the issue under consideration. **Global warming**, for instance, is an issue that contains many distinct questions at issue:

Does global warming exist?

Should the EPA declare global warming a threat to human health?

Are the effects of global warming as serious as some predict?

Should the federal government increase funding for alternative energy?

Is global warming having an effect on our economy?

Is the melting of the polar ice cap a catastrophe for polar bears? For penguins?

A writer who does not focus on one and only one question at issue risks producing a disorganized essay, one that is difficult to follow because the readers will not be sure they understand the point the writer is arguing. Writing on the issue of whether or not global warming will have a significant impact on our economy, one student kept drifting away from that question at issue to whether global warming would affect the weather in her city. Since both her **questions at issue** were part of the **same issue**, global warming, and hence related, she was unaware that her paper was going in two different directions. The result was a disorganized, disjointed essay reflecting muddled thinking.

The following diagram illustrates that a single issue may contain any number of separate and distinct questions at issue. Your task as a writer is to isolate a particular question at issue and stay focused on it.

GLOBAL WARMING

Does global **X**
warming exist?

X Is global warming having an
effect on our economy?

Should the EPA declare **X**
global warming a threat
to human health?

X Should the federal government
increase funding for alternative
energy?

Are the effects of global **X**
warming as serious
as some predict?

X Is the melting of the polar
ice cap a catastrophe for
polar bears? For penguins?

The Thesis

The final step in establishing the focus of an essay is determining the **thesis**. Although the issue and question at issue state the subject and focus of the paper, they are neutral statements; they do not reveal the writer's opinion, nor should they. To encourage objective analysis, the question at issue should be expressed in neutral rather than biased or emotionally charged language. The **thesis**, however, states the writer's position, a response to the question at issue, the *conclusion* of the *argument*, the primary claim being made. Your thesis takes center stage in both the final paper you write and the thinking you do as you conduct your research and prepare drafts. It controls the evidence you gather and clarifies the stand you take.

Suppose you want to write a paper about global warming and you have narrowed the issue to a more focused question at issue:

Should the government take immediate steps to curb global warming?

You might start your paper with a sentence that states the topic but not yet your thesis:

The question of global warming has long been debated, but today most are in agreement that global warming, to some degree, is a reality.

Yes, your reader would say. You've chosen a timely topic, but what about the **argumentative edge**? Where is your opinion? What have you to prove in such a statement? Not much so far. No longer will many people argue with the fact that global warming is a reality. But once you have established a little background on your topic, you need to make a statement about what you want to prove in your paper.

Perhaps you want to convince your reader that it is time for the government to step in with funding.

Thesis:

Although our nation is suffering from deficit spending and budget shortfalls, global warming is too urgent a problem for the government to ignore. Funding is needed immediately.

Or you may want to join those who argue otherwise.

Thesis:

While global warming is a problem, before we start increasing our national debt, we should depend on private initiatives and the individual efforts of us all.

Both of these statements assert a position on a question at issue; both have an argumentative edge. In either case, you need to provide detailed reasoning to support your thesis. With either thesis statement, you will have pinned down your ideas so that you have a road map to guide you as you search for and sift through the evidence necessary to support your position.

You don't necessarily have to arrive at a completely yes-or-no response to the question at issue. To give another example, if the question at issue is whether or not school administrators should have the right to censor student newspapers, your position may not be unequivocal, but a qualified response.

Thesis:

School administrators should not have the right to censor student newspapers unless an article is libelous or clearly obscene.

A thesis is not necessarily restricted to one sentence. In fact, it's not unusual for a thesis to require a paragraph. As your work progresses and new ideas change your thinking, you may need to revise your thesis. You may also find yourself refining the language of your thesis during the final editing process. But a well-thought-out and clearly expressed thesis guides both writer and reader.

IN SUMMARY: You should take the following steps as you prepare to write your argument:

Select an issue that is controversial.

Narrow that issue to a focused question at issue.

Write a thesis that makes an assertion about this question at issue; your thesis states your opinion on the question at issue.

EXERCISE 4A

Identifying the Issue, Question at Issue, and Thesis

Complete the following sets by supplying the missing element.

1. ***Issue:*** _____.

   Question at Issue: Should the federal government ban the use of handheld electronic devices by drivers?

   Thesis: For the safety of all drivers, the federal government should ban handheld electronic devices by drivers.

2. ***Issue:*** Fuel economy standards.

   Question at Issue: Should the government have the right to set fuel economy standards for American automakers?

   Thesis: _____.

3. ***Issue:*** Genetic engineering of crops.

   Question at Issue: _____.

   Thesis: The genetic engineering of crops should continue to have the support of our government and farmers.

4. In the following example, supply two thesis statements.

   Issue: Evolution in high school biology classes.

   Question at Issue: Should evolution be a required component of high school biology classes?

   Thesis: _____.

   Thesis: _____.

SHAPING A WRITTEN ARGUMENT— RHETORICAL STRATEGIES

What do we mean by *rhetorical*? The term **rhetoric** has various shades of meaning, but the following definition from Aristotle provides the most useful approach for our purposes: "The art of using language to good effect, to prove, to convince, to persuade."

And thus to argue. The structure of written argument as we know it today dates back to the orations of the Greeks and Romans. The following features of classical argument, modified by contemporary rhetoric, can serve us well as long as we recognize that they are options, not requisite components. We write to communicate, not to fit a formula or fulfill a set of narrow expectations.

The Introduction

Your introduction may be a single paragraph or run to two or three paragraphs, depending on the strategies you choose and the amount of background required. Usually, you will state your **thesis** somewhere in the introductory paragraphs so that your reader is clear about the purpose of the essay. Some useful strategies:

1. You may begin your essay with a relevant **narrative**, either actual or fictional. For example, if your subject is euthanasia, you may describe a day in the life of a terminally ill patient. Such a scene captures the reader's interest—not a necessity but sometimes a valuable rhetorical technique.

2. An applicable **quotation** can provide an interesting way into your argument.

3. An **opposing view** allows you to build your argument on a **refutation** of what is often the prevailing wisdom on an issue.

4. Some arguments need an expanded **explanation** of the topic, particularly if it's technical in nature.

Look to the three articles in Additional Readings to see how these writers introduce their topics.

The Development of Your Argument

You need to present as many strong **premises** (reasons) in support of your position as necessary. (See Chapter 3.) These in turn have to be explained and defended with as much specific detail as you can provide. You may draw on your own knowledge and personal experience and on research to support your position. Called in classical rhetoric the *confirmation* of your position, this support should be connected explicitly to your thesis. As Plato said in the *Phaedrus*, "What is stated outright will be clearer than what is not."

Sometimes one premise requires a whole paragraph or more. Others may need only a few sentences and can be effectively grouped with additional premises. Here are two examples of paragraphs lifted from the middle of student essays, one that develops a single premise in some detail, another that groups a series of premises together in one paragraph. In both paragraphs, the premises are printed **bold**.

A single-premise paragraph:

Although in 2008 the Supreme Court ruled that the Second Amendment to the Constitution sanctioned the right of Americans to keep loaded handguns in their homes, **the decision should not curtail the right of communities to place constraints on the ownership of guns and their use**. For example, felons must not be authorized to own or use firearms. Communities should still be able to require registration of all guns, including those purchased at gun shows. The ruling leaves open the possibility that all guns could be traceable to their source so that law enforcement can keep track of illegal handguns used on the street.

It left standing the laws that forbid guns from being carried into most Federal Buildings, public schools, or large public gatherings. The increase of rampages on school grounds since Columbine should be evidence enough that guns must be vigilantly controlled, even if the Constitution protects the right to own them. Although this is a hotly debated issue, ammunition should also be traceable. By analogy, most of us support strict controls over who can drive an automobile, another lethal weapon in the wrong hands, yet a cry goes up when the government threatens to limit the use of guns. While many of these limits are opposed by the NRA, I don't believe that the recent Supreme Court ruling means all restrictions are off the table.

A multipremise paragraph:

Although it is a controversial proposition, legalizing drugs has many advantages. First of all, **it will free the now overburdened legal system to do its job dispensing justice.** Cases will be processed with greater speed because the system will not be overwhelmed with drug cases. With the legalization of drugs, **violent drug-related crimes will decrease.** As a result, prisons will be less crowded, which in turn will allow serious offenders to serve longer terms. **Legalizing drugs will free law enforcement officials to combat other serious crimes more effectively.** With the money saved from law enforcement and legal procedures, a more effective campaign of educating the public on the maladies of drugs can be mounted, and more money will be available for the rehabilitation of drug addicts. Finally, **by legalizing drugs, we can slow down the spread of AIDS among HIV drug users**, who will be able to get clean needles and not have to share with other drug addicts, many of whom are infected with the AIDS virus. The positive results of legalizing drugs definitely outweigh the negative consequences.

How Many Premises Should an Argument Have?

It would seem that the greater the number of premises, the stronger the argument, but weak or questionable premises should not be included just to increase the number of premises. It's possible to have a strong argument with only two or three premises if those premises are convincing and are developed in detail.

The Conclusion

We have no simple rule of thumb here other than to suggest you conclude your essay rather than simply stop. If your paper is long and complex, you need to help your reader by briefly summarizing where you have been and what you propose. If, as a result of your argument, you have definite recommendations for action, your conclusion can carry such suggestions.

You and your readers should feel satisfied at the close of your paper. This does not mean that every paper needs a long and redundant formulaic conclusion. We refer you to the sample essays in Exercise 4D for models.

And so your argument assumes its shape. Commenting on effective rhetoric, Plato summed it up in his *Phaedrus*:

> Every discourse, like a living creature, should be so put together that it has its own body and lacks neither head nor feet, middle nor extremities, all composed in such a way that they suit both each other and the whole.

For further discussion of shaping your essay and developing a thesis, see the website mycomplab.com.

A DIALECTICAL APPROACH TO ARGUMENT

Effective argument is more than the straightforward presentation of a thesis, premises, and their support. Persuasive argument depends on **dialectical thinking**. What do we mean by dialectical? Dialectic is the art of arriving at the truth by disclosing the views contrary to your own and overcoming them.

The English philosopher John Stuart Mill was trained by his father to argue both sides of every question and was taught that you had no right to a belief unless you understood the arguments for its opposite.

Eleanor Roosevelt advised women in politics to "argue the other side with a friend until you have found the answer to every point which might be brought up against you."

Cognitive psychologist Piaget maintained that one mark of a maturing mind is the ability to take another's point of view and thus be capable of considering two conflicting views on the same issue.

Clearly Lucy is not a dialectical thinker.

Addressing Counterarguments

To take this dialectical approach to argument, you as a writer must pay careful attention to **counterarguments**, to views contrary to your own. But, one might ask, why aid and abet the opposition by calling attention to their arguments? For a number of good reasons:

1. By **anticipating** your opponent's reasoning, you can often disarm the opposition. The "I recognize that . . ." approach can be very effective.

2. You can make your own position stronger when you state and then **refute** opposing premises by demonstrating their weakness or falseness. Writer Louis Menand recognized this point when he wrote, "Every idea or piece of knowledge worth having is, in part, a response to ideas or knowledge less worth having. Refuting a bad argument makes a good argument stronger."

3. By addressing counterarguments to your position, you also appear more **reasonable**. You show yourself to possess the kind of mind that embraces complexity.

4. When you **acknowledge** the possibility of merit in some of your opponents' reasoning, you have taken the ultimate step in establishing yourself as a knowledgeable, generous thinker.

5. You may even **discover weaknesses and contradictions** in your own thinking as you sort through the reasoning of your opponents. It is not easy to abandon cherished beliefs, but clear thinkers sometimes must.

How Much Counterargument?

How much counterargument should writers include in their papers? There is no precise answer. If the writer has strong refutations for every one of the counterarguments, then she may want to address them all. If, on the other hand, a writer thinks her premises are stronger than her refutation, she may want to include only a minimum of counterargument. In any case, a writer cannot ignore the most compelling opposing views, even if they provide the greatest challenge to the writer's own view. For example, for a paper in favor of the medical use of marijuana, the writer would have to deal with the fact that currently marijuana is a federally controlled drug that, like cocaine and heroin, is subject to legal controls.

Refutation and Concession

As you can see from this discussion, there is more than one way to address counterarguments. But address them you must, since to present a contradictory position and then leave it alone would confuse your reader. Here are two possible responses:

Refutation: Present a counterargument and then explain why this position is false, misleading, or irrelevant; discredit it in some well-reasoned way.

From a student essay in support of a law sanctioning active euthanasia:

Some say death and suffering are in keeping with God's universal plan for humanity. The dying process, no matter how long or how agonizing, has both

Refutation spiritual and moral purpose, functioning to prepare people for the painless eternity of heaven. **To believe this argument though, one must believe there is life after death and many do not. So why can't people live and die in accordance with their own belief system? Let both the religious and secular have some control of their own destiny; give those who choose to die that alternative, while honoring the belief of those who do not.**

Concession

Concession: Recognize the merit of a counterargument and so concede that point. If, for example, you are arguing in favor of euthanasia and want to refute the counterargument that euthanasia is a form of murder, you might begin this way:

Counterargument

Although I also believe that life is sacred and murder is wrong, I don't think that ending the life of a brain-dead patient is equivalent to murder since in the true sense of the word "life," this patient is not living.

Visually, the relationship between counterargument and refutation and concession looks something like this:

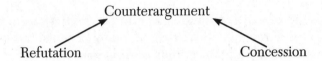

For more examples of counterargument and refutation, see "The Conservative Case for Gay Marriage" by Ted Olsen in Additional Readings.

Rogerian Strategy

For a deeper understanding of concession, we turn to the work of Carl R. Rogers (1902–1987), a psychotherapist and communication theorist. Rogers recognized that people establish barriers and grow more rigid in their beliefs when threatened. In order to be heard, we need to develop *empathy*—the ability, in Rogers' words, "**to see the expressed idea and attitude from the other person's point of view.**" It is through empathy that we can most successfully understand another's position and so concede appropriate points. The reader will feel less threatened as the writer reduces the gap between them and replaces hostile judgment with "mutual communication."

A British politician turned to Rogerian strategy when Iran and Britain were in a political crisis over the publication of Salmon Rushdie's *The Satanic Verses*, a novel that offended Muslims to such a degree that the Ayatollah Khomeini, then the ruler of Iran, called on Muslims around the world to kill Rushdie, sending the author into hiding for 10 years. The British government, while providing the author with continuous police protection, tried to temper Iran's fury. Britain's foreign secretary, Sir Geoffrey Howe, in a BBC radio broadcast meant to be heard by Iran, delivered the following message:

We do understand that the book itself has been found deeply offensive by people of the Muslim faith. We can understand why it has been criticized. It is a book

that is offensive in many other ways as well. We are not upholding the right of freedom to speak because we agree with the book. The book is extremely rude about us. It compares Britain with Hitler's Germany. We don't like that any more than people of the Muslim faith like the attacks on their faith. . . . [But] nothing in the book could justify a threat to the life of the author.

His comments were meant to forge a bond of empathy between the British and the Iranians—both groups, both governments were criticized by Rushdie—so, of course, the British understood the anger of the Iranians. Through this mutual understanding, the foreign secretary hoped to persuade Iran to withdraw its demand that Rushdie be assassinated.

In a more recent example, conservative columnist Stephen Hayes, writing in the *Wall Street Journal*, praised President Obama's rhetorical style. "When he addresses a contentious issue, Mr. Obama almost always begins his answer with a respectful nod in the direction of the view he is rejecting." Soon after being inaugurated, President Obama held an interview with Hisham Melhem of Dubai-based Al Arabiya TV Network. He **conceded** that "we sometimes make mistakes." He condemned Iran's threats against Israel, support of terrorists, and efforts to obtain nuclear weapons, **"but," he conceded**, "it is important for us to be willing to talk to Iran," to find "potential avenues for progress." He went even further when he reminded his audience that "I have Muslim members of my family. I have lived in a Muslim country." He was meeting the opposition half way.

When There Is No Other Side

What makes an issue worth arguing? While there are no fast rules, issues inappropriate for argument fall into three general categories. Some are so personal or so self-evident that they don't lend themselves to intelligent debate. Take for example the following claims:

Chocolate ice cream is far superior to strawberry.

or

Free, quality education should be provided for all children in America.

Neither proposition lends itself to the kind of exploration we have been discussing in this chapter, in the first instance because it concerns a personal and insignificant preference, and in the second because no one could in all seriousness argue against such a proposition.

A third, and more compelling, category is that in which the issue is simply too offensive to the majority of writers or readers. Arguments advocating racial bigotry or denial of the Holocaust, for example, fall into this category. Sometimes there is no other side worth defending.

Columnist Ellen Goodman illustrates how issues with no defensible other side have affected newspaper reporting.

> At the end of the 19th century, when African Americans were strung like "strange fruit" from Southern trees, the *New York Times* required every story about lynching to include a quote from a segregationist justifying the hanging. At some point, the absurdity of that journalistic "evenhandedness" struck home to the editors. Murder is not a story with "another side."
>
> I mention that footnote to my profession's history because I've always found something odd in the notion that "balance" is a seesaw, outfitted with exactly two seats for opponents whose views are carefully and equally weighted. A given story may have 15 sides . . . or one.
>
> When terrorists struck on September 11, there was only one side. No editor demanded a quote from someone saying why it was fine to fly airplanes into buildings . . . .

In a recent interview, veteran television journalist Belva Davis, an African American, remembered a time when she attempted to follow "journalistic 'evenhandedness.'" She and her cameraman were covering a civil rights march in Georgia in the '80s. She told her cameraman that she needed to interview the other side. The cameraman pointed out that the other side consisted primarily of Ku Klux Klan members wearing white sheets. Davis suggested a small group of white women watching the demonstration. When she asked them their opinion of the march, one of the women spat in her face.

LOGICAL CONNECTIONS—COHERENCE

You need to establish a logical sequence of thought in your written argument, both at the sentence level and from paragraph to paragraph.

Joining Words

To incorporate counterargument, refutation, and concession into your written argument, you must signal relationships between ideas. The appropriate choice of conjunctions and transitional phrases can distinguish your position from counterarguments.

In "The Conservative Case for Gay Marriage" by Ted Olsen (see Additional Readings), Olsen makes a concession to those opposed to gay marriage, and then uses "But while" to signal his position on the issue.

> It is true that marriage in this nation traditionally has been regarded as a relationship exclusively between a man and a woman, and many of our nation's multiple religions define marriage in precisely those terms. **But while** the Supreme Court has always previously considered marriage in that context, the underlying rights and liberties that marriage embodies are not in any way confined to heterosexuals.

It is through the different choices of joining words that writers establish their slant on the issue. Let's review these distinctions:

Coordinating Conjunctions	Major Transitions	Subordinating Conjunctions
Counterargument, Refutation	Counterargument, Refutation	Concession
but yet	However on the other hand	While Whereas although though

The degree to which subordinating conjunctions express concession can vary according to the content of the sentence. In some cases you may simply **acknowledge** your opponent's position without really conceding it, as in the following example:

> Although smokers correctly defend their constitutional rights, the health of a non-smoker should come first.

EXERCISE 4B

Making Rhetorical Choices

Take a stance on the issue of general education requirements by combining the first two sentences in number 1, using the appropriate joining word to reflect your position (your argument's **thesis**). Then combine the following pairs of sentences so that the paragraph will be logically "shaped" to support your position and reveal appropriate concessions.

1. Many educators argue for a broad and rigorous series of required general education courses.

   Others claim that students should not have to spend so much time on general courses outside their chosen majors.

2. A general education program often means that students can't graduate in the customary four years and so must delay their careers.

   Graduates with a broad liberal arts background tend to be promoted more consistently than their more narrowly trained competitors.

3. Most students can't afford to prolong their graduation.

   The nation can't afford a workforce of specialists uninformed about the world and unprepared in literacy and thinking skills.

4. Students are not inclined to learn in mandatory classes where they are not interested in the material.

Undergraduates are often unaware of what's available on a college campus or what their interests might be, until they are exposed to a variety of subjects.

More on Coherence

While you can manipulate ideas with joining words to signal relationships between sentences, you also need to develop coherence throughout your paper. The form of your paper can take many shapes, but you want the whole to be held together by an almost invisible glue, the connections clear but not too heavy-handed.

1. Your **thesis** will guide you as you build paragraphs and create a thread that weaves its way from opening sentence to conclusion.

2. Every sentence **should follow** from the sentence before it; each paragraph must follow logically from the one preceding it. As a writer, you take your reader's hand, never letting that reader stray from the flow of your argument. If you were to cut your paper into individual paragraphs, or even sentences, and throw them in the air, a classmate should have no difficulty putting your paper together again.

3. Repeat **key words** to keep your reader focused on your train of thought. Pronouns, those words that refer back to nouns, can help relate one sentence to another, as can synonyms for nouns when repetition becomes monotonous.

4. For more on keeping ideas connected within sentences and paragraphs, see Parallelism and Consistent Sentence Subjects in Chapter 8.

EXERCISE 4C

Identifying Coherence Strategies

Once you have completed Writing Assignment 8, ahead in this chapter, or another writing assignment, make a copy and then cut the paper into separate paragraphs. Shuffle the paragraphs and bring the pieces to class. Exchange your paper with a classmate and see if you can reconstruct each other's work in the order the writer intended. If you encounter difficulties, consult with your partner to see what coherence strategies are needed to provide for a better flow of ideas from paragraph to paragraph.

SAMPLE ESSAYS

To help you see some of the rhetorical features of effective written argument in action, we have selected two examples for you to examine closely.

EXERCISE 4D

Identifying Rhetorical Features of Argument

In the first essay, we identify the elements of written argument presented in this chapter. In the second, we ask you to do the same. We must point out that sometimes these categories overlap: a statement (or statements) may serve as both a refutation and a premise.

thesis   premises

counterarguments   refutations   concessions

Thesis

Could It Be That Video Games Are Good for Kids?

STEVEN JOHNSON

Counter-argument

Dear Sen. Clinton [now Secretary of State]: I'm writing to commend you for calling for a $90-million study on the effects of video games on children, and in particular the courageous stand you have taken in recent weeks against the notorious "Grand Theft Auto" series.   **1**

Refutation

I'd like to draw your attention to another game whose nonstop violence and hostility has captured the attention of millions of kids—a game that instills aggressive thoughts in the minds of its players, some of whom have gone on to commit real-world acts of violence and sexual assault after playing.   **2**

I'm talking, of course, about high school football.   **3**

Counter-argument

I know a congressional investigation into football won't play so well with those crucial swing voters, but it makes about as much sense as an investigation into the pressing issue of Xbox and PlayStation2.   **4**

Refutation

Your current concern is over explicit sex in "Grand Theft Auto: San Andreas." Yet there's not much to investigate, is there? It should get rated appropriately, and that's that. But there's more to your proposed study: You want to examine how video games shape children's values and cognitive development.   **5**

Kids have always played games. A hundred years ago they were playing stickball and kick the can; now they're playing "World of Warcraft," "Halo 2" and "Madden 2005." And parents have to drag their kids away from the games to get them to do their algebra homework, but parents have been dragging kids away from whatever the kids were into since the dawn of civilization.   **6**

Premise

So any sensible investigation into video games must ask the "compared to what" question. If the alternative to playing "Halo 2" is reading "The Portrait of a Lady," then of course "The Portrait of a Lady" is better for you. But it's not as though kids have been reading Henry James for 100 years and then suddenly dropped him for Pokemon.   **7**

Another key question: Of all the games that kids play, which ones require the most mental exertion? Parents can play this at home: Try a few rounds of Monopoly or Go Fish with your kids, and see who wins. I suspect most families will find that it's a relatively even match. Then sit down and try to play "Halo 2" with the kids. You'll be lucky if you survive 10 minutes.   **8**

Premise

The great secret of today's video games that has been lost in the moral panic over "Grand Theft Auto" is how difficult the games have become. That difficulty is not merely a question of hand-to-eye coordination; most of today's games force kids to learn complex rule systems, master challenging new interfaces, follow dozens of shifting variables in real time and prioritize between multiple objectives.   **9**

In short, precisely the sorts of skills that they're going to need in the digital   10
workplace of tomorrow.

Consider this one fascinating trend among teenagers: They're spending less   11
time watching professional sports and more time simulating those sports on Xbox
or PlayStation. Now, which activity challenges the mind more—sitting around root-
ing for the Green Bay Packers, or managing an entire football franchise through a
season of "Madden 2005": calling plays, setting lineups, trading players and ne-
gotiating contracts? Which challenges the mind more—zoning out to the lives of
fictional characters on a televised soap opera, or actively managing the lives of
dozens of virtual characters in a game such as "The Sims"?

On to the issue of aggression, and what causes it in kids, especially teenage boys.   12
Congress should be interested in the facts: The last 10 years have seen the release of
many popular violent games, including "Quake" and "Grand Theft Auto"; that period
also has seen the most dramatic drop in violent crime in recent memory. According to
Duke University's Child Well-Being Index, today's kids are less violent than kids have
been at any time since the study began in 1975. Perhaps, Sen. Clinton, your investigation should explore the theory that violent games function as a safety valve, letting
children explore their natural aggression without acting it out in the real world.

Many juvenile crimes—such as the carjacking that is so central to "Grand Theft   13
Auto"—are conventionally described as "thrill-seeking" crimes. Isn't it possible
that kids no longer need real-world environments to get those thrills, now that the
games simulate them so vividly? The national carjacking rate has dropped substan-
tially since "Grand Theft Auto" came out. Isn't it conceivable that the would-be
carjackers are now getting their thrills on the screen instead of the street?

Crime statistics are not the only sign that today's gaming generation is doing   14
much better than the generation raised during that last cultural panic—over rock
'n' roll. Math SAT scores have never been higher; verbal scores have been climbing
steadily for the last five years; nearly every indicator in the Department of Education study known as the Nation's Report Card is higher now than when the study
was implemented in 1971.

By almost every measure, the kids are all right.   15

Of course, I admit that one charge against video games is a slam dunk. Kids   16
don't get physical exercise when they play a video game, and indeed the rise in
obesity among younger people is a serious issue. But, of course, you don't get exercise from doing homework, either.

(margin annotations, left side:) Premise · Refutation and Premise · Counterargument · Concession

Now identify the same features of argument—thesis, premises, counterargu-   17
ment, and refutation—in the following essay. The writer of this editorial does not
make any concessions to the other side so we're asking you to write one for him.

Elite Colleges, or Colleges for the Elite?

RICHARD D. KAHLENBERG

Today's populist moment, with a growing anger directed at the elites who manipu-   1
late the sytem to their advantage, is an opportune time to examine higher education's biggest affirmative action program—for the children of alumni.

At our top universities, so-called legacy preferences affect larger numbers of stu-   2
dents than traditional affirmative action programs for minority students, yet they have
received a small fraction of the attention. Unlike the issue of racial preferences, advantages of alumni children—who are overwhelmingly white and wealthy—have been
the subject of little scholarship, no state voter initiatives and Supreme Court decisions.

Among selective research universities, public and private, almost three-quarters   3
employ legacy preferences, as do the vast majority of selective liberal arts colleges.
Some admissions departments insist they are used only as tiebreakers among de-
serving applicants. But studies have shown that being the child of an alumnus adds
the equivalent of 160 SAT points to one's application (using the traditional 400-to-
1600-point scale, and not factoring in the writing section of the test) and increases
one's chances of admission by almost 20 percentage points.

At many selective schools, legacies make up 10 percent to 25 percent of the   4
student population. By contrast, at the California Institute of Technology, which has
no legacy preferences, only 1.5 percent of students are the children of alumni.

Legacy preferences are often justified as a way of building loyalty among   5
alumni, sustaining tradition and increasing donations. But there is no hard evidence to prove this. A study by Winnemac Consulting for the Century Foundation
found that from 1998 to 2007, at the nation's top 100 national universities, if one
controls for the wealth of alumni, there is no statistically significant evidence of a
causal relationship between legacy preference policies and total alumni giving."
Moreover, the study found that the seven universities that dropped legacy preferences during the time of the study, their alumni giving didn't decline.

Legacy preferences are "virtually unknown in the rest of the world," according   6
to Daniel Golden, a former reporter for the Wall Street Journal. The paradox is that
while they are an American contrivance, they are also un-American, standing in direct contradiction to Thomas Jefferson's famous call to promote a "natural aristoc-
racy" based on "virtue and talent." The Old World nature of hereditary preferences
may explain why, in a 2004 poll by *The Chronicle of Higher Education*, Americans
opposed such preferences by 75 percent to 23 percent.

Legacy preferences may also be illegal. Although in 1976 a federal court ruled   7
in a passing mention that legacy preferences are constitutional, the issue has never
been properly litigated. Today, new legal arguments have been advanced questioning legacy preferences at both public and private universities.

Steve Shadowen and Sozi Tulante, two lawyers in private practice in Pennsyl-   8
vania, have argued forcefully that preferences violate the equal protection clause

of the 14th Amendment. While the amendment was primarily aimed at prohibiting discrimination against blacks, it also extends to what Justice Potter Steward called "preferences based on lineage." In the past, the Supreme Court has read the amendment to prohibit laws that judge individuals on the parents' actions or behaviors such as those that punish children born out of wedlock.   9

Legacy preferences at private institutions may also violate the 1866 Civil Rights Act, which prohibits discrimination on the basis of "ancestry" as well as race.   10

Affirmative action policies are controversial because they pit two fundamental principles against each other—the anti-discrimination principle, which says we should not classify people by ancestry, and the anti-subordination principle, which says we must address a brutal history of discrimination. Legacy preferences, by contrast, advance neither principle—they simply classify individuals by bloodline.   11

Congress should outlaw alumni preferences at all universities and colleges receiving federal financing, just as the Civil Rights Act of 1964 outlaws racial discrimination at them. Or lawmakers could limit the tax deductibility of alumni donations at institutions that favor legacy children on the principle that tax-deductive donations are not supposed to enrich the giver. If legislators don't act, it will fall to lawyers to bring suit to enforce the 14th Amendment and the 1866 Civil Rights Act and put an end to this form of discrimination in higher education.

A TWO-STEP PROCESS FOR WRITING A COMPLETE ARGUMENT

The next two writing assignments provide steps in completing a polished argument.

WRITING ASSIGNMENT 7

Arguing Both Sides of an Issue

The Approach

Below is a list of proposals advocating a position on a social issue. Choose **one** and write two separate arguments, one **defending** and one **refuting** the proposal. For **each** argument:

1. Write a short **thesis** at the top of each page.

2. For each position, provide **relevant premises (reasons)** that are, to the best of your knowledge, accurate although not fully developed yet.

3. You will have two separate papers with **a paragraph for each premise**. Although each paragraph should be written coherently with fluent sentences, you don't, at this stage, need to provide logical transitions between paragraphs for a coherent whole.

4. You need not provide an introduction or conclusion. All this will come later in Writing Assignment 8.

The Topics

Choose carefully because your topic will be the same for the expanded argument you'll write for Writing Assignment 8.

1. Parents should be permitted to withhold vaccines from their school-age children.

2. Schools should make it a requirement of admission that parents vaccinate their children against common childhood diseases such as measles.

3. The use of electronic devices while a driver is in motion should be prohibited in every state.

"This one's too hard to type on while I'm driving."

4. Schools should have the right to ban cell phone use during the school day.

5. The military draft should be reinstated.

6. Public service should be required for all people between the ages of 18 and 25.

7. Medical research on animals should be forbidden by law.

8. Athletes who have used performance-enhancing drugs should be permitted to hold the records they have achieved.

9. All restaurants should be required to post the calories of their menu items.

10. Girls 17 and under should be required to obtain parental permission before having an abortion.

11. Nationwide standardized tests throughout elementary and secondary school have a negative effect on education.

12. Torture is justified when the security of the nation is at stake.

13. Women in the military should serve in combat.

If another issue interests you more, be sure the issue is one worth arguing from both sides and can be expressed as a proposal similar to those above. Consult your instructor before selecting an alternative topic.

Audience

A wide range of your peers: those who might take one side or the other and those who have not, as yet, formed any opinion.

Purpose

To present both sides of a controversial issue so you and your readers are forced to consider opposing views. Here is an example:

In a recent edition, the *Wellness Letter* of the University of California, Berkeley, addressed the question at issue, "Who needs Alzheimer's testing?" Summarizing their findings, they presented premises for and against in the same format we propose for Writing Assignment 7.

Who Needs Alzheimer's Testing?

Some arguments made for universal screening:

An early diagnosis of Alzheimer's or another type of dementia allows the family and patient to prepare financially and emotionally. While still competent, the patient can make a will and other legal arrangements.   1

As the disease progresses, the patient can be urged to give up driving, cooking, traveling alone, and other potentially dangerous activities.   2

Medications can be administered. There are five FDA-approved drugs. They neither prevent nor cure dementia, but in some people they produce temporary slowing of mental decline.   3

Public awareness would increase, which might lead to an upsurge in research spending.   4

If we develop reliable tests now, we'll be ahead of the curve when we do have good treatments.   5

Screening may uncover dementias with other causes, such as certain thyroid problems, depression, or vitamin B-12 deficiency, which can be treated.   6

On the con side:

Universal screening would include many people with no memory problems at all. Apart from the waste of time and money, testing can lead to worry, depression, and family disruption.   7

There's no sure way to differentiate between mild age-related cognitive impairment, which may never get worse, and early Alzheimer's. If the test tells you that you're okay now but may develop dementia later, what can you do with that information?   8

Diagnostic tests for early dementia are not reliable, especially in people under 70. Misdiagnoses could be devastating. People might lose their jobs, driver's licenses, or even their potential caregivers, and be unable to get medical or life insurance. 9

Alzheimer's medications are expensive, and their benefits are very limited and of short duration. They are prescribed only for people who are already exhibiting clear signs of dementia. 10

Early diagnosis would benefit the drug companies more than the public, according to some critics. And for some researchers and doctors, there's money to be made from devising and administering the tests. 11

WRITING ASSIGNMENT 8

Taking a Stand

In this essay, take a stand on one side of the issue you debated in Writing Assignment 7, constructing as persuasive an argument as possible.

1. Your **thesis** should express your **own position** on the proposition you addressed in the previous assignment.

2. To support **your position**, draw on the **premises** you presented in Writing Assignment 7, discarding reasoning that seems weak or irrelevant, adding reasons where you find gaps in your earlier paper. Strengthen your argument with as much data as you think necessary to make your case for a skeptical audience.

3. Address significant **opposing views**, acknowledging, conceding, and refuting in the manner best suited to your stand on the issue. Do not elaborate the opposing views in the same way you develop your own premises.

4. Include an introduction and a conclusion.

5. Revise your paper for coherence, at both the sentence and paragraph level.

For help in organizing your paper, refer to the sample essays in Exercise 4D. **Important:** To complete the assignment, include the following attachment typed out on a separate sheet as an introductory page:

a. Your **issue**, **question at issue**, and **thesis**

b. Your principal argument set out in **standard form** (see Chapter 3)

Audience

A wide range of your peers: those who would agree with you, those who would disagree, and those who have not, as yet, formed any opinion.

Purpose

To present a convincing, balanced argument for your position on a controversial issue in order to persuade your readers to adopt your point of view.

A FINAL CHECKLIST FOR AN EFFECTIVE ARGUMENT

Choose an issue worth arguing.

Express your thesis clearly.

Support your own position as thoroughly as possible.

Anticipate relevant opposing views (counterarguments).

Provide appropriate concessions and refutations.

Develop empathy with your audience.

Create a coherent flow.

SUMMARY

Convincing arguments usually contain an introduction to the topic, a stated **thesis**, well-supported **premises**, acknowledgment of **opposing views**, and a conclusion. Successful written argument depends on a **dialectical approach** in which writers address both their own position and the views of others.

A well-written argument requires joining sentences for logic and fluency and developing coherent links between paragraphs to express relationships.

KEY TERMS

Concession   a statement that grants the opposing view.

Counterargument   an opposing view in an argument.

Dialectic   a method of argument that systematically weighs contradictory ideas.

Empathy   the ability to see and understand an idea or issue from the other person's point of view.

Issue   any topic of concern and controversy.

Question at issue   a particular aspect of the issue under consideration.

Refutation   an explanation of why a position is false or weak.

Rhetoric   the art of using language to good effect: to prove, to convince, to persuade.

Rogerian strategy   an explicit effort to see ideas from an opponent's point of view; the cultivation of empathy with the opposition; a concept derived from the research of psychologist Carl Rogers.

Thesis   a statement of a writer's position; in argument, a response to the question at issue.

CHAPTER 5

The Language of Argument— Definition

> *"When I use a word," Humpty Dumpty said in rather a scornful tone, "it means just what I choose it to mean—neither more nor less."*
> —Lewis Carroll, *Alice Through the Looking Glass*

> *"If you would argue with me, first define your terms."*
> —Voltaire

> *"Every word has its story."*
> —Antoine Meillet

In Chapter 4, we discuss the large building blocks of written arguments—thesis statements, premises, counterarguments, refutations and concessions—and how they fit together. In this chapter, we concentrate on the smaller building blocks: words. It is important that we know the meaning and the power of the words we use, and that when we write, our readers share our understanding of these words. When we cannot assume that our readers share an understanding of our terms, we need to define them.

DEFINITION AND PERCEPTION

Who Controls the Definitions?

Ellen Willis, writing in *Rolling Stone*, admonishes us, "Find out who controls the definitions, and you have a pretty good clue who controls everything else." Toni Morrison, in her novel *Beloved*, illustrates the brutal oppression of slavery with the story of the slave Sixo. When the schoolteacher accused him of stealing the shoat (a piece of pork), Sixo claimed he wasn't *stealing* but *improving his property*. The teacher beat Sixo "to show him that definitions belonged to the definers—not the defined."

Alice responded to Humpty Dumpty's claim in the opening quotation of this chapter with, "The question is, whether you *can* make words mean so many different things." Humpty Dumpty continued, "The question is, which is to be master—that's all."

In her book *Waiting for Daisy*, Peggy Orenstein chronicles her experience with infertility. She learns that 90 percent of women in their late thirties will conceive a child in two years (if their partner has a viable sperm count), but the medical establishment defines infertility as one year of trying but failing to get pregnant. Who benefits from this definition?

Nowhere is the precision of language more important than in politics. Yet nowhere is meaning more likely to be manipulated. Writing in the *New York Times Magazine*, political writer Matt Bai explained how the Republican party controlled the language of debate during recent elections using terms like "tax relief" and "partial-birth abortions" to cast a favorable aura around its policies of low taxes and opposition to abortion.

Defining Ourselves

Through the centuries, people have been defining what they consider themselves to be, using the term *man* in a number of inventive ways.

Plato

First, he put man in the class "biped" and differentiated him from others in the class by describing him as "a featherless biped." When his rival, Diogenes, produced a plucked chicken, Plato had to add "having broad nails" as a further distinguishing characteristic.

Shakespeare

"What a piece of work is a man, how noble in reason, how infinite in faculties; in form and moving how express and admirable, in action how like an angel, in apprehension how like a god: the beauty of the world, the paragon of animals! And yet, to me, what is this quintessence of dust? Man delights not me—nor woman neither..." (*Hamlet*)

Ambrose Bierce

"An animal so lost in rapturous contemplation of what he thinks he is as to overlook what he indubitably ought to be. His chief occupation is extermination of other animals and his own species, which, however, multiplies with such insistent rapidity as to infest the whole habitable earth and Canada." (*Devil's Dictionary*)

Our definitions can reveal how we see people—as individuals and collectively. In his book *Days of Obligation*, writer Richard Rodriguez points out that American feminists appropriated the word *macho* "to name their American antithesis," a man who is "boorish" and "counterdomestic." But Rodriguez tells us that in Mexican Spanish "*machismo* is more akin to the Latin *gravitas*. The male is serious. The male provides. The Mexican male never abandons those who depend upon him." As this example illustrates, when different cultures share languages, *shifts in meaning often occur, reflecting cultural bias.*

In his article "Understanding Corruption," Professor Lawrence Rosen discovers that the West and the Middle East define the words "corruption" and "nepotism" differently.

> *corruption*: morally degraded, debased in character (in the West); the failure to share any largess you have received with those with whom you have formed ties of dependence (in the Middle East)

> *nepotism*: favoritism shown to relatives, especially in appointments to desirable positions (in the West); family solidarity (in the Middle East)

Feminist Gloria Steinem pointed out our culture's sexual bias in its traditional definitions of the following terms, definitions that have played crucial roles in determining how women and men view themselves and others:

> *work:* something men do, go to; as distinguished from housework and childcare, which is what women do

> *art:* what white men produce

> *crafts:* what women and ethnic minorities do

For more on the relationship between language and culture, see "You Are What You Speak" by Guy Deutscher in Additional Readings.

Shifting Definitions

Fortunately, these definitions are changing. Indeed, we have historical precedent for scientific definitions shifting to conform to new ways of thinking. In the 19th century, alcoholism was defined as criminal behavior. When the term was redefined as an illness after World War I, considerable progress in treatment became possible. Conversely, when the American Psychological Association stopped classifying homosexuality as an illness, the homosexual community was understandably gratified by the revision of a definition unjust and damaging.

In 2005, three astrophysicists surprised the scientific community when they identified what they thought to be a tenth planet, later named *Eris*. But more surprising, the smallest of the nine known planets, *Pluto*, was then determined to be too small to qualify. Heated debate erupted over the definition of what constituted a planet. If it was size, then Pluto had to go. In fact, Pluto and Eris are currently considered "dwarf planets." After 78 years of counting nine planets, we now have only eight, not ten as it seemed for a year or two. One astronomer cast the controversy this way: "Like continents, planets are defined more by how we think of them than by someone's after-the-fact pronouncement." Even in fact-based science, precise definitions can be slippery.

A look at a few familiar words can illustrate how meaning can migrate. For example:

> ***elite***: Once a French word carrying an accent over the *é*, it referred to the privileged who had power, taste, and money and were looked up to or envied. Gradually it moved in a less favorable direction, until today the right-wing

"Elitist!"

media use the term "the liberal elite" to denigrate liberals, especially celebrities, journalists, and academics.

brand: Formerly the term meant simply the company name for a product. Nike was just the name of an athletic shoe. Today, a website offers instructions to companies on marketing their product and defines *brand* as the "proprietary visual, emotional, rational, and cultural image" associated with a company, a product, or even a person. Soccer player David Beckham is considered a brand. During the 2008 presidential campaign, Frank Rich in the *New York Times* commented, "Obama-branded change is snowballing . . . ," while according to the *San Francisco Chronicle*, McCain was building "his brand." People appeared to be "identifying more with Brand McCain" rather than "Obama's hope brand." "Candidates are brands . . . the key to all branding is to get people to identify with the candidate." "Selling voters on the brand is crucial to closing the deal," claimed the headline. Painter Andy Warhol foresaw this phenomenon, first with his portraits of Campbell's soup cans and then with his multiple images of Marilyn Monroe, Jackie Kennedy, and Elizabeth Taylor. The image is the brand; people become objects.

market: Originally, it was a place where one bought and sold agricultural products and food in general. Now anything or even a person can be a *market*, the target for anyone trying to sell anything.

When meaning shifts, it can both reflect and influence changes in the culture.

Definition: the Social Sciences and Government

In a study on child abuse and health, which we cite in an exercise in Chapter 7, the researchers first had to define child abuse before they could determine its effect on women's health. They separated child abuse into three categories—emotional, physical, and sexual. Then they defined each category.

emotional abuse: repeated rejection or serious physical threats from parents, tension in the home more than 25 percent of the time, and frequent violent fighting among parents.

physical abuse: strong blows from an adult or forced eating of caustic substances; firm slaps were excluded.

sexual abuse: any non-voluntary sexual activity with a person at least five years older.

Researchers interviewed 700 women from a private gynecological practice and tabulated their responses according to these categories. Without **clear-cut definitions** to guide them, social scientists would be left with subjective impressions rather than quantifiable results.

In law, definitions often need to be revised to avoid unfair applications as society changes. Such was the case when SUVs slipped though a giant loophole in the tax code inadvertently left gaping. To help small businesses and farmers, the government provided tax credits and accelerated depreciation for small trucks, vehicles defined not by function but by their weight—more than 6,000 pounds. Into this provision slipped the SUV, once rare for personal use but for many years now a popular family vehicle. A variety of professional people could receive a tax break for driving very large, very expensive SUVs to work and around town. To achieve fairness, we need new definitions: "work vehicles" and "passenger vehicles."

Texas politicians and educators understand the role of definition. In 2004 the Texas Board of Education approved new definitions of marriage for the state's high school and middle school textbooks. Where formerly the texts used terms like *married partners*, the board agreed to rewrite the definition of marriage as a "life-long union between a husband and a wife," thus conforming to Texas law banning gay marriage.

LANGUAGE: AN ABSTRACT SYSTEM OF SYMBOLS

Abstract words can present particular difficulties when it comes to stipulating precise meaning. But language itself, whether it refers to an **abstraction** (politics) or a **concrete** object (a given politician), is an abstract system of symbols. The word is not the thing itself, but a *symbol* or *signifier* used to represent the thing we refer to, which is the *signified*. For example, the word *cat* is a symbol or signifier for the animal itself, the signified.

"Cat"

THE SYMBOL or SIGNIFIER
(the word)

THE SIGNIFIED
(the thing being referred to)

But meaning is made only when the signified is processed through the mind of someone using or receiving the words. Whenever a speaker, writer, listener, or reader encounters a word, a lifetime of associations renders the word, and thus the image it conjures up, distinct for each individual.

As literary theorist Stanley Fish points out, meaning is dependent not only on the individual but also on the context, situation, and interpretive community. To illustrate this point, let's look at the word *host*. It means one thing if we are at a party, something different if we're discussing parasites with a biologist, and something else entirely if we are at a Christian church. Hence, the context or situation determines our understanding of *host*.

If, however, you are not a member of a religion that practices the ritual of communion or are not conversant with parasitology, then you may understand the meaning of *host* only as the giver of a party. You are not part of the interpretive community, in this case a religious community or a scientific discipline, that understands *host* as a consecrated wafer, a religious symbol, or as an organism on which another lives.

Even when the signified is concrete, individual experience and perception will always deny the word complete stability; the range of possible images will still be vast. Take the word *table*. Nothing of the essence of table is part of the word *table*. Although most words in English (or any modern language) have roots and a history in older languages, the assignation of a particular meaning to a given term remains essentially arbitrary. While all English speakers share a general understanding of the word *table*, each user or receiver of this word, without having considerably more detail, will create a different picture.

If the symbolic representation of a **concrete**, visible object such as a table is as unstable as our discussion suggests, think how much more problematic **abstract** terms must be. Were we to substitute the abstraction *freedom* for the concrete *table*, the range of interpretations would be considerably more diverse and much more challenging to convey to others. This becomes particularly evident when political issues are at stake. For example, some saw the war in Iraq as bringing "**freedom**" to Iraqis; others saw it as an unlawful "**occupation**" of a foreign country.

Visual pictures, which arise when concrete objects are signaled, don't come to mind as readily when we refer to abstractions, a distinction that led Shakespeare to explain why poets must give "to airy nothing a local habitation and a name."

In the following poem, Thomas Lux explores the instability of language as readers, even when reading the same text, make it uniquely their own.

THE VOICE YOU HEAR WHEN YOU READ SILENTLY

The voice you hear when you read silently
is not silent, it is a speaking
out-loud voice in your head: it is spoken,
a voice is saying it
as you read. It's the writer's words,

of course, in a literary sense
his or her "voice" but the sound
of that voice is the sound of your voice.
Not the sound your friends know
or the sound of a tape played back
but your voice
caught in the dark cathedral
of your skull, your voice heard
by an internal ear informed by internal abstracts
and what you know by feeling,
having felt. It is your voice
saying, for example, the word "barn"
that the writer wrote
but the "barn" you say
is a barn you know or knew. The voice
in your head, speaking as you read,
never says anything neutrally—some people
hated the barn they knew,
some people love the barn they know
so you hear the word loaded
and a sensory constellation
is lit: horse-gnawed stalls,
hayloft, black heat tape wrapping
a water pipe, a slippery
spilled chirrr of oats from a split sack,
the bony, filthy haunches of cows . . .
And "barn" is only a noun—no verb
or subject has entered into the sentence yet!
The voice you hear when you read to yourself
is the clearest voice: you speak it
speaking to you.

EXERCISE 5A

Reading Language

1. In this poem, what is the difference between the voice of the writer and the voice of the reader?

2. What is the significance of the exclamation mark at the end of the following lines?

    And "barn" is only a noun—no verb

    or subject has entered into the sentence yet!

3. What is Lux saying about language and the act of reading?

The Importance of Concrete Examples

Semanticist S. I. Hayakawa discussed the idea of an **abstraction ladder** in which language starts on the ground, so to speak, with an object available to our sense of perception, and moves up to concepts abstracted from, derived from, the concrete source—for example, from a specific cow (Bessie) to cow to livestock to farm assets to asset and finally to wealth. Liberally adapted from Hayakawa, such a ladder would look like this:

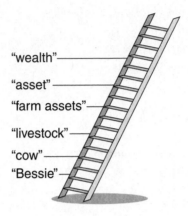

"wealth"
"asset"
"farm assets"
"livestock"
"cow"
"Bessie"

He stressed that our powers of abstraction are indispensable. "The ability to climb to higher and higher levels of abstraction is a distinctively human trait without which none of our philosophical or scientific insights would be possible." But he cautioned against staying at too high a level of abstraction. The kind of "thinking" we must be extremely wary of is that which *never* leaves the higher verbal levels of abstraction, the kind that never points *down* the abstraction ladder to lower levels of abstraction and from there to the extensional world:

> "What do you mean by *democracy*?"
> "Democracy means the preservation of human *rights*."
> "What do you mean by *rights*?"
> "By rights I mean those privileges God grants to all of us—I mean man's inherent privileges."
> "Such as?"
> "Liberty, for example."
> "What do you mean by *liberty*?"
> "Religious and political freedom."
> "And what does that mean?"
> "Religious and political freedom is what we enjoy under a democracy."

The writer never moves down to the essential lower levels on the abstraction ladder, and a discourse consisting only of abstractions, devoid of concrete details and examples, is necessarily vague, often difficult for the reader to understand, and, in this definition of democracy, circular.

To avoid the confusion that abstractions can generate, Hayakawa suggested pointing down "to extensional levels wherever necessary; in writing and speaking, this means giving **specific examples** of what we are talking about," grounding our arguments in the **concrete**.

Compare the empty, circular definition of **democracy** Hayakawa quotes above with the **concrete illustrations** that illuminate E. B. White's celebrated World War II definition of the same term:

> We received a letter from the Writers' War Board the other day asking for a statement on "The Meaning of Democracy." It presumably is our duty to comply with such a request, and it is certainly our pleasure. Surely the Board knows what democracy is. It is the line that forms on the right. It is the don't in don't shove. It is the hole in the stuffed shirt through which the sawdust slowly trickles; it is the dent in the high hat. Democracy is the recurrent suspicion that more than half of the people are right more than half of the time. It is the feeling of privacy in the voting booths, the feeling of communion in the libraries, the feeling of vitality everywhere. Democracy is a letter to the Editor. Democracy is the score at the beginning of the ninth. It is an idea that hasn't been disproved yet, a song the words of which have not gone bad. It's the mustard on the hot dog and the cream in the rationed coffee. Democracy is a request from a War Board, in the middle of a morning in the middle of a war, wanting to know what democracy is.

Such specificity is what writer Annie Dillard values when she says, "This is what life is all about: salamanders, fiddle tunes, you and me and things . . . the fizz into **particulars**." And what novelist Vladimir Nabokov prizes when he asks us to "Caress the details, the divine **details**."

EXERCISE 5B

Levels of Specificity

Good writing requires that general concepts or categories be illustrated by specific examples. To practice providing the kind of concrete, specific detail Dillard and Nabokov talk about in the paragraph above, rank the words and phrases in the following lists, giving a *1* to the most general, with higher numbers moving through each level of specificity. You may find more than one item on a given level.

Example:	2	1	4	3	2
	actors;	performers;	Will Smith;	movie actors;	singers;

	4	4	3
	Mariah Carey;	Jennifer Aniston;	pop singers

1. painting
   work of art
   Whistler's Mother
   American painting
   painting by Whistler

2. shuffle
   move
   amble
   walk slowly
   travel on foot
   drive
   walk

3. sport
   doubles
   five-card draw
   boxing
   card games
   activity
   poker
   tennis
   bridge
   singles
   welterweight fight

4. negative characteristic
   characteristic

   cheating
   unethical characteristic
   plagiarism

5. novel
   American novel
   reading
   The Grapes of Wrath
   fiction
   literature
   novel by Steinbeck
   modern novel

6. vertebrates
   Alaskan huskies
   biped
   Chris Rock
   woman
   dogs
   animals
   quadruped
   Beyonce Knowles
   man
   cat
   Siamese cats
   Basset Hounds

Abstractions and Evasion

Sometimes people use abstractions and evasive language, consciously or unconsciously, to confuse, distort, conceal, or avoid; in short, to manipulate others—a practice Hemingway laments in his war novel *A Farewell to Arms:*

> I was always embarrassed by the words sacred, glorious, and sacrifice and the expression in vain. We had heard them, sometimes standing in the rain almost out of earshot, so that only the shouted words came through, and had read them, on proclamations that were slapped up by billposters or other proclamations, now for a long time, and I had seen nothing sacred, and the things that were glorious had no glory and the sacrifices were like the stockyards at Chicago if nothing was done with the meat except to bury it. There were many words that you

could not stand to hear and finally only the names of places had dignity. Certain numbers were the same way and certain dates and these with the names of the places were all you could say and have them mean anything. Abstract words such as glory, honor, courage, or hallow were obscene beside the concrete names of villages, the numbers of roads, the names of rivers, the numbers of regiments and the dates.

Hemingway eloquently indicates the power of concrete nouns to honor the dead.

Orville Schell, dean of the Graduate School of Journalism at the University of California at Berkeley, refers to the **obfuscation** (lack of clarity) of much political discourse: "When a country's democratic leaders lose the ability to describe reality accurately, its people become handicapped in their quest to understand and solve their problems."

In Britain, a government spokesman explained why British officials chose to avoid the term *war on terror.* They recognized that "this isn't us against one organized enemy with a clear identity and a chosen set of objectives" as the term *war on terror* implies. They saw that such an abstract term is "vague and simplistic" and that terrorism is a tactic, not an enemy force.

British writer George Orwell addressed the political significance of language in his celebrated essay "Politics and the English Language," claiming that:

> If thought corrupts language, language can also corrupt thought. To think clearly is a necessary first step towards political regeneration: so that the fight against bad English is not frivolous and is not the exclusive concern of professional writers. . . . Political speech and writing are largely the defense of the indefensible. . . . Defenseless villages are bombarded from the air, the inhabitants driven out into the countryside, the cattle machine-gunned, the huts set on fire with incendiary bullets: this is called *pacification*.

Pacification is an example of a **euphemism** that deliberately obscures the concrete reality of war.

Euphemism and Connotation

Euphemisms—indirect, less expressive words or phrases for sensitive ideas— are sometimes justified as a means of sparing feelings: someone *passed away* rather than *died*, or a fat person is referred to as *big-boned*. But we must be particularly wary of language that **deliberately** camouflages precise meaning. A few years ago, when opposition to building the controversial MX missile grew heated, the proponents began to call the missiles "peacemakers," hoping to deflect public reaction away from the notion of an arms buildup.

As suggested by the elephants' conversation in the cartoon that follows, euphemisms can give a positive connotation to a negative experience. Many words carry both a denotative and a connotative meaning.

Denotation refers to the basic dictionary meaning of a word, separate from its emotional associations.

" 'Born in conservation,' if you don't mind. 'Captivity' has negative connotations."

Connotation means the suggestive or associative implications beyond the literal, explicit sense of a word.

For example, think of the words *bachelor* and *spinster*. Both refer to (denote) an unmarried adult. But now consider the connotation. In our culture, one word carries a positive connotation, the other a negative one. The two words *slender* and *skinny* both mean thin. But one would be a compliment, the other not. On a more serious level, Susan Jacoby, in her book *The Age of American Unreason*, points to politicians and the media, who substitute *troop* for *soldier*, turning "an individual . . . into an anonymous-sounding troop," encouraging "the public to think about war and its casualties in a more abstract way."

EXERCISE 5C

Beware the Euphemism

Below is a list of paired terms or phrases. For each, briefly explain how the euphemism dulls or deflects the meaning of the term, and discuss why you think such euphemistic language replaced the original term.

EUPHEMISM	/	TERM
1. offshore	/	foreign
2. revenue enhancement	/	taxes

3. tax relief	/	tax cuts
4. collateral damage	/	civilian losses
5. "somatic cell nuclear transfer"	/	cloning
6. friendly fire	/	shot by a fellow soldier
7. laugh lines	/	face wrinkles
8. information extraction	/	torture
9. enhanced interrogation	/	waterboarding
10. Healthy Forests Restoration Act	/	timber industry legislation allowing forest exploitation

THE LOCKHORNS

"IT'S NOT GOSSIP....IT'S ORAL HISTORY!"

DEFINITION IN WRITTEN ARGUMENT

Appositives—A Strategy for Defining Terms Within the Sentence

As we have illustrated in this chapter, abstract terms need illustration with specific, concrete examples, and words that might be obscure to a general audience need defining so that our readers understand what we mean. How does a writer define terms without derailing the organization and flow of the paper or paragraph? Often, the answer is to use **appositives—noun phrases placed beside other nouns to elaborate on their meaning within the sentence**. We illustrate this relationship in the examples below with **an arrow pointing from the appositive to the noun it modifies**.

Appositives usually follow the nouns they modify:

The next topic will be <u>muscular dystrophy</u>, *a chronic disease* in which patients suffer from a wasting of the muscles.

To understand the topic, students need a definition of the technical term *muscular dystrophy.*

Writer Susan Jacoby is deeply concerned about <u>debased speech</u>, "*a kind of low-level toxin*" she sees as coarsening our discourse and reflecting fuzzy thinking.

Jacoby explains what she means by *debased speech* in order to continue with an extended argument on the subject.

The <u>Sacramento River</u>, *the main source of surface water in California*, has its headwaters in the far northern ranges of Siskiyou County.

By placing important detail in an appositive, writer Joan Didion describes a California river and identifies its origins, all in one fluent sentence. But writers may also introduce a sentence with an appositive:

An expression of frustrated rage, <u>rap</u> tries to be outrageous in order to provoke strong reactions.

The phrase *an expression of frustrated rage* modifies *rap.* Such additions allow a writer to include essential information or background details that may not warrant separate sentences.

EXERCISE 5D

Recognizing Appositives

In the three passages that follow, identify the appositives and the nouns they modify by underlining the appositives and drawing an arrow pointing to the nouns or pronouns they modify.

1. Definition

As Baranczak points out, Nobel Prize–winning poet Milosz rejects symbols in favor of metonymy and synecdoche, those figures of speech which represent a whole by a thing allied to it or by a part of it.

—HELEN VENDLER IN *THE NEW YORKER*

2. Identification

Cotton Mather was an exception, one who so fully accepted and magnified the outlook of his locality that he has entered folklore as the archetypal Puritan, not only a villainous figure in the pages of *Hawthorne*, William Carlos Williams and Robert Lowell, but an object of parody even to his fellow townsmen in 18th-century Boston.

—LARZER ZIFF, *THE NEW YORK TIMES BOOK REVIEW*

3. A descriptive passage with examples

The Evertons are introduced to a second national peculiarity, one they will soon recognize on the streets of Ibarra and in towns and cities beyond. It is something they will see everywhere—a disregard for danger, a companionship with death. By the end of a year they will know it well: the antic bravado, the fatal games, the coffin shop beside the cantina, the sugar skulls on the frosted cake.

—HARRIET DOERR, *STONES FOR IBARRA*

Appositives and Argument

Appositives in arguments are useful, allowing you to define terms, expand and emphasize ideas, and show opposing points of view in the same sentence, as illustrated in the following example:

A <u>unilateral attack</u> on a foreign enemy, *a policy that was considered difficult and dangerous by many, but one that was vigorously promoted by a number of hardline strategists,* means the US would strike without the support of other nations.

Two views on American foreign policy are juxtaposed in one strong sentence.

You will also find appositives helpful when identifying sources within the text of your paper:

S. I. Hayakawa, *a noted semanticist,* points out that advertising and poetry are alike.

Punctuation of Appositives

Punctuation choices are simple and logical. In most cases, the appositive phrase is set off from the noun it modifies with commas, as we illustrate above. If you want greater emphasis, you can do as Harriet Doerr did and use a dash: "It is something they will see everywhere—*a disregard for danger, a companionship with death.*"

Occasionally, when an appositive ends a sentence, a colon is appropriate for even sharper emphasis. This is a good choice when you're concluding a sentence with a list.

The stimulus package contained many components: *funds to banks, to small businesses, to schools, for tax relief, for homeowners' relief, to cite a few examples.*

EXERCISE 5E

Creating Appositives

Most of you already use appositives to some extent in your writing whether you recognize them or not. But a little conscious practice may expand your use of this handy device.

A. Combine the following sets of sentences by reducing one or more sentences to appositives. You may find more than one way to combine them.

> ### *Example:*
>
> A unilateral attack on a foreign enemy was considered difficult and dangerous by many. It means the US would strike without the support of other nations.
>
> becomes
>
> A unilateral attack on a foreign enemy means the US would strike without the support of other nations, *a policy that was considered difficult and dangerous by many.*
>
> or
>
> A unilateral attack on a foreign enemy, *a policy that means the US would strike without the support of other nations,* was considered difficult and dangerous by many.

1. New York has long been the destination of America's adventurous young. It is a city of danger and opportunity.

2. Punk was a return to the roots of rock 'n' roll. It was a revolt against the predictability of disco.

3. People have very different ideas about the meaning of poverty. It is a condition that to some suggests insufficient income, to others laziness, and to still others a state of unwarranted discomfort.

4. Writing ability can have far-reaching effects on a college graduate's future accomplishments. Writing ability is the capacity to generate and organize relevant ideas, compose coherent sentences, choose precise diction, control mechanics.

5. According to the lieutenant's testimony during his court-martial, he was simply following orders as any military man is trained to do. These orders came from his commanding officers.

6. When the Soviets sent troops into Vilnius, Vytautas Landsbergis isolated himself and members of his government in a fortified parliament building. Vilnius is the capital of Lithuania, and Landsbergis was the Lithuanian president.

7. Over time, psychiatrists have expanded the definition of the term *addiction*. It is a word whose meaning has undergone revision to cover a broader range of compulsive behaviors. These compulsions now include sex, television viewing, designer clothes, shopping, computers. These extend to a whole spectrum of dependencies.

8. Concrete has spread over wider and wider areas of the American landscape. It has covered not just the weed patches, deserted lots, and infertile acres but whole pastures, hillsides, and portions of the sea and sky.

B. Write a sentence about your major, your job, or another interest, being sure to include a related technical term. Then add an appositive that defines or illustrates the term.

C. In your next essay or in a revision of a previous assignment, write and identify at least four appositives.

Extended Definition

An appositive is a valuable device for defining a word or a person, but sometimes an entire argument rests on a definition. Before you take a position on abortion for instance, you need to define when you think life begins. Before mounting an argument on gun control, you need to define what you think the wording of the Second Amendment means and stipulate the particular firearms you're considering.

You must also consider your audience, what terminology might be unfamiliar to them. Note how student Nathan Yan (see Chapter 3) defines the high school AP test early in his essay. If he were writing this piece for an AP class, he would not need to define "advanced placement," but writing for a newspaper, he knows many readers will be unfamiliar with such tests and thus, without clarification, will not continue reading his argument. Note how smoothly he has integrated his definition into the flow of his paper:

> The AP tests are nationwide standardized tests administered by the private College Board Association. Successfully passing an AP test will count toward college credit and, depending on the college or university, may grant exemptions from certain general education courses. For many high schools it represents the highest class level for students taking a particular course.

In the following editorial, writer Virginia Heffernan takes a fresh look at the term "addiction," building an entire argument on the term "Internet addiction."

Miss G: A Case of Internet Addiction

VIRGINIA HEFFERNAN

There are certain popular diversions—television, video games, the Internet—that   1
we pursue so deliriously we end up hating ourselves for loving them. Others we brightly recast as the duties of citizenship: newspapers, public radio, sports.

All the while, cottage industries crop up to freak us out about our every last   2
cultural pursuit. In recent years, it's Internet use that's been styled as potentially sick, and "Internet addiction" a new reason for self-hatred.

If you're inclined to worry about your habits, you may have already stumbled   3
onto a strange and influential self-evaluation questionnaire by Dr. Kimberly Young,

a professor of business at St. Bonaventure University. Though Dr. Young developed the test in 1998, early in Web life, it still dominates the Google returns for "Internet addiction" and steadily stirs up anxiety.

Dr. Young told me she believes the Internet is addictive in part because it "allows us to create new personalities and use them to fulfill unmet psychological needs"—which sounds worrying except that art, entertainment and communications systems are designed explicitly to permit self-exploration and satisfy psychological needs. 4

The way the test loads the cultural dice in favor of reality over fantasy should make hearts sink. In the hierarchy of the test, any real-world task or interaction, no matter how mundane or tedious, is more important—and, worse, ought to be more fulfilling—than online fantasy, research or social life. "Do you neglect household chores to use the Internet?" one question asks, and undone laundry is later cited as a warning sign. "How often do you block out disturbing thoughts about your life with soothing thoughts of the Internet?" goes another question. 5

Can this really be science? (And might another psychologist find something to admire in the person who quiets his mind with mere thoughts of the Internet?) I wondered whether other habits of cultural consumption were considered pathological enough to inspire tests. The Web carries a few tests for television addiction, and none for movies. Over on operaaddiction.com, there are no tests, only recordings to order. 6

In general, if a pastime is not classy, those who love it are "addicted." Opera and poetry buffs are "passionate." 7

Virtually all non-work activities have, at one time or another, been represented as craven and diseased. Opera obsession leads to delinquency in Jean-Jacques Beineix's 1981 film "Diva"; an intense movie habit deepens the alienation of the hero of Walker Percy's 1961 novel "The Moviegoer." 8

Novels themselves, now the signature pursuit of the sound and literate mind, have also been considered toxic, as in the 1797 analysis, "Novel Reading, a Cause of Female Depravity." The 18th-century worry about female literacy is not unlike the contemporary anxiety that Web use above all makes girls vulnerable to "predators": "Without this poison instilled, as it were, into the blood, females in ordinary life would never have been so much the slaves of vice." Taken together, these warnings against the very stuff that makes life worth living often seem either like veiled boasts (I'm addicted to the symphony!") or just absurd. 9

So why are authors and educators hellbent on using this shopworn rhetoric when it comes to Internet use? 10

Two weeks ago, I met a professed Internet addict, a 20-year-old college student in New York named Gabriela. (Like many addicts, she preferred that only her first name be used.) One of Gabriela's professors had told me she slept with her laptop, and was wired in the extreme. She told me she had taken Dr. Young's test and was worried about her Internet habits. 11

In e-mail, Gabriela struck a note between irony and concern as she described her symptoms. She told me she keeps an extremely late bedtime, sometimes 4 a.m., because she's up noodling around online. 12

She then described a typical surfing session: "I'll be on Facebook and see a   13
status update of song lyrics, and I'll Google them and find the band name, that
I will subsequently Wikipedia and discover that the lead singer is interesting and
briefly look at his Twitter and try his music on Grooveshark"—a music search engine with streaming service—"while looking at pictures of him on Tumblr"—the
multimedia microblogging platform—"that will lead me to a meme I've never
heard of that I'll explore until I find hilarious photos I will subsequently share with
friends of mine on Facebook." Gabriela, who sometimes dresses in the futuristic
Victoriana known as steampunk, also loves Webcomics, a site for graphic novels
and comic books, and Neopets, a game that lets players care for virtual pets.

She indeed sleeps with her laptop in her bed, "partly so I can have my iTunes   14
play my Sleep playlist." Even on the Sabbath, when she refrains from Internet use
for religious reasons, she talks and thinks about the Internet. She told me she considers surfing the Web not so much a regimen but "a state of being" that, like a
meditative state, took her years to achieve.

Aha, I'm no addiction expert, but Gabriela strikes me as a bright, self-effacing,   15
religious young woman who keeps student hours and prefers logic games, jokes,
graphic novels, trivia quizzes, music, Victoriana and socializing on Facebook to pre-
fab pop bands.

This kind of Internet use isn't usefully described as an addiction, even if there's   16
some shirking of chores and insomnia to it. Fantasy life and real life should, ideally,
be brought into balance—but no student who's making decent grades needs to
get off the Internet just because it would look more respectable or comprehensible
to be playing chess, throwing a Frisbee or reading a George Orwell paperback. The
Internet as Gabriela uses it simply is intellectual life, and play. She's just the person
I'd want for a student, in fact—or a friend, or a daughter.

It's no accident that "search" is the dominant metaphor of the Internet. And it's   17
no accident that the Internet attracts a certain kind of young, dreamy mind at some
liberty to find itself—the type that in earlier eras might have been drawn to novels or
movies. As Binx Bolling puts it in "The Moviegoer": "What is the nature of the search?
you ask. Really it is very simple; at least for a fellow like me. The search is what anyone
would undertake if he were not sunk in the everydayness of his own life."

EXERCISE 5F

Defining Internet Addiction

1. What does writer Heffernan mean when she says, "This kind of Internet use
   isn't usefully described as an addiction"? What kind of Internet use is she talking about?
2. How does Heffernan defend her postion?
3. What do you think of Gabriela's example of a typical surfing session?
4. How would you define Internet addiction? How much time would you estimate you spend "searching"?

WRITING ASSIGNMENT 9

Composing an Argument Based on a Definition

> *"Words usually have something to hide—you have to shake them until the top pops off and some revelation tumbles out. . . ."*
>
> —GEOFFREY NUNBERG

Step 1

Choose a word from the list of abstract terms below, think about its implications for a few minutes, and then start writing a definition that captures its meaning and significance for you. Using a freewriting approach (see Chapter 1), keep going for about twenty minutes. If time and your instructor permit, do this in class; you will find the combination of spontaneity and structure imposed by writing during class to be an aid to composing. You can't get up to make a phone call or make a sandwich. Volunteers can enlighten (and entertain) the class by reading these drafts aloud.

addiction	identity
alcoholism	law
art	leader
cool	maturity
courage	political correctness
cult	politician
defeat	pornography
depression	progress
education	terrorism
elite	the middle class
gossip	torture
heroism	

Step 2

With more time for reflection and revision, take the spontaneous draft you have written and expand and edit your definition. In the process of defining your term, arrive at a significant point and support your position.

You need to argue your point, to use the term you are defining as a springboard for a complete written argument. As the discussion in this chapter has emphasized, you must include specific detail to animate your abstraction.

Here are some possible strategies for writing an extended definition; do not feel compelled to use them all:

- Stipulate your precise meaning, but don't begin with a dictionary definition unless you plan to use it or disagree with it.
- Provide examples of the term.

- Explain the function or purpose of the term.
- Explore etymology (origin and history of a word). The most fruitful source for such explorations is the *Oxford English Dictionary*, a multivolume work available online and in most college libraries and a dictionary well worth your acquaintance. Use the history of a term to help make a point.
- Examine the connotations of the term.
- Discuss what it is not (use this sparingly).
- Draw analogies. Here you will want to be precise; be sure the analogy really fits. (See references to analogy in Chapters 1 and 6 and Malcolm Gladwell's use of analogy in "The Order of Things" in Additional Readings.)

Audience

The instructor and other members of the class.

Purpose

To make the definition of a term the focal point of an argument.

An Alternative

According to your instructor's preference, you may choose to write a shorter version of your definition in the manner of the two student examples and one by *New York Times* columnist Maureen Dowd below.

Different Approaches to the Same Term

Radical 1

The word "radical" has been defined in the *Oxford English Dictionary* as "going to   1
the root or origin, touching or acting upon what is essential and fundamental."
Thus, a radical reform is said to be a fundamental, "thorough reform." In a political sense, an advocate of "radical reform" was described as "one who holds the
most advanced views of political reform on democratic lines, and thus belongs to
the extreme section of the Liberal party." While this may have been a commonly
accepted usage of the term in England at the time, the word "radical" has drifted
away from its original specific meaning to a rather vague term for anyone who
appears to be trying to disrupt the status quo.

In the late 1800s and early 1900s, socialists, Communists, and anarchists alike   2
were popularly categorized by the general American public with the term "radical."
With the controversy surrounding the political goals of these different activists, "a
radical" was at the very least a controversial figure. More often than not, the word
"radical" brought to mind some sort of disruptive character, a nonspecific image
of an extremist, most probably from the far left. On the political spectrum the
"radical" is still viewed as an individual on the extreme left, opposite the "right" or
"conservative" parties. "Conservatives" holding radically different views and goals
are not normally termed "radicals"; they are merely part of the "ultraright."

The term "radical" today is used less as a description of political intent and   3
more as a critique of overall manner and appearance. While many of the "radicals"
in the 1960s did indeed advocate numerous political reforms, the general public
was more impressed by their personal character and style of advocacy. It is not
surprising that when asked to define "a radical," most individuals conjure up a
vague image of some young person wearing ragged clothes and long hair. It is a
pity that in this society, where progressive change is so essential, the term "radical"
has been imbued with so much negativity, so many connotations that really have
nothing to do with political reform.

Radical 2

A radical is an algebraic symbol that tells a person to carry out a certain mathemati-   1
cal operation. The end result of this operation will tell a person the root or origin of
a number or problem.

Recently, while in Los Angeles, I overheard someone describe a car as radical.   2
I immediately thought to myself, something is wrong here. Radicals do not have
engines. They may contain a number, like 32, underneath their top line, but never
a stock Chevy 302 engine. It simply would not fit. When I asked this person why he
called the car a radical, he replied, "Because the car is different and unusual." Once
again, I thought to myself, he has made a mistake. Radicals are quite common. In
fact, they are an essential part of most algebraic theories. I had to infer that this
man knew nothing about algebra. If he did, he would have realized that radicals
are not different or unusual at all, and would not have called the car one.

While I was in New York this past summer, I happened to see a group of peo-   3
ple carrying signs of protest in front of the United Nations Building. As I watched
them, a man came over to me, pointed at the group and muttered, "Radicals." I
thought to myself, man are you ever wrong. Radicals do not carry signs saying,
"Feed the Poor." They may carry a number, like 2, in their top right hand corner,
but this number only means to find the root of a problem. It does not mean, "Feed
the Poor."

These two events show that there is a great deal of misunderstanding through-   4
out the country in regard to what a radical is. At their simplest level, radicals tell us to
find the root of a problem. At their most complex level, they tell us the same thing.

Slut

MAUREEN DOWD

After eons of being a summary judgment that a woman is damaged goods, the   1
word slut has shifted into more ambiguous territory. It can still be an insult, especially since there is no pejorative equivalent to suggest that a man has sullied himself with too many sexual partners. Men are players, women are sluts, just the way
men are tough and women are bitchy.

Republicans denigrated the prim law professor Anita Hill by painting her, in   2
David Brock's memorable phrase, as "a little bit nutty and a little bit slutty." Clinton
defenders demonized Monica Lewinsky the same way.

But as women express themselves more, sexually and professionally, and no   3
longer need to "use their virginity as a meal ticket," as the anthropologist Helen
Fisher puts it, the slur may have lost some sting. *The Times's* Stephanie Rosenbloom
writes that the word has morphed into a term of endearment and teasing, with
teenage girls greeting each other with "Hi slut!"—the way "queer" and "pimp"
took on different coloration, and the way "girl" went from an insult in early feminist days to a word embraced by young women. The gangsta rap characteriza-
tions of women that some found offensive are now being embraced by many
young women.

"Slut" is a faddish appellation for everything from lip balm to cocktails, and ap-   4
plies to voracious behavior of all kinds; *Cosmopolitan* recently ran a quiz on how to
tell if you're an "attention slut."

"It's just a really fun word to say," explains my classy 26-year-old girlfriend.   5
"Usually women only call someone a slut if she's not slutty, but if you do call a
slutty friend a slut, you can get away with it because, oh, it was just a *joke*, even
when it's not. So, yet another way for mean girls to flourish."

It was probably inevitable, once women began discovering their inner slut with   6
microminis and other provocative outfits, and with high school and college girls reporting a much more blasé attitude about performing oral sex, that they'd turn the
word itself inside-out. But, semantics aside, have attitudes really changed much?

Studies show that superiors, men and women, may penalize female executives   7
who dress in too sexy a manner—proving that it's not always safe to strut as a slut.
And Don Reisinger, a student in Albany, told Ms. Rosenbloom, "When I think of the
word slut, I think of a woman who has been around the block more times than my
dad's Chevy. I might date a slut, but I certainly wouldn't marry one."

That men are counting those spins around the block is a fact that's not lost on   8
women. The late-night comic Craig Ferguson dryly observed that women often get
back with their exes because they don't want their total number to go up.

One 24-year-old Washington reporter agreed that "redos" of previous partners   9
can keep your number below the slut threshold, defined by two of her male friends
as "less than 20." She thinks she is "chaste" with a number of six, but admits she
sometimes subtracts one or two when telling a guy her romantic history. She said
she kept dating Mr. Six after she'd lost interest simply because she didn't want to
up the number to Mr. Seven.

One 25-year-old writer in D.C. said his ideal girl's number is one or two fewer   10
than his. When he had "the numbers talk" with one date, she gave him an answer
that he found both satisfactory and sexy: "Enough to know what I'm doing."

INVENTING A NEW WORD TO FILL A NEED

Alice Walker, author of the *The Color Purple*, sought to rectify some of the linguistic imbalance in gender representation when she coined the term *womanist* for her
collection of nonfiction *In Search of Our Mothers' Gardens: Womanist Prose*. Why,
we might ask, did she need to invent such a word? We can assume that she experienced a condition for which there was no term, so she created one. Her word stuck,

turning up in a 2008 book review: "Amy Richards serves on the boards . . . of such blue-chip **'womanist'** organizations as *Ms. Magazine* . . . and Planned Parenthood." A student came up with *strugglesome*, a term we're often tempted to use ourselves. Writer Douglas Coupland suggests these new words:

> *Frankentime*—What time feels like when you realize that most of your life is spent working with and around a computer and the Internet.
>
> *me goggles*—The inability to accurately perceive oneself as others do.
>
> *omniscience fatigue*—The burnout that comes with being able to know the answer to almost anything online.

Writer and performer Rich Hall created the word *sniglet* for "any word that doesn't appear in the dictionary, but should." Two examples from his collection:

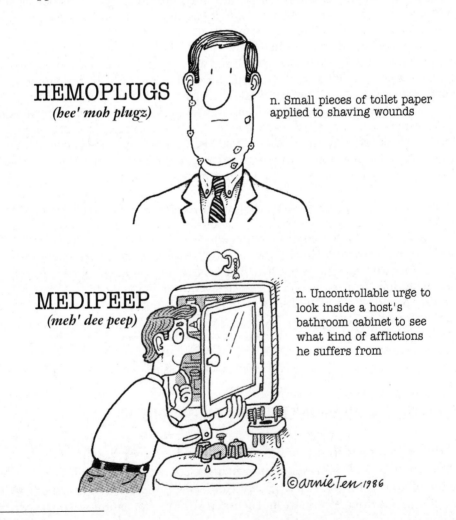

HEMOPLUGS
(hee' moh plugz)

n. Small pieces of toilet paper applied to shaving wounds

MEDIPEEP
(meh' dee peep)

n. Uncontrollable urge to look inside a host's bathroom cabinet to see what kind of afflictions he suffers from

©arnieTen 1986

WRITING ASSIGNMENT 10

Creating a New Word

Now it's your turn to create a new word. Give the word an extended definition so that those in your class can see how to use it and why our culture needs such an addition to the language. Here you have an opportunity to develop an argument while using your imagination. Your new word will serve as a springboard.

Audience
The instructor and other members of the class.

Purpose
To identify a meaning in need of a name.

SUMMARY

It is important that our readers understand the meaning of the words we use when we write.

Controlling the **definitions** is important, particularly in politics. Definitions can affect how people view themselves and others, *alcoholism* being one example of many such terms.

Language is an abstract system of symbols.

The assignation of a particular meaning to a given term remains essentially arbitrary. Meaning is dependent to a large degree on the individual, the context, and the interpretive community.

Political systems and advertising often manipulate abstract language for their own purposes. The power to abstract is what makes us human. **Concrete, specific details** are what flesh out our ideas so our readers can grasp, visualize, and retain meaning.

We must beware of evasive language and euphemisms.

Appositives define terms at the sentence level.

KEY TERMS

Appositives noun phrases placed beside nouns to elaborate on their meaning, useful for defining, identifying, explaining, and describing terms within the sentence.

Connotation the suggestive or associative implications beyond the literal, explicit sense of a word.

Denotation the basic dictionary meaning of a word, separate from its emotional associations.

Euphemism an indirect, less expressive word or phrase for a sensitive or controversial idea.

Obfuscation lack of clarity.

CHAPTER 6

Fallacious Arguments

Her reasoning is full of tricks
And butterfly suggestions,
I know no point to which she sticks;
She begs the simplest questions,
And, when her premises are strong
She always draws her inference wrong.

—*Upon Lebia Arguing* by Alfred Cochrane (1865–?)

WHAT IS A FALLACIOUS ARGUMENT?

Short people do not make good presidents.
The Democratic candidate is short.
Therefore, the Democratic candidate will not be a good president.

Senator Smith was expelled from college for cheating on an exam.
His wife divorced him because of his numerous affairs.
Therefore, he is a man without honor, a politician who cannot be
    trusted, and we should not support his National Health Bill.

Which of these two arguments is more persuasive? Technically, the line of reasoning in the first argument is logical because the two premises lead inescapably to the conclusion. There is nothing fallacious in the *form* of this argument. The difficulty lies in the first premise; it is an absurd claim and an unacceptable premise. This argument is not persuasive and would convince no one. (Look ahead to Chapter 7, "Deductive and Inductive Argument," for a detailed explanation of form and acceptability of premises.)

But what about the second argument? Would you be in favor of a National Health Bill created by such a man? Some might find it persuasive, believing that he could not propose worthwhile legislation. But because nothing in the premises indicates flaws in the bill—only flaws in the man—the conclusion is not logically supported. The bill may be worthwhile despite the nature of the man who proposes it. This then is a **fallacious argument**, an argument that is persuasive but does not logically support its conclusion.

Because fallacious arguments are both appealing and abundant, we as critical readers and writers must guard against them. The first step in this defense is to familiarize ourselves with the most common fallacies. Fallacious reasoning may be intentional, as is sometimes the case with unscrupulous merchandisers and politicians, or it may be an innocent mistake resulting from fuzzy thinking or unexamined bias. In any case, if we are familiar with fallacies we can avoid them in our own thinking and writing. We can also spot them in the arguments of others, a skill that makes us wiser consumers and citizens.

There are many fallacies, a number of which tend to overlap. In one sense, the Latin term **non sequitur—it does not follow**—covers most fallacies. Our intention here is not to overwhelm you with an exhaustive list of fallacies and a complex classification scheme. Instead, we offer a list of the more common fallacies, presented in alphabetical order for easy reference.

Appeal to Authority

The opinion of an authority can support an argument only when it reflects his special area of expertise; the authority must be an expert on the subject being argued, as is the case in the following examples:

> The surgeon general warns that smoking is injurious to health.
> Vladimir Horowitz, the internationally acclaimed pianist, preferred the Steinway piano.
> Studies conducted by the *Washington Post,* the *Los Angeles Times,* and CNN suggest that increasing numbers of parents object to video game violence.

But if the appeal is to an authority that is not appropriate, the appeal is fallacious, as is the case in the following example:

> Abortion to save the life of a mother is an irrelevant issue because a former surgeon general, a well-known pediatric surgeon, claimed that in all his years of surgical practice he had never seen a case in which such a dilemma had arisen.

The problem here is that a pediatric surgeon is not an appropriate authority on an issue involving obstetrics, a different medical specialty.

Fallacious appeals to authority are bountiful in advertising, which employs well-known actors and athletes to sell us everything from banking services to automobiles to coffee. Since many of these celebrities have no specialized knowledge—no authority—on the particular service or product they are promoting, they are not credible sources. For example, George Foreman, a boxer, gave his name to an appliance, the George Foreman Grill, though he has never been a chef or worked in the food industry.

Appeals to authority also appear in the form of **snob appeal** or **appeal to the authority of the select few**. The following advertisement for a resort hotel illustrates this fallacy, which appeals to people's desire for prestige and exclusivity:

Palmilla's not for everyone. The best never is.

Keep in mind that fallacious appeals to authority should not cause us to doubt all authorities but rather should encourage us to distinguish between reliable and unreliable sources. In constructing your own arguments, be prepared to cite, explain, and, if necessary, defend your sources when relying on authority.

Appeal to Fear

An appeal to fear attempts to convince by implicitly threatening the audience. Its efforts to persuade are based on emotion rather than reason. An ad for a business college uses this approach:

Will there be a *job* waiting when *you* leave college?

The ad attempts to frighten students by implying that unless they attend this business college, they will be unable to get a job after attending a four-year traditional college.

The following ad for "structural reinforcing" was published during the 2008 recession and stock market decline:

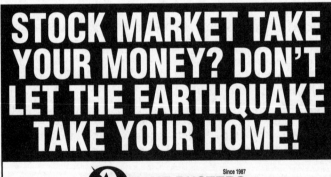

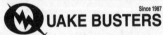

Appeal to Pity

An appeal to pity attempts to win our sympathy in order to convince us of the conclusion. Like an appeal to fear, it appeals to our emotions rather than our intellect. Some students use this approach when arguing for a particular grade.

> Professor Hall, I must get an A in your course. If you don't give me an A, I won't be able to go to law school.

As we know, a student's work in a course—papers, exams, participation—determines the final grade. The consequences of a grade, no matter how dire they may be, should have no effect in determining that grade.

Emotion may play a part in argument, but its role must be secondary, a backdrop to logical reasoning. In fact, effective arguments often begin with frightening statistics—"If nothing is done about global warming, the earth's temperature will increase 10 degrees by the year 2015 with disastrous consequences for our environment." Or they may begin with an emotional illustration. For example, an argument for mandatory fencing around all private swimming pools may open with a description of a mother caring for a child who is brain damaged as a result of almost drowning in a private pool. Either of these introductions will capture the emotions and interest of the audience, but they should be followed by facts, appropriate appeals to authority, and logical reasoning.

Begging the Question

When a person **begs the question**, he offers no actual support for his conclusion while appearing to do so. Instead, he may argue in a circle, just restating, as a premise, his conclusion in different words:

> "The reason he's so strong is because of his strength." (a TV commentator at an NCAA basketball tournament)

The writer is simply stating that the basketball player is strong because he's strong. He does not offer reasons for the player's strength. He begs the question. Some classic examples:

> Parallel lines will never meet because they are parallel.

> . . . your noble son is mad.
> Mad call I it, for to define true madness,
> What is't but to be nothing else but mad?
>
> —POLONIUS TO QUEEN GERTRUDE IN *HAMLET*, II.II

We can discern something of Polonius's character from the manner of his argument.

> Money is better than poverty, if only for financial reasons.
>
> —WOODY ALLEN

Even a president can be guilty of circular reasoning:

> The reason I keep insisting that there was a relationship between Iraq and al Qaeda [is] because there was a relationship between Iraq and al Qaeda.
> —FORMER PRESIDENT GEORGE W. BUSH

Columnist Jon Carroll notes that the term "beg the question" is often misused and that his own understanding of the term needed refreshing:

> I was helping a friend with a writing chore she had, and I noticed that she had used the phrase 'beg the question.' I knew it was wrong because I hang around with word people a lot, and they are always insisting that 'beg the question' is constantly misused. I realized it didn't mean 'raise the question,' which is how it's often used, but I realized the leaky part of my brain had lost the real meaning of 'beg the question.'
>
> Perhaps some of you are with me on this. Maybe you have leaky brains, too. So I went to the dictionary and discovered this definition: 'to assume the truth of the very point raised in the question.' It's sort of like a circular argument—'This is true because this is true,' only tarted up with clauses and phrases and fancy words.
>
> Example pulled from the Internet: 'Person A: Bob is annoyed right now. Person B: Why do you say that? Person A: Well, because he is really angry.'
>
> An actual answer to the question would be more like, 'Because his wife ran away with his best friend and took the dog and the car and his collection of fossilized femurs.' The question would thus not have been begged. I'm making a big deal of this so I'll remember, and maybe you'll remember, and the word people will be briefly happy until another outrage stirs their blood.

Some such fallacious arguments beg the question not by restating the conclusion but by supporting the conclusion with assumptions, stated or hidden (see Chapter 3), that are as much in need of proof as is the conclusion. For example, those opposed to rent control argue that rent control should be removed in order to boost construction and thus increase the number of affordable rental units. A letter to the editor points out the weakness:

> Editor: In your editorial concerning the housing crisis, you rely on one of the oldest rhetorical tricks of accepting as a given that which you could not possibly prove, that is, "There can be little question that removal of rent controls would result in a boom in apartment house construction . . ." If rent control is such an important factor, construction should have been booming in the '80s before rent control laws existed in our state. It wasn't. . . .

Before we can accept the conclusion, the "truth" of the premise—that construction of new housing will increase if rent control laws are abolished—must be established.

"You know what I like about power? It's so damn empowering."

We can also encounter question begging (avoiding the issue) in the form of an actual question, a **loaded question**. An example:

Have you started paying your fair share of taxes yet?

First, the questioner would have to establish what he means by "fair share" and then establish that the person to whom he addressed the question had not been paying it.

In some arguments, just a single word—*reactionary, negligent, warmonger, deadbeat*—can beg the question. Be on the alert for such prejudicial language.

Double Standard

When an argument contains the fallacy of **double standard** (sometimes referred to as special pleading), it judges and labels the same act differently, depending on the person or group who performs the act.

Shannon Faulkner, the first woman ever admitted to the Citadel, a military college in South Carolina, dropped out in her first year. The other cadets cheered as she departed the campus, and the media covered her departure in great detail. What the jeering male cadets and the media ignored were the 34 other first-year students, all men, who also dropped out. Shannon Faulkner and her classmates made the same decision, but she was subjected to ridicule and close media scrutiny while her 34 male classmates were not; a double standard was applied.

Editorialist Cynthia Tucker accuses our government of having a double standard in its dealings with China and Cuba:

> If diplomatic relations and free trade are a sound policy toward China, which restricts religious freedoms, limits free speech, builds nuclear weapons, and poses a threat to its neighbors, doesn't the same apply to Cuba, which restricts religious freedoms, limits free speech, and has no nuclear weapons and poses no threat to its neighbors?

A California city was recently accused of a double standard of enforcement when a local newspaper uncovered a city memo that "directed parking officers to issue tickets to cars parked in the wrong direction or on sidewalks anywhere in the city except for two wealthy neighborhoods. Cars in those neighborhoods were not tagged but instead received courtesy notices when they violated either of two parking laws." Once the policy was made public, the city abandoned it and applied a single standard to the two violations.

Sometimes a double standard can be applied subtly through the manipulative use of language. A well-known defense lawyer, while discussing legal strategies on television, stated that he "prepares" his witnesses while the prosecution "coaches" theirs. "Prepares" suggests professional legal preparation for the courtroom, whereas "coaches" suggests that a witness is encouraged to say what the lawyer tells her to whether it is true or not. Both lawyers are working with their clients before trial, but the defense lawyer's subtle use of language casts a negative slant on opposing counsel.

Equivocation

Equivocation is the shifting of the meaning of a given term within an argument. This fallacy stems from the often ambiguous nature of language. A term may be ambiguous because it has more than one meaning; for instance, the word *affair* may mean a party, a controversial incident, or an extramarital relationship. Look at this example:

> We are told by the government that to discriminate against a person in employment or housing is wrong and punishable by law. But we must discriminate when

we hire an individual (Does he have the necessary experience?) or when we rent an apartment (Does he have sufficient income?). Discrimination is a necessary part of making such decisions.

The word *discriminate* is the culprit. In the first sentence, "discriminate" refers to prejudice, to denying an individual employment or housing because of his or her race, sex, or religion. In the second sentence, "discriminate" refers to making careful distinctions between applicants on the basis of relevant issues.

60 Minutes correspondent Morley Safer is guilty of equivocation in the following email he wrote to fellow members of a private New York club that wanted to sever its ties with an all-male London club:

> If we were to place embargoes on all entities that continue to discriminate, we would have to dissolve our own Association. We practice economic discrimination—our dues are prohibitive to a good part of the population. . . . We elect a Committee on Admissions, which by its very nature, is charged with the responsibility to "discriminate."

Again, these kinds of discrimination are not the same as excluding all women because they are women.

To equivocate means to use equivocal terms in order to deceive or mislead; we can avoid this by defining all ambiguous terms and being consistent in our use of them (see Chapter 5).

False Analogy

One creative way to mount an argument can be through analogy (see Chapter 1). An argument by analogy compares two or more things, alike in certain respects, and suggests that since they share certain characteristics, they probably share other characteristics as well. By comparing the brain to the heart, a doctor argues effectively for drug therapy over psychotherapy as the best treatment for schizophrenia or severe depression. "The brain is an organ, like the heart, and like that organ, can malfunction as a result of biochemical imbalances."

But in a **false analogy**, one compares two things in which the key features are different. A mountain climber offers this analogy to minimize the danger of his sport:

> I don't want to die falling off a rock. . . . But you can kill yourself falling in the bathtub, too.
>
> —John Bachar

He is comparing two extremely dissimilar acts: climbing a mountain and taking a bath, one a sport, the other a daily routine. And while it is possible to kill oneself slipping in the bathtub, if we were to compare the number of deaths in proportion to the number of bathers and the number of mountain climbers, we would surely find a higher incidence of deaths resulting from mountain climbing than from bathing. To construct a more convincing analogy, the mountain climber should compare the risk in mountain climbing with that in another high-risk sport such as race car driving.

A *Dear Abby* reader writes in response to Abby's recommendation that young people use contraceptives for premarital sex: "We know that premarital sex is wrong, just as we know shoplifting is wrong." Dear Abby's reply points out the fallaciousness of this comparison.

> One of the most powerful urges inborn in the human animal is the sex drive. Nature intended it to ensure perpetuation of our species. It is not comparable with the temptation to swipe a candy bar or a T-shirt.

Writer Alice Walker compares the genital mutilation of female children in some parts of Africa to the plastic surgery performed on women in the West. But is this an accurate analogy? Young girls have no say in the surgery performed on them, while adult women choose to have surgery to enhance their appearance.

The following letter to *Miss Manners* argues on the basis of analogy, an analogy that in her reply Miss Manners shows to be false:

> Dear Miss Manners:
>   If I were to entertain someone at dinner whom I knew to be a vegetarian, I would make certain there would be plenty of things on the menu that a vegetarian could eat. Besides my lamb chop, there would be plenty of vegetables, breads, salads, etc. I would not feel compelled to become a vegetarian myself for the occasion.
>   Were I to dine at the home of vegetarians, I would expect of them a similar accommodation, so that in addition to their usual fare, they might serve me a small steak, perhaps, though of course they wouldn't need to partake of it themselves.

Miss Manners replies:

> Gentle Reader:
>   You lose the argument. Here is the problem: Serving vegetables to guests does not violate your principles, nor does it make you a vegetarian. However, expecting your vegetarian friends to serve you something that they exclude from their households would require their violating their principles.

Reasoning by analogy is appealing because it is vivid and accessible and thus can be an effective argument strategy. But we must not accept analogies without careful examination. We must ask if the two things being compared are similar in ways that are significant to the point being made. Turn to Malcolm Gladwell's article "The Order of Things" in Additional Readings, in which he compares the ranking of cars to the ranking of colleges. Is the analogy effective and logical?

False Cause

The fallacy of **false cause** is also called **post hoc reasoning**, from the Latin *post hoc, ergo propter hoc*, which means "after this, therefore because of this." As this translation indicates, the fallacy of false cause assumes a cause–effect relationship between two events because one precedes another. It claims a causal relationship solely on the basis of a chronological relationship. Mark Twain uses this relationship for humorous effect:

> I joined the Confederacy for two weeks. Then I deserted. The Confederacy fell.

We know, as Twain did, that his desertion did nothing to end the Civil War, but this fallacy is not always so obvious. Look at the following example:

> Governor Robinson took office in 2006.
> In 2008, the state suffered a severe recession.
> Therefore, Governor Robinson should not be reelected.
> (Hidden assumption: The governor caused the recession.)

Elected officials are often credited with the success or blamed for the failure of the economy. But in fact, anything as complex as the economy is affected by numerous factors. A federal investigation into the 2008 financial crisis concluded (in 2011) that the crisis was caused by regulatory neglect, corporate bungling, and excessive risk-taking by Wall Street. Some disagreed with this official conclusion and blamed cheap money and the desire for homeownership. Is it possible both are right?

In another example of post hoc reasoning, an author attributes his nephew's autism to a vaccination. A doctor criticizes the writer's conclusion in a letter to the *New York Times Book Review*:

> To the Editor:
> There will always be people who are convinced that because the signs of mental retardation or a seizure disorder or autism first became evident after an immunization, then certainly the immunization caused their problems; millions of dollars have been awarded in damages because some such people served on juries.
> For those people of reason who remember that **post hoc, ergo propter hoc** is a logical fallacy and not a standard of proof, let me state categorically that careful review of the literature confirms that a DPT shot might result in a fever or a sore leg or an irritable child. But it will not cause retardation, it will not precipitate epilepsy, and it never has and never will lead to autism.
>
> DIANE LIND FENSTER, M.D.
> GREEN BAY, WIS.

Some have argued that the atomic bombs we dropped on Hiroshima and Nagasaki caused Japan to surrender at the end of World War II. Others argue that this is a case of post hoc reasoning, that other factors such as Russia's threat to enter the war against Japan caused Japan to surrender, so that the killing of 110,000 Japanese, many of them women and children, was unnecessary.

Determining the cause of all but the simplest events is extremely difficult. Post hoc reasoning is appealing because it offers simple explanations for complex events.

False Dilemma

A **false dilemma** presents two and only two alternatives for consideration when other possibilities exist. For this reason, a false dilemma is often referred to as **either/ or reasoning**.

In his essay "Love One, Hate the Other," movie critic Mick LaSalle rails against what he calls "false polarities." He offers the following examples: Lennon *or* McCartney, Monroe *or* Bardot, Hemingway *or* Fitzgerald, Freud *or* Jung. He calls them false "because, in each case, two elements are arbitrarily set apart as opposites when they are not opposite at all, and the idea is that we must choose between the two when there's no legitimate need to do that."

Narrowing to two choices is a strategy designed to forestall clear thinking and force a quick decision. This kind of reasoning can be seductive because it reduces the often difficult decisions and judgments we must make by narrowing complex problems and issues to two simple options.

"Damn it, Eddie! If you don't believe in nuclear war and you don't believe in conventional war, what the hell kind of war do you believe in?"

What alternative has the speaker completely overlooked?

Columnist Ellen Goodman offers an example of one young critical thinker who refused to accept the limits of either/or thinking:

Remember the story of Heinz, the man whose wife was dying for lack of medicine or the funds to buy it? Children are asked to decide whether it's OK for Heinz to steal the drugs. On the one hand it's wrong to break the law, on the other, it's wrong to let the woman die.

What I remember most about the Heinz dilemma is the response of an 11-year-old little girl named Amy, as described in Carol Gilligan's book, *In a Different Voice*. Amy didn't think that Heinz should steal the drugs because if he did he might end up in jail—and what would happen next time his wife needed the pills? Nor did Amy think she should die.

This 11-year-old refused to choose from column A or column B. She thought they should "talk it out," get a loan, or find another way out of the dilemma. Traditional moralists thought Amy was "illogical." But the truth was that she took the long, wide moral view—six steps down the road, up a side road, and back to the main road. Amy stepped outside the multiple-choice questionnaire.

Hasty Generalization

A **hasty generalization** is a conclusion based on a sample that is too small or in some other way unrepresentative of the larger population.

> Students in Professor Hall's eight o'clock freshman composition class are often late. There's no doubt that people are right when they claim today's college students are irresponsible and unreliable.

In this case the sample is both unrepresentative and too small; unrepresentative because we would expect an eight o'clock class to have more late students than classes offered later in the day, and too small because one section can't represent an entire freshman class.

In Chapter 7, we ask students to collect hasty generalizations. Here are some of our favorites:

> Jocks can't type.
> Women in bridal departments are airheads.
> Anyone who listens to heavy metal is not intelligent.
> Older guests always arrive early.
> Everyone in the South is gun crazy.
> Everyone in Germany dances by themselves.
> Women who work full time have unsuccessful marriages.

It is impossible to avoid making generalizations, nor should we try. But we must examine the basis for our generalizations to determine their reliability (see Chapter 7).

One way to avoid this fallacy is to qualify your generalizations with words such as *many* or *some*. Most of us would accept the claim that "some women are bad drivers" but would reject and be offended by the claim that "women are bad drivers."

Personal Attack

Often called by its Latin name, ***ad hominem*** ("against the man"), the fallacy of personal attack substitutes for a reasoned evaluation of an argument, an attack against the person presenting the argument. The person is discredited, not the argument.

When Rachel Carson's *Silent Spring*, a seminal work on the health hazards of insecticides and pesticides, was published in 1962, a leading scientist (male) questioned her concern for future generations because she was a spinster who had no children. He attacked her personally, not her argument that certain commonly used chemicals caused cancer.

As a newspaper columnist, writer Jon Carroll often receives mail from readers who disagree with him. One such reader called him a "bunny hugger" for his protect-the-environment point of view. Carroll's response:

> . . . here's a little rule: If you hurl ad hominems at people, you are forcing them to shut their ears. You could be Albert Bloody Einstein, and if you start your note with "Dear Idiot," your message will not come through.

The website Politics Daily (politicsdaily.com) recently sent the following message to all its readers:

> We are reading all comments before publishing them. Personal attacks (on writers, other readers, Nancy Pelosi, George W. Bush, or anyone at all) and comments that are not productive additions to the conversation will not be published, period, to make room for a discussion among those with ideas to kick around.

Those given to Latin names like to label a particular kind of personal attack as *tu quoque*—"you also." In this instance, a person and thus his arguments are discredited because his own behavior does not strictly conform to the position he holds. We've all heard about the parent who drinks too much but admonishes his child about the dangers of drinking.

Anti-gun-control groups were delighted when Carl Rowan, a prominent Washington columnist and a staunch advocate of gun control, used an unregistered pistol to wound a young man who broke into his backyard. But Rowan's failure to follow his own beliefs does not necessarily make his argument for gun control a weak one.

Poisoning the Well

A person **poisons the well** when he makes an assertion that precludes or discourages an open discussion of the issue. This assertion will intimidate the listener, who fears that any resistance on his part will lead to a personal disagreement rather than a critical discussion.

> Every patriotic American supports legislation condemning the desecration of the flag.

The listener must now prove his patriotism rather than express his doubts about the legislation, and the speaker avoids having to defend his conclusion with relevant premises.

Or take this comment from a movie critic: "Essential viewing for serious moviegoers." What does that make us if we decide not to see the film under discussion?

Red Herring

The term **red herring** comes to us from fox hunting. The strong-smelling fish, red after being smoked, was used to throw hunting dogs off the trail of the fox. Mystery writers often throw red herrings in their readers' path, leading them away from the real culprit by making them suspect other characters. In argument, a red herring is a distraction from the issue under discussion; a different, irrelevant topic. For example:

> While the hospital bond issue has merit, there are too many bond issues on this ballot.

Attention is being diverted from the merits of a particular bond issue to another topic—the number of bond issues on the ballot.

Don't confuse red herring with *straw man* on the next page. Straw man is a distortion of an opponent's argument, while red herring introduces a completely different topic in order to divert attention from the topic under discussion.

Slippery Slope

We know the **slippery slope** fallacy by other names too: the domino theory, the ripple effect, the snowball effect, the doomsday scenario, or opening the floodgates.

One thing leads to another. People often claim that an action should be avoided because it will inevitably lead to a series of extremely undesirable consequences. Sometimes such a chain reaction is possible, but often it can be exaggerated for effect.

Writer Wendy Kaminer, reviewing *Under Fire: The NRA and the Battle for Gun Control*, presents one group's position on gun control:

> What seems like reasonable restrictions on guns with no legitimate civilian purpose (assault rifles, for example) will lead inevitably to total prohibition of gun ownership that ends in virtual slavery at the hands of a totalitarian regime.

The argument here is that if we allow the government to take one step—the banning of assault weapons—the next step will be the banning of all guns, and the final step, loss of all freedom for all citizens. In this argument, the downward slope is more precipitous than the evidence warrants, leading to an erroneous conclusion.

For another example of slippery slope, we return to an email from *60 Minutes* correspondent Morley Safer cited above under Equivocation. Safer, opposed to his private New York club's decision to break its ties with a private, all-male London club, poses a rhetorical question:

> What will be next? Disassociation with clubs that do not cater to vegans on their menus? Kosher dining rooms? Special facilities for nudists and transsexuals?

Linguist Geoffrey Nunberg notes that slippery slope is a "convenient way of warning of the dire effects of some course of action without actually having to criticize the action itself, which is what makes it a favorite ploy of hypocrites: 'Not that there's anything wrong with A, mind you, but A will lead to B and then C, and before you know it we'll be up to our armpits in Z.'" Nunberg also notes that this fallacy is used to protect the status quo, the existing state of affairs. English legal scholar Glanville Williams would agree, calling slippery slope "the trump card of the traditionalist, because no proposal for reform is immune to [it]."

Columnist William Safire points out that "Logicians are very cautious about *slippery slope* arguments because it is impossible to know beforehand, with absolute deductive certainty, that an 'if-then' statement is true." Careful reasoning helps us distinguish between probable and outrageous claims.

Straw Man

In a **straw man** argument, a person creates and then attacks a distorted version of the opposition's argument:

> The candidate wants the federal government to house everyone, feed everyone, care for everyone's children, and provide medical care for everyone. And he's going to take 50 percent of every dime you make to do it.

This argument overlooks the candidate's proposal to reduce defense spending to meet his goals. Hence, this is an unfair presentation of the opposing view, but one that could be extremely effective in discouraging votes for the candidate. This is the purpose of a straw man argument: to frighten supporters away from the opponent's camp and into one's own. Columnist Ellen Goodman comments on this strategy in an essay titled "The Straw Feminist":

> The straw man has been a useful creature throughout history. Whenever people argued, he could be pulled together quickly out of the nearest available haystack, and set up as an opponent. The beauty of the straw man was that he was easily defeated. The straw man was also useful as a scarecrow. The arguments attributed to him were not only flimsy, they were frightening. . . .
>
> The straw feminist wanted to drive all women out of their happy homes and into the workforce. The straw feminist had an abortion as casually as she had a tooth pulled. The straw feminist was hostile to family life and wanted children warehoused in government-run day and night care. At times, the straw feminist was painted slightly pinko by the anticommunists or rather lavender by the anti-lesbians. But it was generally agreed upon that she was a castrating—well, you fill in the blank.
>
> This creature was most helpful for discrediting real feminists but also handy for scaring supporters away.

A caution: German philosopher Arthur Schopenhauer (1788–1860) pointed out that "it would be a very good thing if every trick could receive some short and obviously appropriate name, so that when a man used this or that particular trick, he could at once be reproved for it." Fallacies provide us with those short and appropriate names for tricks or errors in reasoning, but we must not assume that all such errors can be labeled. Whenever we find fault with a particular line of reasoning, we should not hesitate to articulate that fault, whether or not we have a label for it. On the other hand, we must be careful not to see fallacies everywhere, perhaps even where they don't exist.

EXERCISE 6A

Identifying Fallacies

Identify by name the fallacies in each of the following arguments and justify your responses. You may want to turn to the end of the chapter for a chart of the fallacies.

Competition and collaboration: An interesting approach to this exercise combines competition and cooperation. The class is divided into two teams who compete in identifying the fallacies, with team members cooperating on responses as an option.

1.

"It could go badly, or it could go well, depending on whether it goes badly or well."

2. "A group of self-appointed 'life-style police' are pushing to control many aspects of our daily lives. If they succeed, we lose our basic right to free choice. Today they're targeting smoking. What's next? Red meat? Leather? Coffee? If fifty million smokers can lose their rights anyone can." (From an ad for the National Smokers Alliance.)

3. America: Love it or leave it.

4. You can't expect insight and credibility from the recent book *The Feminist Challenge* because its author David Bouchier is, obviously, a man.

5. Politicians can't be trusted because they lack integrity.

6. "We would not tolerate a proposal that states that because teenage drug use is a given we should make drugs more easily available." (Archbishop John R. Quinn in response to a National Research Council's recommendation that contraceptives and abortion be made readily available to teenagers)

7. How long must we allow our courts to go on coddling criminals?

8. "I'm firm. You are stubborn. He's pig-headed." (Philosopher Bertrand Russell)

9. Anyone who truly cares about preserving the American way of life will vote Republican this fall.

10. "Why is it okay for people to choose the best house, the best schools, the best surgeon, the best car, but not try to have the best baby possible?" (A father's defense of the Nobel Prize winners' sperm bank.)

11. Socrates, during his trial in 399 B.C.: "My friend, I am a man, and like other men, a creature of flesh and blood, and not of wood or stone, as Homer says;

and I have a family, yes, and sons, O Athenians, three in number, one almost a man, and two others who are still young; and yet I will not bring any of them hither in order to petition you for an acquittal." (Plato, *The Apology*)

12.

MUTTS by Patrick McDonnell

13. Mark R. Hughes, owner of Herbalife International, was questioned by a Senate subcommittee about the safety of the controversial diet products marketed by his company. Referring to a panel of three nutrition and weight-control authorities, Hughes asked: "If they're such experts, then why are they fat?"

14. The Black Panthers—Were they criminals or freedom fighters? (From a television ad promoting a documentary on the 1960s radical group.)

15. When the Supreme Court ruled that school officials need not obtain search warrants or find "probable cause" while conducting reasonable searches of students, they violated freedoms guaranteed under the Bill of Rights. If you allow a teacher to look for a knife or drugs, you'll soon have strip searches and next, torture.

16. Since I walked under that ladder yesterday, I've lost my wallet and received a speeding ticket.

17. Sometimes, the *best* is not for everyone. (An ad for a "Parisian boutique.")

18. "I'm being denied the right to own a semiautomatic firearm simply because someone doesn't like the way it looks. If you look at all the different automobiles out there, the majority of them travel on regular roads. So how do you explain the dune buggies or off-road vehicles? They're different, but you don't hear anybody saying, 'Why does anyone need to have a dune buggy or an off-road vehicle? What's wrong with your regular run-of-the-mill traditional automobile?' It's all a matter of personal preference." (Marion Hammer, president of the National Rifle Association)

19. We are going to have to ease up on environmental protection legislation or see the costs overwhelm us.

20. Any rational person will accept that a fetus is a human being.

21. A tax loophole is something that benefits the other guy. If it benefits you, it is tax reform.

22. Heat Wave Blamed for Record Temperatures Across U.S. (A *Grass Valley Union* headline.)

23. The erosion of traditional male leadership has led to an increase in divorce because men no longer possess leadership roles.

24. "Just as instructors could prune sentences for poor grammar, so the principal was entitled to find certain articles inappropriate for publication—in this situation because they might reveal the identity of pregnant students and because references to sexual activity were deemed improper for young students to see."

25.

26. Now, all young men, a warning take, And shun the poisoned bowl; [alcohol] 'Twill lead you down to hell's dark gate, And ruin your own soul. (Anonymous, from Carl Sandburg, ed., *The American Songbag*)

27. While our diplomats in France were gathering intelligence, their diplomats in Washington were practicing espionage.

28. I recently read about a homeless man with a burst appendix who was turned away from a hospital emergency room to die in the street. It's obvious that hospitals don't care about people, only money.

29. Do the vastly inflated salaries paid to professional athletes lead them into drug abuse?

30. The Nuclear Freeze movement was misguided and dangerous from the beginning, dependent as it was on "unilateral" disarmament. (This is a common argument of the movement's opponents. Those supporting the Nuclear Freeze movement actually proposed "bilateral" disarmament.)

31. *Haemon:* So, father, pause, and put aside your anger. I think, for what my young opinion's worth, that, good as it is to have infallible wisdom, since this is rarely found, the next best thing is to be willing to listen to wise advice.

    Creon: Indeed! Am I to take lessons at my time of life from a fellow of his age? (Sophocles, *Antigone*)

32. S & W vegetables are the best because they use only premium quality.

33. In the presidential election of 2000, Al Gore challenged George W. Bush's victory on grounds of voter fraud in Florida. The electoral college votes, deciding the winner, hung in the balance, even though Gore held the lead in the popular vote. Some asserted that Gore should concede, just as Nixon did when John F. Kennedy won in 1960. In that election, votes for Kennedy in Illinois were said to have been fraudulently earned, although without the Illinois electoral votes, Kennedy still held his lead as he also held the lead in the popular vote.

34. Reading test scores in public schools have declined dramatically. This decline was caused by the radical changes in teaching strategies introduced in the 1960s.

35. Howard Dean, as head of the Democratic National Committee, claimed that the Republican party consisted of white Christians.

36. "I give so much pleasure to so many people. Why can't I get some pleasure for myself?" (Comedian John Belushi to his doctor in justification of his drug use.)

37. "Editor: Now that it has been definitely established that nonsmokers have the right to tell smokers not to pollute their air, it follows that people who don't own cars have the right to tell car owners not to drive. Right?" (Jim Hodge, *San Francisco Chronicle*)

38. We must either give up some of our constitutional liberties to ensure that the government can protect us against terrorism or we will again fall prey to terrorists.

39. "Students should not be allowed any grace whatsoever on late assignments. Before you know it, they will no longer complete their work at all. If they don't do their assignments, they will be ignorant. If the students who are being educated are ignorant, then all of America will become more ignorant." (Thanks to a former student.)

40. I think there is great merit in making the requirements stricter for graduate students. I recommend that you support it, too. After all, we are in a budget crisis and we do not want our salaries affected.

41. Potential customer to cosmetics saleswoman: "What is the difference between the daytime moisturizer and the nighttime moisturizer?"

  Saleswoman: "You put the daytime moisturizer on in the daytime and the nighttime moisturizer on at nighttime."

42.

Tom Meyer/San Francisco Chronicle.

EXERCISE 6B

Analyzing a Short Argument

The following letter is not a genuine letter to the editor but a critical thinking test devised by educators. Test yourself by writing a paragraph by paragraph critique of this deliberately flawed argument. It contains at least seven errors in reasoning, some of them fallacies that you have studied in this chapter, some of them weaknesses that can be identified and described but not labeled.

230 Sycamore Street
Moorburg
April 10

Dear Editor:
  Overnight parking on all streets in Moorburg should be eliminated. To achieve   1
this goal, parking should be prohibited from 2 a.m. to 6 a.m. There are a number
of reasons why an intelligent citizen should agree.

For one thing, to park overnight is to have a garage in the streets. Now it is ille-   2
gal for anyone to have a garage in the city streets. Clearly then it should be against
the law to park overnight in the streets.

Three important streets, Lincoln Avenue, Marquand Avenue, and West Main   3
Street, are very narrow. With cars parked on the streets, there really isn't room
for the heavy traffic that passes over them in the afternoon rush hour. When
driving home in the afternoon after work, it takes me thirty-five minutes to
make a trip that takes ten minutes during the uncrowded time. If there were no
cars parked on the side of these streets, they could handle considerably more
traffic.

Traffic on some streets is also bad in the morning when factory workers are on   4
their way to the 6 a.m. shift. If there were no cars parked on these streets between
2 a.m. and 6 a.m., then there would be more room for this traffic.

Furthermore there can be no doubt that, in general, overnight parking on the   5
streets is undesirable. It is definitely bad and should be opposed.

If parking is prohibited from 2 a.m. to 6 a.m., then accidents between parked   6
and moving vehicles will be nearly eliminated during this period. All intelligent citizens would regard the near elimination of accidents in any period as highly desir-
able. So we should be in favor of prohibiting parking from 2 a.m. to 6 a.m.

Last month the Chief of Police, Burgess Jones, ran an experiment which proves   7
that parking should be prohibited from 2 a.m. to 6 a.m. On one of our busiest
streets, Marquand Avenue, he placed experimental signs for one day. The signs
prohibited parking from 2 a.m. to 6 a.m. During the four-hour period there was *not
one accident* on Marquand. Everyone knows, of course, that there have been over
four hundred accidents on Marquand during the past year.

The opponents of my suggestions have said that conditions are safe enough   8
now. These people don't know what "safe" really means. *Conditions are not safe if
there's even the slightest possible chance for an accident.* That's what "safe" means.
So conditions are not safe the way they are now.

Finally let me point out that the director of the National Traffic Safety Council,   9
Kenneth O. Taylor, has strongly recommended that overnight street parking be
prevented on busy streets in cities the size of Moorburg. The National Association
of Police Chiefs has made the same recommendation. Both suggest that prohibiting parking from 2 a.m. to 6 a.m. is the best way to prevent overnight parking.

I invite those who disagree as well as those who agree with me to react to my   10
letter through the editor of this paper. Let's get this issue out in the open.

Sincerely,

Robert R. Raywift

WRITING ASSIGNMENT 11

Analyzing an Extended Argument

Choose one of the two following editorials (or find one in a newspaper or periodical)
on which to write an essay evaluating the argument.

The Approach

1. Analyze each paragraph of your chosen editorial in order. Compose a list of the fallacies you find in each paragraph—give names of fallacies or identify weaknesses in reasoning (not all weaknesses can be precisely named) and illustrate with specific examples from the editorial. Avoid the trap of being too picky; you won't necessarily find significant fallacies in every paragraph.

2. During this paragraph-by-paragraph analysis, keep the argument's conclusion in mind and ask yourself if the author provides adequate support for it.

3. Next, review your paragraph-by-paragraph analysis to determine the two or three major problems in the argument. Then group and condense your list of faults or fallacies and, in a coherently written essay organized around these two or three principal categories, present your evaluation of the argument. For example, if you find more than one instance of personal attack, devote one of your paragraphs to this fallacy and cite all the examples you find to support your claim. Follow the same procedure for other weaknesses. Identify each specific example you cite either by paraphrase or direct quotation, imagining as you write that the reader is not familiar with the editorial you are critiquing. In your introduction, briefly discuss the issue of the editorial you've chosen, possibly supplying background information not covered in the editorial itself.

Audience

College-age readers who have not read the editorial and who are not familiar with all of the fallacies listed in the text.

Purpose

To illustrate to a less critical reader that published arguments written by established professionals are not necessarily free of fallacious reasoning.

On Date Rape

CAMILLE PAGLIA

Humanities professor and cultural critic, *San Francisco Examiner*

Dating is a very recent phenomenon in world history. Throughout history, women   1
have been chaperoned. As late as 1964, when I arrived in college, we had strict rules. We had to be in the dorm under lock and key by 11 o'clock. My generation was the one that broke these rules. We said, "We want freedom—no more double standard!" When I went to stay at a male friend's apartment in New York, my aunts flew into a frenzy: "You can't do that, it's dangerous!" But I said, "No, we're not going to be like that anymore." Still, we understood in the '60s that we were taking a risk.

Today these young women want the freedoms that we won, but they don't   2
want to acknowledge the risk. That's the problem. The minute you go out with a
man, the minute you go to a bar to have a drink, there is a risk. You have to accept
the fact that part of the sizzle of sex comes from the danger of sex. You can be
overpowered.

So it is women's personal responsibility to be aware of the dangers of the   3
world. But these young feminists today are deluded. They come from a protected,
white, middle-class world, and they expect everything to be safe. Notice how it's
rarely black or Hispanic women who are making a fuss about this in the media or
on campus—they come from cultures that are fully sexual, and they are fully realistic about the dangers of life. But many of these other women are nice, genteel,
sexually repressed white girls coming out of pampered homes, and when they arrive at college and suddenly hit raw male lust, the go, "Oh, no!"

These girls say, "Well, I should be able to get drunk at a fraternity party and go   4
upstairs to a guy's room without anything happening." And I say, "Oh, really? And
when you drive your car to New York City, do you leave your keys on the hood?"
My point is that if your car is stolen after you do something like that, yes, the police should pursue the thief and he should be punished. But at the same time, the
police—and I—have the right to say to you, "You stupid idiot, what the hell were
you thinking?"

I mean, wake up to reality. This is male sex. Guess what, it's hot. Male sex is   5
hot. There's an attraction between the sexes that we're not totally in control of.
The idea that we can regulate it by passing campus grievance committee rules
is madness. My kind of feminism stresses personal responsibility. I've never been
raped, but I've been very vigilant—I'm constantly reading the signals. If I ever got
into a dating situation where I was overpowered and raped, I would say, "Oh well,
I misread the signals." But I don't think I would ever press charges.

Boxing, Doctors—Round Two

LOWELL COHN

Sportswriter, *San Francisco Chronicle*

Before I went on vacation a few weeks ago, I wrote a column criticizing the   1
American Medical Association for its call to abolish boxing. As you might have
expected, I have received letters from doctors telling me I'm misinformed and sci-
entifically naive. One doctor even said I must have had terrible experiences with
doctors to have written what I wrote.

That just shows how arrogant doctors are. It never would occur to them that I   2
might have a defensible position. If I disagree with them, it's because I'm ignorant.

Doctors are used to being right. We come into their offices sick and generally   3
not knowing what's wrong with us. We are in awe of their expertise and afraid for
our well-being. We have a tendency to act like children in front of them. "If you
can only make me well, Doc, I will love you for life." Doctors, who start out as regular human beings, come to expect us to worship them. They thrive on the power
that comes from having knowledge about life and death.

Which brings us to their misguided stand against boxing. Doctors are offended   4
by injuries in boxing, although they don't seem as mortified by the people who die
skiing or bike riding or swimming every year. You rarely hear a peep out of them
about the many injuries football players sustain—that includes kids in the peewee
leagues and high school. Why the outrage over boxing?

Because many doctors are social snobs. They see people from ethnic minori-   5
ties punching each other in a ring and they reach the conclusion that these poor,
dumb blacks and Latinos must be protected from themselves because they don't
know any better. The AMA is acting like a glorified SPCA, arrogantly trying to prevent cruelty to animals. They would never dare preach this way to football players,
because most of them went to college. Nor would they come out against skiing,
because many doctors love to ski.

Boxers know the risks of taking a right cross to the jaw better than doctors,   6
and they take up the sport with a full understanding of its risks. A man should have
the right to take a risk. Doctors may want to save us from adventure, but there still
is honor in freely choosing to put yourself on the line. Risk is why race-car drivers
speed around treacherous tracks. Danger is why mountain climbers continue to
explore the mystery of Mount Everest. Yet doctors do not come out against auto
racing or mountain climbing.

One physician wrote a letter to the *Sporting Green* saying the AMA's position   7
against boxing is based on medical evidence. As I read the letter's twisted logic, I
wondered if the AMA causes brain damage in doctors. "Skiing, bicycle riding and
swimming kill more people each year [than boxing]," he writes. "Obviously, far
more people engage in those activities than enter a boxing ring."

Does his position make sense to you? We should eliminate boxing, the sport   8
with fewer negative consequences, but allow the real killer sports to survive.
Amazing.

If this doctor were really concerned with medical evidence, as he claims, he   9
would attack all dangerous sports, not just boxing.

But he doesn't. The truth is, boxing offends the delicate sensibilities of doc-   10
tors. They don't like the idea that two men *intentionally* try to hurt each other.
They feel more comfortable when injuries are a byproduct of a sport—although ask
any batter who has been beaned by a fastball if his broken skull was an innocent
byproduct.

In other words, doctors are making a moral judgment, not a medical judg-   11
ment, about which sports are acceptable. Every joker is entitled to ethical opinions,
but doctors have no more expertise than you or I when it comes to right and
wrong. If preaching excites them, let them become priests.

What if the AMA is successful in getting boxing banned? Will the sport disap-   12
pear? No way. As long as man is man, he will want to see two guys of equal weight
and ability solve their elemental little problem in a ring. If the sport becomes illegal,
it will drift off to barges and back alleys, where men will fight in secret without
proper supervision. And then you will see deaths and maiming like you never saw
before.

Whom will the AMA blame then?   13

KEY TERMS

Term	Description	Example
Appeal to authority (2 forms)	1. Appeals to an authority who is not an expert on the issue under discussion.	Abortion to save the mother is irrelevant because a pediatric surgeon has never seen a case in which such a dilemma has arisen.
Snob appeal	2. Appeals to people's desire for prestige and exclusivity.	Pamilla's not for everyone. The best never is.
Appeal to fear	Implicitly threatens the audience.	Will there be a *job* waiting when *you* leave college?
Appeal to pity	Attempts to win sympathy.	Professor Hall, I must get an A in your course. If you don't give me an A, I won't be able to go to law school.
Begging the Question (3 forms)	1. Offers no actual support; may restate as a premise the conclusion in different words.	The reason he is so strong is because of his strength.
Loaded question	2. Asks a question that contains an assumption that must be proven.	Have you started to pay your fair share of taxes yet?
Question-begging epithet	3. Uses a single word to assert a claim that must be proven.	Reactionary, negligent, warmonger, deadbeat.
Double standard	Judges and labels the same act differently depending on the person or group who performs the act.	China and Cuba both restrict religious freedoms and limit free speech. China has favored-nation status whereas Cuba is not recognized by the United States.
Equivocation	Shifts the meaning of a term within a single argument.	We are told that to discriminate in employment or housing is punishable by law. But we must discriminate when we hire an individual or rent an apartment.

Term	Description	Example
Fallacious argument	Persuasive but does not logically support its conclusion.	Senator Smith was expelled from college for cheating on an exam. His wife divorced him because of his numerous affairs. Therefore, he is a man without honor, a politician who cannot be trusted, and we should not support his National Health Bill.
False analogy	Compares two or more things that are not in essence similar and suggests that since they share certain characteristics, they share others as well.	I don't want to die falling off a rock. But you can kill yourself falling in the bathtub too.
False cause [Latinname: *post hoc, ergo propter hoc*]	Claims a causal relationship between events solely on the basis of a chronological relationship.	I joined the Confederacy for two weeks. Then I deserted. The Confederacy fell.
False dilemma	Presents two and only two alternatives for consideration when other possibilities exist.	Lennon *or* McCartney, Monroe *or* Bardot, Hemingway *or* Fitzgerald, Freud *or* Jung.
Hasty generalization	Generalizes from a sample that is too small or in some other way unrepresentative of the target population.	Students in Professor Hall's eight o'clock freshman composition class are often late. Today's college students are irresponsible and unreliable.
Personal attack [Latin name: *ad hominem*] (2 forms)	1. Attacks the person representing the argument rather than the argument itself.	Because Rachel Carson has no children, she cannot have concern for the effect of insecticides and pesticides on future generations.
Tu quoque ("you also")	2. Discredits an argument because the behavior of the person proposing it does not conform to the position he's supporting.	A teenager to his father: Don't tell me not to drink. You drink all the time.

Term	Description	Example
Poisoning the well	Makes an assertion that will intimidate the audience and therefore discourage an open discussion.	Every patriotic American supports legislation condemning the desecration of the flag.
Red herring	Shifts the discussion from the issue to a different topic.	While the hospital bond issue has merit, there are too many bond issues on this ballot.
Slippery slope	Claims that an action should be avoided because it will lead to a series of extremely undesirable consequences.	What seems like reasonable restrictions on guns with no legitimate civilian purpose will lead inevitably to total prohibition of gun ownership that ends in virtual slavery at the hands of a totalitarian regime.
Straw man	Creates and then attacks a distorted version of the opposition's argument.	The Democratic candidate wants the federal government to house everyone, feed everyone, care for everyone's children, and provide medical care for everyone. And he's going to take 50 percent of every dime you make to do it.

CHAPTER 7

Deductive and Inductive Argument

There is a tradition of opposition between adherents of induction and deduction.
In my view, it would be just as sensible for the two ends of a worm to quarrel.
—ALFRED NORTH WHITEHEAD

Sometimes arguments are classified as deductive or inductive. Deduction and induction are modes of reasoning, particular ways of arriving at an inference. Different logicians tend to make different distinctions between deductive and inductive reasoning, with some going so far as to declare, as Whitehead did, that such a distinction is spurious. But classifications, if carefully made, help us to understand abstract concepts, and scientists and humanists alike often refer to patterns of reasoning as deductive or inductive. This classification also helps us to distinguish between conclusions we must accept and those we should question, a valuable skill for both reading critically and writing logically.

KEY DISTINCTIONS

The key distinctions between deduction and induction are generally seen as falling into two categories.

(1) Necessity Versus Probability

In a **deductive argument**, the conclusion will follow by **necessity** from the premises if the method of reasoning is valid, as in this familiar bit of classical wisdom:

1. All men are mortal.
2. Socrates is a man.
∴ Socrates is mortal.

In an **inductive argument**, the conclusion can follow only with some degree of **probability** (from the unlikely to the highly probable). British philosopher Bertrand Russell made the point implicitly but emphatically in *The Problems of Philosophy*: "The man who has fed the chicken every day throughout its life at last wrings its neck instead." The chicken reasons thus:

1. He has fed me today.
2. He has fed me this next day.

3. He has fed me this day too.

4. He has fed me yet another day, etc.

∴ He will feed me tomorrow.

The poor chicken has made a prediction, and a reasonable one, based on its past experience.

A related distinction here becomes clear. The premises of a deductive argument contain all the information needed for the conclusion, whereas the conclusion of an inductive argument goes beyond the premises. For this reason, some prefer the certainty of deduction to the probability of induction.

Ambroise Paré, a French Renaissance physician, revealed his distrust of induction when he defined inductive diagnosis as "the rapid means to the wrong conclusion." One assumes that he would have argued for the value of a few well-learned principles behind one's observations. In contrast, 19th-century Harvard professor and scientist Louis Agassiz urged his students to practice induction, to observe before making generalizations, believing that: "[A] physical fact is as sacred as a moral principle."

(2) From General to Specific, Specific to General

In a ***deductive*** argument, the inference usually moves from a generalization to a particular, specific instance or example that fits that generalization. Two examples:

1. All students who complete this course successfully will fulfill the critical thinking requirement.

2. Jane has completed this course successfully.

∴ Jane has fulfilled the critical thinking requirement.

1. Children born on a Saturday will "work hard for a living."

2. Nick was born on a Saturday.

∴ Nick will work hard for his living.

You may not believe this folk wisdom, especially if you were born on a Saturday, but the line of reasoning is still deductive.

In an ***inductive*** argument, the inference usually moves from a series of specific instances to a generalization.

1. Droughts have been more frequent in some areas.

2. Skin cancers related to ultraviolet rays have been increasing.

3. The tree line is moving north about 40 meters a year.

4. Polar ice has been melting more rapidly than in the past.

5. Oceans have been rising at measurable annual rates around the globe.

∴ Clearly, global warming is upon us.

Sometimes in inductive reasoning, we begin with a **hypothesis, an unproved theory or proposition**, and gather the data to support it. For instance, when Jonas Salk thought his vaccine would cure polio, he first had to test it inductively by administering it to a broad sample before concluding that the vaccine prevented polio.

THE RELATIONSHIP BETWEEN INDUCTION AND DEDUCTION

In Exercise 7B we ask you to distinguish between inductive and deductive reasoning, but in reality the two are inextricable. Consider the source for the generalizations upon which deductions are based. In some cases they seem to be the laws of nature, but more often than not we arrive at these generalizations by means of repeated observations. Throughout history, people have observed their own mortality, so we can now take that generalization—all people are mortal—as a given from which we can deduce conclusions about individual people. Induction has, in this case, led to a trusted generalization that in turn allows us a "necessary," or deductive, inference.

Humorists have sometimes turned these concepts on their heads. Here's Woody Allen reflecting on deduction: "All men are Socrates." And Lewis Carroll, in "The Hunting of the Snark," on induction: "What I tell you three times is true." While studying logic in college, Steve Martin was inspired by Lewis Carroll's wacky arguments. One example of Carroll's logic:

1. Babies are illogical.
2. Nobody is despised who can manage a crocodile.
3. Illogical persons are despised.
∴. Babies cannot manage crocodiles.

Martin began closing his show by announcing: "I'm not going home tonight. I'm going to Bananaland, a place where only two things are true, only two things: one, all chairs are green; and, two, no chairs are green."

In a more serious approach, Robert Pirsig, in his philosophical novel *Zen and the Art of Motorcycle Maintenance*, attempts to explain deduction, induction, and the relationships between them in language we can all understand. These terms were never intended to be the exclusive domain of academics but, rather, descriptive of the ways in which we all think every day.

Note how the following excerpt from Pirsig's novel explains both the differences between induction and deduction and their dependence on one another.

Mechanics' Logic

Two kinds of logic are used (in motorcycle maintenance), inductive and deductive. Inductive inferences start with observations of the machine and arrive at   1 general conclusions. For example, if the cycle goes over a bump and the engine misfires, and then goes over another bump and the engine misfires, and then goes over another bump and the engine misfires, and then goes over a long smooth stretch of road and there is no misfiring, and then goes over a fourth bump and the engine misfires again, one can logically conclude that the misfiring is caused by the bumps. That is induction: reasoning from particular experiences to general truths.

Deductive inferences do the reverse. They start with general knowledge and   2
predict a specific observation. For example, if, from reading the hierarchy of facts about the machine, the mechanic knows the horn of the cycle is powered exclusively by electricity from the battery, then he can logically infer that if the battery is dead the horn will not work. That is deduction.

Solution of problems too complicated for common sense to solve is achieved   3
by long strings of mixed inductive and deductive inferences that weave back and forth between the observed machine and the mental hierarchy of the machine found in the manuals. The correct program for this interweaving is formalized as scientific method.

Actually I've never seen a cycle-maintenance problem complex enough really   4
to require full-scale formal scientific method. Repair problems are not that hard. When I think of formal scientific method an image sometimes comes to mind of an enormous juggernaut, a huge bulldozer—slow, tedious, lumbering, laborious, but invincible. It takes twice as long, five times as long, maybe a dozen times as long as informal mechanic's techniques, but you know in the end you're going to *get* it. There's no fault isolation problem in motorcycle maintenance that can stand up to it. When you've hit a really tough one, tried everything, racked your brain and nothing works, and you know that this time Nature has really decided to be difficult, you say, "Okay, Nature, that's the end of the *nice* guy," and you crank up the formal scientific method.

For this you keep a lab notebook. Everything gets written down, formally, so   5
that you know at all times where you are, where you've been, where you're going and where you want to get. In scientific work and electronics technology this is necessary because otherwise the problems get so complex you get lost in them and confused and forget what you know and what you don't know and have to give up. In cycle maintenance things are not that involved, but when confusion starts it's a good idea to hold it down by making everything formal and exact. Sometimes just the act of writing down the problems straightens out your head as to what they really are.

The logical statements entered into the notebook are broken down into six   6
categories: (1) statement of the problem, (2) hypotheses as to the cause of the problem, (3) experiments designed to test each hypothesis, (4) predicted results of the experiments, (5) observed results of the experiments and (6) conclusions from the results of the experiments. This is not different from the formal arrangement of many college and high-school lab notebooks but the purpose here is no longer just busy-work. The purpose now is precise guidance of thoughts that will fail if they are not accurate.

The real purpose of scientific method is to make sure Nature hasn't misled you   7
into thinking you know something you don't actually know. There's not a mechanic

or scientist or technician alive who hasn't suffered from that one so much that he's not instinctively on guard. That's the main reason why so much scientific and mechanical information sounds so dull and so cautious. If you get careless or go romanticizing scientific information, giving it a flourish here and there, Nature will soon make a complete fool out of you. It does it often enough anyway even when you don't give it opportunities. One must be extremely careful and rigidly logical when dealing with Nature: one logical slip and an entire scientific edifice comes tumbling down. One false deduction about the machine and you can get hung up indefinitely.

In Part One of formal scientific method, which is the statement of the problem, the main skill is in stating absolutely no more than you are positive you know. It is much better to enter a statement "Solve Problem: Why doesn't cycle work?" which sounds dumb but is correct, than it is to enter a statement "Solve Problem: What is wrong with the electrical system?" when you don't absolutely *know* the trouble is *in* the electrical system. What you should state is "Solve Problem: What is wrong with cycle?" and *then* state as the first entry of Part Two: "Hypothesis Number One: The trouble is in the electrical system." You think of as many hypotheses as you can, then you design experiments to test them to see which are true and which are false. 8

This careful approach to the beginning questions keeps you from taking a major wrong turn which might cause you weeks of extra work or can even hang you up completely. Scientific questions often have a surface appearance of dumbness for this reason. They are asked in order to prevent dumb mistakes later on. 9

Part Three, that part of formal scientific method called experimentation, is sometimes thought of by romantics as all of science itself because that's the only part with much visual surface. They see lots of test tubes and bizarre equipment and people running around making discoveries. They do not see the experiment as part of a larger intellectual process and so they often confuse experiments with demonstrations, which look the same. A man conducting a gee-whiz science show with fifty thousand dollars' worth of Frankenstein equipment is not doing anything scientific if he knows beforehand what the results of his efforts are going to be. A motorcycle mechanic, on the other hand, who honks the horn to see if the battery works is informally conducting a true scientific experiment. He is testing a hypothesis by putting the question to Nature. The TV scientist who mutters sadly, "The experiment is a failure; we have failed to achieve what we had hoped for," is suffering mainly from a bad scriptwriter. An experiment is never a failure solely because it fails to achieve predicted results. An experiment is a failure only when it also fails adequately to test the hypothesis in question, when the data it produces don't prove anything one way or another. 10

Skill at this point consists of using experiments that test only the hypothesis in question, nothing less, nothing more. If the horn honks, and the mechanic concludes that the whole electrical system is working, he is in deep trouble. He has reached an illogical conclusion. The honking horn only tells him that the battery and horn are working. To design an experiment properly he has to think very rigidly in terms of what directly causes what. This you know from the hierarchy. The horn doesn't make the cycle go. Neither does the battery, except in a very indirect 11 way. The point at which the electrical system *directly* causes the engine to fire is at the spark plugs, and if you don't test here, at the output of the electrical system, you will never really know whether the failure is electrical or not.

To test properly the mechanic removes the plug and lays it against the engine   12
so that the base around the plug is electrically grounded, kicks the starter lever and watches the spark-plug gap for a blue spark. If there isn't any he can conclude one of two things: (a) there is an electrical failure or (b) his experiment is sloppy. If he is experienced he will try it a few more times, checking connections, trying every way he can think of to get that plug to fire. Then, if he can't get it to fire, he finally concludes that *a* is correct, there's an electrical failure, and the experiment is over. He has proved that his hypothesis is correct.

In the final category, conclusions, skill comes in stating no more than the ex-   13
periment has proved. It hasn't proved that when he fixes the electrical system the motorcycle will start. There may be other things wrong. But he does know that the motorcycle isn't going to run until the electrical system is working and he sets up the next formal question: "Solve Problem: What is wrong with the electrical system?"

He then sets up hypotheses for these and tests them. By asking the right ques-   14
tions and choosing the right tests and drawing the right conclusions the mechanic works his way down the echelons of the motorcycle hierarchy until he has found the exact specific cause or causes of the engine failure, and then he changes them so that they no longer cause the failure.

An untrained observer will see only physical labor and often get the idea that   15
physical labor is mainly what the mechanic does. Actually the physical labor is the smallest and easiest part of what the mechanic does. By far the greatest part of his work is careful observation and precise thinking. That is why mechanics some-times seem so taciturn and withdrawn when performing tests. They don't like it when you talk to them because they are concentrating on mental images, hierar-chies, and not really looking at you or the physical motorcycle at all. They are using the experiment as part of the program to expand their hierarchy of knowledge of the faulty motorcycle and compare it to the correct hierarchy in their mind. They are looking at underlying form.

EXERCISE 7A

Analyzing Pirsig

1. According to Pirsig, what is the most important part of the mechanic's work?

2. How does Pirsig define induction and deduction?

3. Which method of reasoning—induction or deduction—does the scientific method rely on?

4. Return to the statement by mathematician and philosopher Alfred North Whitehead (1861–1947), which begins this chapter, and explain its meaning.

EXERCISE 7B

Distinguishing Inductive from Deductive Reasoning

Read the following passages carefully to determine which are based on inductive reasoning and which on deductive. Briefly explain your answers.

1. Only 18-year-old citizens can vote, and Felix is not a citizen, so he can't vote in the upcoming presidential election.

2. The United States Supreme Court nominee received excellent grades throughout his school career and made law review at Harvard Law School. Add to these excellent credentials the fact that everyone who has ever known him says that he is kind and fair. I think he will make an excellent Supreme Court justice.

3. Sophie must be ill. I haven't seen her in class, and she hasn't answered her cell or responded to my text messages.

4. Cat lovers do not care for dogs, and since Colette had numerous cats all of her life, I assume she did not care for dogs.

5. According to polls taken prior to the national convention, the candidate I support held a substantial lead in the presidential race. I am now confident that he will win in November.

6. Every Frenchman is devoted to his glass of *vin rouge*. Philippe is a Frenchman, so he too must be devoted to that glass of red wine.

7. George W. Bush lied to the American people about weapons of mass destruction in Iraq. Bill Clinton lied about his relationship with a White House intern. Richard Nixon lied about Watergate. Lyndon Johnson lied about the Gulf of Tonkin and the Vietnam War. I'll let you draw your own conclusion.

8. As an expert testified on the *NewsHour* following the *Challenger* space shuttle disaster, the solid rocket booster had proved safe in more than 200 successful launchings of both space shuttles and Titan missiles. It was reasonable to conclude that the same rocket booster would function properly on the *Challenger* mission.

9. Over time the only investment to keep pace with inflation is an investment in the stock market. So despite the current economic crisis, responsible retirement fund managers should continue to buy stocks.

10. When people are confident and cheerful, they are generally inclined to spend more freely. With this in mind, we have designed these ads to project a feeling of cheerful confidence that should encourage viewers to spend more freely on your product. (Ad agency pitch to a potential client.)

DEDUCTIVE REASONING

Class Logic

Having established the differences between deductive and inductive reasoning, we can now examine each in greater detail. Underlying both forms of reasoning is an understanding of class logic. In fact, good reasoning in general often depends on seeing relationships between classes. **A class in logic is all of the individual things—persons, objects, events, ideas—that share a determinate property, a common feature.** What is that determinate property? Anything under the sun. A class may consist of any quality or combination of qualities that the classifier assigns to it. A class may be vast, such as a class containing everything in the universe, or it may be small, containing only one member, such as Nick's last girlfriend. Making classes and assigning members to those classes is an essential part of everyday reasoning—it's how we order our experience. Indeed, each word in the language serves as a class by which we categorize and communicate experience. We can then take these words in any combination to create the categories or classes that serve our purpose.

A recent article in the *Journal of the American Medical Association*, for example, features a piece titled "Risk of Sexually Transmitted Diseases Among Adolescent Crack Users in Oakland and San Francisco." This title, which identifies one class (and the subject of the article), was created by combining seven classes: the class of things involving risk, the class of things that are sexually transmitted, the class of disease, the class of adolescents, the class of crack users, the class of persons living in Oakland, and the class of persons living in San Francisco.

Relationships Between Classes

There are three possible relationships between classes: **inclusion**, **exclusion**, and **overlap**.

INCLUSION   One class is included in another if every member of one class is a member of the other class. Using letters, we can symbolize this relationship as all As are Bs. Using circle diagrams, also called Euler diagrams after Leonhard Euler, an eighteenth-century mathematician, we can illustrate a relationship of inclusion this way:

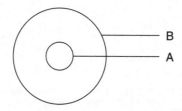

For example, the class of professional basketball players is included in the class of professional athletes because all professional basketball players are also professional athletes. The following diagram illustrates this relationship:

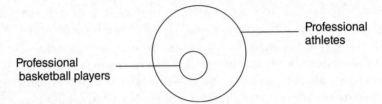

EXCLUSION   One class excludes another if they share no members, that is, if no As are Bs. Such a relationship exists between handguns and rifles:

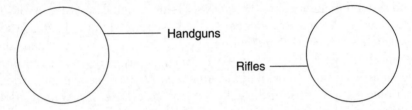

OVERLAP   One class overlaps with another if both have at least one member in common—if at least one A is also a B—for example, students at this university and students who like classical music:

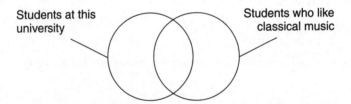

Cartoonist Ariel Molvig has fun with the relationship of overlap between classes:

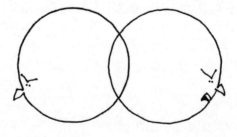

"At least we agree to disagree."

The way our public institutions classify relationships between groups of people can have a significant impact on their lives. The federal Department of Housing and Urban Development (HUD) is authorized to allocate housing funds to individuals with disabilities. People with AIDS argued that they were entitled to such funds, but HUD, until recently, had denied them any such subsidy. Clearly, HUD saw the relationship between disabilities and AIDS as one of exclusion, whereas those with AIDS saw their relationship to those with disabilities as one of inclusion, a relationship they were, over time, able to convince HUD of.

EXERCISE 7C

Identifying Relationships Between Classes

Using circle diagrams, illustrate the relationships between the following pairs of classes:

1. witches and women
2. hedgehogs and foxes
3. judges and lawyers
4. BMWs and convertibles
5. mollusks and amphibians
6. cosmetics and hairspray
7. the homeless and the mentally ill
8. euthanasia and suicide
9. concession and Rogerian strategy (see Chapter 4)
10. What is the meaning of the following diagram, which appeared on the *New York Times*'s editorial page?

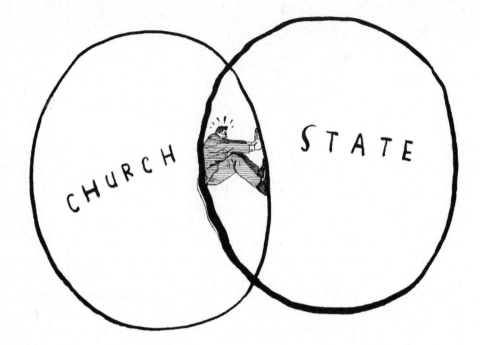

Now create your own classes:

1. Identify two classes, one of which is inclusive of the other.
2. Identify two classes that are exclusive of one another.
3. Identify two classes that overlap one another.

Class Logic and the Syllogism

Both inductive and deductive reasoning often depend on supporting a conclusion on the basis of relationships between classes. Let's look first at deduction. Deductive arguments usually involve more than two classes; in fact, the simplest form of deductive argument involves three classes. Remember this famous argument?

All men are mortal.

Socrates is a man.

∴ Socrates is mortal.

The three classes are *men*, *mortality*, and *Socrates*. We can use circle diagrams to illustrate the relationship between these three classes. The first premise asserts that the class of men is included in the class of mortality. The second premise asserts that the class of Socrates is included in the class of men; and thus the conclusion can claim that Socrates is included in the class of mortality.

This type of argument is called a **categorical syllogism**—a deductive argument composed of three classes; such an argument has two premises and one conclusion derived from the two premises.

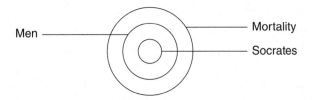

THE SUBJECT AND THE PREDICATE   To help identify the three classes of a categorical syllogism, you may want to identify the subject and predicate of each premise. Categorical propositions, and indeed all English sentences, can be broken down into two parts—the subject and predicate. These terms are shared by both grammar and logic and mean the same thing in both disciplines. The subject is that part of the sentence about which something is being asserted, and the predicate includes everything being asserted about the subject. In the first premise above, *all men* is the subject and *are mortal* is the predicate; in the second premise, *Socrates* is the subject and *is a man* is the predicate. The subject identifies one class; the predicate, the other.

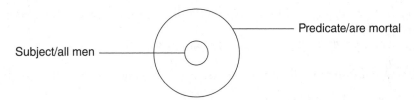

Note: If the premise stated *men are mortal* rather than *all men are mortal*, the meaning would be the same because, if a class is not quantified in some way—*some, many, few, one*—it is assumed that the assertion refers to the entire class.

TRUTH, VALIDITY, AND SOUNDNESS   If the conclusion follows of necessity, inescapably, from the premises, as it does in the syllogism about Socrates, then it is a **valid** argument.

We frequently use the term *valid* in everyday language. For example, we say, "That's a valid point." But in logic, **validity** has this very precise meaning: The conclusion follows of necessity from the premises, the form of the argument is correct, the line of reasoning conforms to the rules of logic. When we learn to evaluate the validity of a deductive argument, we can see what it means for a conclusion to follow inescapably from the premises.

Validity, however, is not the only requirement for a successful deductive argument; the premises must also be **true** or **acceptable**. Logicians use the term *true*, appropriate when a proposition can be evaluated by absolute or mathematical standards. But proof must often fall short of what can be claimed as true, an absolute term too imposing, even intimidating, for many assertions that we would nonetheless be inclined to accept. In most of our arguments, we must settle for what is **reasonable to believe**, what has been adequately supported and explained. Oliver Wendell Holmes, Supreme Court Justice (1841–1935), skirted the issue when he said, "What is true is what I can't help believing." We prefer the term *acceptable* to *true*.

An important point here is that to evaluate an argument successfully, we must begin by evaluating the premises, one by one, rather than moving in on the conclusion first. The conclusion will only be as acceptable as the sum of its premises.

To summarize, **two requirements must be met for us to accept the conclusion of a deductive argument**:

1. The structure of the argument must be valid—that is, the conclusion must follow of necessity from the premises.

2. The premises must be **_acceptable_** (true).

A deductive argument whose premises are acceptable and whose structure is valid is a **sound** argument—**a successful deductive argument**. Put another way, if the argument is valid and the premises are acceptable, then the conclusion cannot be false. Keep in mind that the terms *validity* and *soundness* can refer only to the argument as a whole. In contrast, individual statements can only be described as acceptable or unacceptable (true or false). In logic, we don't describe an argument as being true or a premise as valid.

Some examples of sound and unsound arguments:

1. A sound argument—the premises are acceptable and the structure valid.
   Drift-net fishing kills dolphins.
   Mermaid Tuna uses drift nets.
   ∴ Mermaid Tuna kills dolphins.

2. An unsound argument—one of the premises (in this example the first one) is false or not acceptable, even though the structure is valid.
   All Greeks are volatile.
   Athena is a Greek.
   ∴ Athena is volatile.

3. An unsound argument—the premises are acceptable but the structure is invalid.
   All athletes are people.
   All football players are people.
   ∴ All football players are athletes.

Note that in example 3, all the statements are acceptable, both the premises and the conclusion, but because the structure of the argument is invalid—the premises do not lead inescapably to the conclusion—the argument is unsound. Sketch this argument with circle diagrams to illustrate the principle.

Unreliable syllogisms turn up as accident and as humorous intent in a variety of places. Writer and critic Donald Newlove once claimed that, because he fell asleep while reading Harold Brodkey's *Runaway Soul*, which he also did his first time through literary classics *Moby Dick* and *Ulysses, Runaway Soul* must also be a great work of literature. Writer Ian Frazier found the following graffiti on a library table at Columbia University:

Bono is supreme.

God is supreme.

∴ Bono is God.

GUILT BY ASSOCIATION   Let's look at another example of an invalid argument with acceptable premises.

Members of the Mafia often have dinner at Joe's Place in Little Italy.

My neighbor frequently dines there.

∴ My neighbor is a member of the Mafia.

Most of us would reject this argument, but this pattern of reasoning, erroneous as it is, is fairly common. One famous example took place in 1950 when communism was referred to as the "red menace," and Senator Joseph McCarthy and the House Un-American Activities Committee were beginning their witch hunt against anyone who had ever had an association, no matter how slight or distant, with communism. It was in this climate of national paranoia that Republican Richard Nixon, running against Democrat Helen Gahagen Douglas for a California senate seat, presented the following argument, allowing the voters to draw their own conclusions:

Communists favor measures x, y, and z.

My opponent, Helen Gahagen Douglas, favors these same measures.

∴ [Helen Gahagen Douglas is a Communist.]

This kind of reasoning, based on guilt by association, is faulty (but often effective—Douglas lost the election) because it assumes that if two classes share one quality, they share all qualities. Such reasoning is a source of much sexism and racism; it assumes that if two people are of the same sex or race, they share not only that characteristic but an entire set of characteristics as well. Simple diagrams can illustrate where the logic fails:

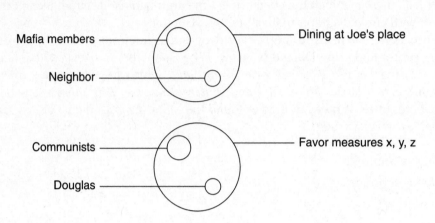

Faulty as this logic is, it was used in the 2008 presidential race. Those against Obama publicized the fact that he and Bill Ayers, a former 60s radical involved in terrorist activities, sat on the same board, implying that Obama was also a radical and a terrorist. This time the guilt by association strategy ultimately failed. Barack Obama was elected. But many voters believed that Obama was tainted by his association with Ayers even though the president was eight years old when Ayers was engaged in radical activities.

Plans to build a Muslim community center and mosque two blocks from the site of the World Trade Center has enraged many New Yorkers as well as many other Americans, including former Alaskan governor Sarah Palin. They see the proposed 13-story complex as an insult to the almost three thousand people who died at the World Trade Center on 9/11. The mayor of New York, Michael Bloomberg, disagrees. He sees the proposed building as a symbol of America's religious tolerance: "We would betray our values if we were to treat Muslims differently than anyone else."

These opposing viewpoints are based on the relationship they see between two classes: Muslims and terrorists. Those opposed to the project see the relationship between these two groups as one of inclusion:

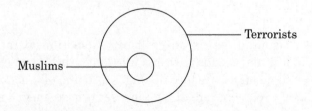

All Muslims are terrorists.

Those in favor of the project see the relationship as one of overlap:

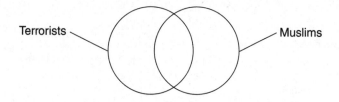

Some Muslims are terrorists or not all Muslims are terrorists. The converse is also true: not all terrorists are Muslims. The Oklahoma City bomber was not a Muslim. Members of the Independent Republican Army of Ireland, which conducted a long campaign of terrorism against the British in Ireland and England, were not Muslims.

MORE ON SYLLOGISMS   Before you examine some syllogisms on your own, we need to look once again at exclusion, overlap, and inclusion. Examine the following example and use circle diagrams to illustrate the relationship between each of the classes to determine the validity of the reasoning.

All Alice's friends are business majors.

Deborah is not a business major.

∴ Deborah is not a friend of Alice.

Were you able to illustrate by exclusion that this is a valid argument? Can you do the same for this one?

None of Alice's friends are business majors.

Deborah is not a friend of Alice.

∴ Deborah is not a business major.

Can you illustrate why this reasoning is not reliable, why the argument is invalid?

So far we have been dealing with what we call a **universal proposition**, an assertion that refers to all members of a designated class. What happens when we qualify a premise with *some* and then have what logicians call a **particular proposition**? Let's look at an example:

All gamblers are optimists.

Some of my friends are gamblers.

∴ Some of my friends are optimists.

A diagram illustrates that because the conclusion is qualified, it can follow from one qualified, or *particular*, premise. Although it's possible for some friends to fall outside the class of gamblers and thus, perhaps, outside the class of optimists, the second premise guarantees that some (at least two) of my friends are included in the class of gamblers.

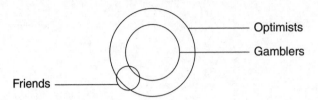

> Five steps to determine the soundness of a categorical syllogism:
>
> 1. **Identify three classes:** subject and predicate in the first premise, subject in the second premise.
>
> 2. Represent the relationship between the three classes by drawing **circle diagrams.**
>
> 3. **Compare** the circle diagram to the conclusion. If they match, the structure of the argument is valid. If not, the structure is invalid.
>
> 4. Determine the **acceptability** of the premises.
>
> 5. If the structure is valid and the premises acceptable, the argument is **sound.** If both criteria are not met, the argument is **unsound.**

EXERCISE 7D

Determining the Soundness of Categorical Syllogisms

First use Euler diagrams to determine the validity of the following categorical syllogisms. Then determine if the premises are acceptable or not. If the structure of the argument is valid and the premises acceptable, the argument is sound.

Example

1. Stealing is a criminal act.

   Shoplifting is stealing.

   ∴ Shoplifting is a criminal act.

VALID inclusion and the premises are acceptable, so argument is SOUND

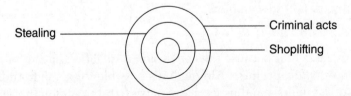

1. Liberals want to ban offshore drilling.
   Conservationists want to ban offshore drilling.
   ∴ Conservationists are liberals.

2. A cautious pilot wouldn't drink before a flight.
   Maxine is a cautious pilot.
   ∴ Maxine wouldn't drink before a flight.

3. All Jose's parrots understand Spanish.
   Pepe is his favorite parrot.
   ∴ Pepe understands Spanish.

4. Gauguin's paintings of Tahiti have brilliant and unrealistic colors.
   Starry Night has brilliant and unrealistic colors.
   ∴ *Starry Night* is a Gauguin painting of Tahiti.

5. Young men with shaven heads and swastikas tattooed on their arms are racists.
   John is a young man who doesn't shave his head or have a swastika tattooed on his arm.
   ∴ John is not a racist.

6. Nations that do not respect their citizens' civil liberties shouldn't receive favored nation status.
   China's censorship of the Internet demonstrates China's lack of respect for the civil liberties of its citizens.
   ∴ China doesn't deserve its favored nation status.

7. Every pediatrician knows that each child develops at his own rate.
   Dr. Haskell knows that each child develops at his own rate.
   ∴ Dr. Haskell is a pediatrician.

8. Some artists are completely self-absorbed.
   Frida Kahlo was an artist.
   ∴ Frida Kahlo was completely self-absorbed.

9. Members of the Christian Coalition believe in family values.
   Carlos and Maria believe in family values.
   ∴ Carlos and Maria are members of the Christian Coalition.

10. Killing the innocent is morally wrong.

    Modern warfare always involves killing the innocent.

    ∴ Modern warfare is always morally wrong.

Create three categorical syllogisms of your own—one valid but unsound, one invalid, and one sound.

EXERCISE 7E

Evaluating Deductive Arguments in Everyday Language

Determine whether the following arguments are sound or unsound. For each argument, follow these steps: first, reduce each argument to a categorical syllogism (supplying any unstated premises or conclusions—see "Hidden Assumptions in Argument" in Chapter 3); then use circle diagrams to determine validity; and finally, discuss the truth or acceptability of each premise.

1. Plagiarism is wrong, and paraphrasing the words of others without proper acknowledgment is the same as plagiarism, so paraphrasing the words of others without proper acknowledgment is wrong.

2. Mafia member Joe Bonano was guilty of criminal activities because he claimed the Fifth Amendment in the course of his trial. The Fifth Amendment, you will recall, is the privilege of a witness not to testify on the grounds that the evidence called for might be incriminating. One may choose not to testify against oneself, but there is a risk attached to this privilege. For we cannot avoid the fact that people who take the Fifth Amendment have something to hide—their guilt. In the case of Joe Bonano, that something to hide was his criminal activities.

HYPOTHETICAL ARGUMENTS

Another common type of deductive argument is the hypothetical or conditional argument which, unlike the categorical syllogism, is concerned not with classes but with conditions. For example:

If Maria drops that glass, it will break.

A condition is established that, if met, will lead to a specified consequence. The condition is called the **antecedent**; the consequence or result is called, appropriately enough, the **consequent**. The second premise, or minor premise, establishes whether or not that condition has been met.

Maria dropped the glass.

In this case, the antecedent has been affirmed. The conclusion then follows of necessity: The glass broke. The argument pattern looks like this:

If A, then B.

A.

∴ B.

The Valid Hypothetical Argument

This argument pattern *affirms the antecedent* (logicians refer to this argument pattern as *modus ponens*), and any argument that conforms to this pattern is valid; though of course, whether or not the argument is sound, whether or not we accept the conclusion, depends on the acceptability of the premises as well as the validity of the argument.

Another valid argument pattern is one in which the minor premise *denies the consequent*. Logicians refer to this argument pattern as *modus tollens*.

If Maria drops that glass, it will break.

It did not break.

∴ Maria did not drop it.

It follows that if the glass didn't break, Maria didn't drop it. Here's the form of this argument.

If A, then B.

Not B.

∴ Not A.

The rule governing the validity of a hypothetical argument is really quite simple: *The minor premise must either affirm the antecedent or deny the consequent.*

The Invalid Hypothetical Argument

Conversely, to deny the antecedent or affirm the consequent leads to invalidity.
For example:

If Maria drops the glass, it will break.	[If A, then B.
Maria did not drop the glass.	Not A.
∴ The glass did not break.	∴ Not B.]

It does not follow that if Maria does not drop it, it won't break, since there are many other ways for the glass to break: Jack may drop it or someone may pour very hot liquid into it, just to name two possibilities.

To affirm the consequent will also produce an invalid argument.

If Maria drops the glass, it will break.	[If A, then B.
It broke.	B.
∴ Maria dropped it.	∴ A.]

If the glass did break, it doesn't necessarily follow that Maria was the cause, since, once again, there are many ways for a glass to meet such a fate.

To summarize: These two hypothetical argument patterns are valid.

If A, then B.	If A, then B.
A.	Not B.
∴ B.	∴ Not A.

These two hypothetical argument patterns are invalid.

If A, then B.	If A, then B.
Not A.	B.
∴ Not B.	∴ A.

Determining the validity of hypothetical reasoning reminds us that many conditions or causes can lead to the same result; we can't assume only one specific condition for a particular consequence unless we are told that this is the case.

Necessary and Sufficient Conditions

When there is a condition essential for a particular consequence or result, that condition is called a **necessary condition**—a condition without which something cannot happen. Fire, for example, cannot occur without oxygen; oxygen then is a necessary condition of fire. But oxygen alone cannot start a fire—there must be matter to burn as well as something to ignite it—so oxygen is not a **sufficient condition**. While it is necessary, it is not enough.

Logicians sometimes express a necessary cause as "if and only if." If, and only if, oxygen is present can fire start. Or, as writer Tobias Wolff (in *This Boy's Life*) remembers his mother warning him: "She said I could have the rifle if, and only if, I promised never to take it out or even touch it"—a necessary condition he failed to honor, unfortunately.

"He is physically able to wag his tail—given sufficient cause."

Hypothetical Chains

Hypothetical arguments may also consist of entire chains of conditions, as in the following example:

> If gun control advocates mount a very strong, well-funded campaign, then Congress will pass a law banning handguns.
>
> If Congress passes a law banning handguns, then fewer people will be able to purchase them.
>
> If fewer people are able to purchase them, then there will be fewer guns.
>
> If there are fewer guns, then there will be less violence in our society.
>
> ∴ If gun control advocates mount a very strong, well-funded campaign in the fall, then there will be less violence in our society.

The pattern is apparent:

If A, then B.

If B, then C.

If C, then D.

If D, then E.

∴ If A, then E.

If, in such a chain, the first condition is affirmed, the other conditional claims, like falling dominoes, lead us inescapably to the conclusion—providing, of course, that we accept the truth of the claims.

Hypothetical Claims and Everyday Reasoning

As you prepare to do the following exercise on hypothetical arguments, keep in mind that such reasoning is not limited to logic texts. Hypothetical relationships also play a central role when computer programmers design software, and hypothetical reasoning is, in fact, a common feature of the thinking we do every day. For example:

> If I miss that review session, I won't be prepared for the midterm.
>
> If I don't stop at the grocery store on my way home, I won't have anything to eat for dinner.

As these examples indicate, we continually make conditional claims and decisions based on these claims and the outcome we desire. In the examples above, if the "I" of the sentences fails to affirm the antecedent, he must be prepared to accept the less-than-desirable consequences.

EXERCISE 7F

Determining the Validity of Hypothetical Arguments

Use argument patterns to determine the validity of the following hypothetical arguments. (Keep in mind that you are not evaluating the acceptability of each premise, so even the valid arguments could be unsound according to the principles of reasoning discussed earlier in this chapter.)

1. If the burglar came in through the window, it would be unlocked. We found the window unlocked. We all agreed that the burglar must have come in through the window.

2. If most nations view ethnic cleansing in Darfur as a crime against humanity, then military action against the aggressors should be stepped up. Indeed, most nations do view ethnic cleansing as a crime against humanity, so military action against the aggressors should be increased.

3. Doctors claim that if you eat barbecued meats on a regular basis, you increase your risk of developing cancer. Fortunately, Calvin is a vegetarian and thus doesn't eat barbecued meats, so he is not at increased risk for cancer.

4. If the burglar came in through the window, it would be unlocked. We found the window locked, leading us to believe that the burglar couldn't have come in through the window.

5. If you respected my opinion, you would seek my advice. You don't seek my advice, so I can only conclude that you don't respect my opinion.

6. If the government doesn't balance the budget, the deficit will increase. The facts speak for themselves: the deficit is increasing. Clearly, the government is not balancing the budget.

7. If the governor makes a strong speech on the necessity of conserving water, he will be able to convince people to do so. Fortunately, he has scheduled a press conference for that purpose, so people will conserve water.

8. All the sportswriters agreed that if the Patriots didn't play well against the Giants, the Patriots were destined to lose the all-important game. As we all remember, they lost in the closing minutes, leaving me with the unhappy knowledge that they didn't play well that day.

9. If the paint is oil-based, the paintbrush cannot be cleaned with water, but the brush is being cleaned with water, so the paint must not be oil-based.

10. If oil supplies from the Persian Gulf are reduced, the price of oil will rise in the United States. If the price of oil in the United States rises, manufacturing costs will rise, and if this happens, an economic recession could develop. So if an economic recession does develop, we can certainly attribute it to reduced oil supplies from the Persian Gulf.

EXERCISE 7G

Analyzing a Timeless Argument

Reduce the following poem by Andrew Marvell (1621–1678) to a hypothetical argument containing two premises and a conclusion, and determine its validity. Hint: The first two stanzas contain the first and second premises, respectively, and the last contains the conclusion.

TO HIS COY MISTRESS

Had we but world enough, and time,
This coyness, Lady, were no crime.
We would sit down, and think which way
To walk, and pass our long love's day.
Thou by the Indian Ganges' side
Shouldst rubies find; I by the tide
Of Humber would complain. I would
Love you ten years before the Flood,
And you should, if you please, refuse
Till the Conversion of the Jews.
My vegetable love should grow

Vaster than empires and more slow;
An hundred years should go to praise
Thine eyes, and on thy forehead gaze;
An age at least to every part,
And the last age should show your heart.
For, Lady, you deserve this *state*,   (dignity)
Nor would I love at lower rate.

But at my back I always hear
Time's winged chariot hurrying near;
And yonder all before us lie
Deserts of vast eternity.
Thy beauty shall no more be found,
Nor, in thy marble vault, shall sound
My echoing song; then worms shall try
That long-preserved virginity,
And your *quaint* honor turn to dust,   (proud)
And into ashes all my lust:
The grave's a fine and private place,
But none, I think, do there embrace.

Now therefore, while the youthful hue
Sits on thy skin like morning dew,
And while thy willing soul *transpires* (breathes out)
At every pore with instant fires,
Now let us sport us while we may
And now, like amorous birds of prey,
Rather at once our time devour
Than languish in his slow-*chapped* power. (jawed)
Let us roll all our strength and all
Our sweetness up into one ball,
And tear our pleasures with rough strife
Thorough the iron gates of life:
Thus, though we cannot make our sun
Stand still, yet we will make him run.

EXERCISE 7H

Evaluating an Argument for Peace

Using your own words, reduce this poem by Wilfred Owen (1893–1918) to a hypothetical argument and determine its validity. Hint: The first premise is stated in the last stanza, but the minor premise and the conclusion are implicit.

DULCE ET DECORUM EST

Bent double, like old beggars under sacks,
Knock-kneed, coughing like hags, we cursed through sludge,
Till on the haunting flares we turned our backs
And toward our distant rest began to trudge.
Men marched asleep. Many had lost their boots.
But limped on, blood-shod. All went lame; all blind;
Drunk with fatigue; deaf even to the hoots
Of tired, outstripped Five Nines that dropped behind.

Gas! Gas! Quick, boys!—An ecstasy of fumbling,
Fitting the clumsy helmets just in time;
But someone still was yelling out and stumbling
And flound'ring like a man in fire or lime. . . .
Dim, through the misty panes and thick green light,
As under a green sea, I saw him drowning.
In all my dreams, before my helpless sight,
He plunges at me, guttering, choking, drowning.

If in some smothering dreams you too could pace
Behind the wagon that we flung him in,
And watch the white eyes writhing in his face,
His hanging face, like a devil's sick of sin;
If you could hear, at every jolt, the blood
Come gargling from the froth-corrupted lungs,
Obscene as cancer, bitter as the cud
Of vile, incurable sores on innocent tongues,
My friend, you would not tell with such high zest
To children ardent for some desperate glory
The old Lie: *Dulce et decorum est*
Pro patria mori.*

INDUCTIVE REASONING

The fundamental distinction between deductive and inductive reasoning lies in the relative certainty with which we can accept a conclusion. The certainty guaranteed when a deductive argument is validly reasoned from acceptable premises cannot

*"It is sweet and fitting to die for one's country." From the Latin poet Horace.

Biographical note: This poem is especially poignant because its author, Wilfred Owen, died on the battlefield in the last week of the First World War at the age of 25.

be assumed in an inductive argument, no matter how carefully one supports the inference. The terms most appropriate for inductive arguments then are **strong** and **weak**, **reliable** or **unreliable**, rather than valid and invalid.

Some logicians prefer the categories *deductive* and *nondeductive* to *deductive* and *inductive*, given the varied forms arguments can take when they don't conform to the rigorous rules of inference required for deduction.

Generalization

Determining cause and effect, formulating hypotheses, drawing analogies, and arriving at statistical generalizations are examples of nondeductive reasoning, or, as we have chosen to call it, inductive reasoning. In this section, we concentrate on the statistical generalization. **Statistical generalizations** are best characterized as predictions, as claims about the distribution of a **projected property** in a given group or population, the **target population**. From the distribution of such a property in *part* of the target population, the **sample**, we infer a proposition, a conclusion that is either strong or weak depending on how carefully we conduct our survey. We make a prediction, an inference, about the unknown on the basis of the known; on the basis of our observations of the sample, we make a generalization about all of the population, including that part we have not observed closely.

Suppose we want to determine whether New York taxpayers will support a tax designated specifically for building shelters for the homeless. Here **the projected property would be the willingness to support this particular tax (what we want to find out). The target population would be New York taxpayers. The sample would be that portion of New York taxpayers polled. From their answers, we would draw a conclusion, make a generalization about New York taxpayers in general:** unanimous support, strong support, marginal support, little support, no support—whatever their answers warrant. But no matter how precise the numbers from the sample, we cannot predict with absolute certainty what the entire population of New York taxpayers will actually do. When we make an inference from some to all, the conclusion always remains logically doubtful to some degree.

Let's look at another example:

For several years now, scientists and health officials have alerted the public to the increased risk of skin cancer as the thinning of the ozone layer allows more of the harmful ultraviolet rays to penetrate the atmosphere. Imagine that the student health center at your school wanted to find out if students were aware of this danger and were protecting themselves from it. In this case, **the projected property would be taking preventive measures to protect oneself from the sun. The target population would be all the students attending your school, and the sample would be the number of students polled.** Once again, any conclusions reached by the health center on the basis of its survey would be tentative rather than certain, with the certainty increasing in proportion to the size of the sample—the greater the number of students polled, the more reliable is the conclusion, assuming the sample is representative as well.

The Direction of Inductive Reasoning

The direction of inductive reasoning can vary. We may start by noting specific instances and from them make general inferences, or we may begin with a general idea and seek specific examples or data to support it. The following example moves from specific cases to a generalization:

> Observing a sudden increase in the number of measles cases in several communities, public health officials inferred that too many infants were going unvaccinated.

You may notice that our ability to think both deductively and inductively has a way of intertwining the two modes of thought, but the structure of this argument is still inductive, the conclusion being probable rather than guaranteed.

Often we start with a tentative generalization, a possible conclusion called a **hypothesis, an assertion we are interested in proving**.

> Roussel-Uclaf, the French manufacturers of a revolutionary new pill to prevent pregnancy and avoid abortion, hoped to prove that it was both effective and safe. To do so, they had to conduct elaborate studies with varied groups of women over time. Until they had gathered such statistical support in a sample population, their claim that it was effective and safe was only a hypothesis, not a reliable conclusion. But once they had tested their product, RU-486, on 40,000 women in several European countries and found only two "incidents" of pregnancies and no apparent harm, they were ready to claim that RU-486 is reasonably safe and statistically effective.

Even here, the conclusion remains inductive—it is a highly probable conclusion but not a necessary one as it would be in deduction. Unfortunately, there are examples of such inductive reasoning leading to false (and disastrous) conclusions.

Approved for use in Europe, the drug thalidomide, given to pregnant women for nausea in the 1960s, caused many children to be born with grave deformities. And the Dalkon Shield, an intrauterine birth control device of the 1970s, although tested before being made available, caused sterility in many of its users.

Given the degree of uncertainty inherent in any conclusion based on a sample, the Japanese take no chances when it comes to their nation's beef supply. According to the *New York Times*, "Japan tests all the cows it slaughters each year, 1.2 million," while the United States Department of Agriculture relies on a sample, testing approximately one hundred cows a year.

Testing Inductive Generalizations

With inductive arguments, we accept a conclusion with varying degrees of probability and must be willing to live with at least a fraction of uncertainty. But the question always remains, how much uncertainty is acceptable?

CRITERIA FOR EVALUATING STATISTICAL GENERALIZATIONS   *How* we infer our conclusions, the way in which we conduct our surveys, is crucial to determining the strength of an inductive argument. Whether we are constructing our own arguments or evaluating those of others, we need to be discriminating. Many of our decisions on political, economic, sociological, even personal issues depend on inductive reasoning. Scarcely a day goes by without an inductive study or poll reaching newspapers, television news, and the Internet: surveys show the president's popularity is rising or falling, Americans favor socialized medicine, girls are doing as well as boys in math. A few principles for evaluating such generalizations can help us all examine the conclusions with the critical perspective necessary for our self-defense.

In order to accept a conclusion as warranted or reliable, we need to control or interpret the conditions of the supporting survey.

Two features of the sample are essential:

1. The *size* must be adequate. The proportion of those in the sample must be sufficient to reflect the total size of the target population. Statisticians have developed complex formulas for determining adequate size proportionate to a given population, but for our general purposes common sense and a little well-reasoned practice will serve. The Gallup Organization polls 2,500 to 3,000 people to determine how 80 million will vote in a presidential election and allows for only a 3 percent margin of error. This suggests that the size of a survey can often be smaller than we might initially assume.

2. The sample must be *representative*. It must represent the target population in at least two different ways.

   a. The sample must be selected *randomly* from the target population.

   b. It must also be *spread* across the population so that all significant differences within the population are represented. Such a contrived approach might seem contradictory to a random sample, but some conscious manipulation is often necessary to ensure a sample that is genuinely typical of the target population.

Examine the following diagram to see these principles illustrated:

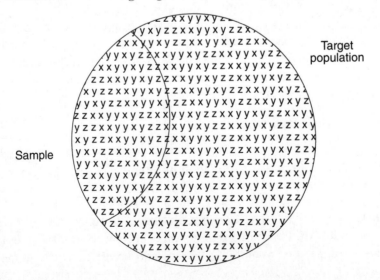

As you can see, we are back to classes (see "Class Logic" earlier in this chapter). The sample is a subclass included in the larger class of the target population. As we make inferences, we move from a conclusion about the smaller class, the sample, to a conclusion about the larger class, the target population.

> If they remove all the fools from Congress, it wouldn't be a representative Congress.
>
> —POLITICAL COMMENTATOR MOLLY IVINS

Let's evaluate the reasoning in the following argument:

A visitor of modest means from a midwestern city comes to San Francisco for five days and is instructed by her friends to assess the prices of San Francisco's restaurants; some of them are considering a trip there in the near future. Our tourist, let's call her Kate, picks up a guidebook and takes the first five restaurants listed in the book: Boulevard, Campton Place, Masa's, Quince and the Ritz Carlton, all of which are located downtown. Verging on bankruptcy, poor Kate returns home with the report that restaurants in San Francisco are staggeringly expensive. For a resident of San Francisco, the error in her conclusion and the flaw in the reasoning that led to her false conclusion are easy to spot—she has inadvertently chosen five of the most expensive restaurants in the city. Before selecting her restaurants, she should have examined her guidebook carefully to be sure that her survey of restaurants was, to some degree, representative. The book clearly began with a list of the major splurges, and that was as far as Kate went.

With only five days, she was necessarily limited when it came to the *size* of her sample, and thus she would have to place a strong qualifier on any conclusions she drew. But, with a little care, she could have aimed for a more ***random*** sample by investigating different sections of her guidebook, referring to more than one guide, and visiting various geographical areas of San Francisco. Such a sampling would also have helped her arrive at examples spread more effectively over different types of cuisines. A visitor intent on savoring the best fare regardless of cost would have done well following Kate's approach, but one interested in the prices was doomed to a distorted picture.

Can you identify the projected property, the target population, the sample, and the conclusion for this inductive argument?

HASTY GENERALIZATIONS   When, like Kate, we leap to an unwarranted conclusion, we commit the common logical fallacy of hasty generalization. If, for example, after one semester at a university as a student having had two professors who failed to return work, often missed class, or arrived late, you concluded that the university had a rotten faculty, you would be guilty of hasty generalization. The sample is clearly too small to warrant such a conclusion. Newspaper columnist Jon Carroll "remember[s] one [East Coast] writer who came to California, stayed in the Beverly Hills Hotel for three days and concluded that all Californians were stupid, narcissistic and in the movie business." To discredit this hasty generalization, all one would have to do is find a **counterexample**, one Californian who wasn't stupid, narcissistic, and in the movie business. What mistake did the East Coast writer make with his sample? For further discussion of this familiar fallacy, see Chapter 6.

COUNTEREXAMPLES

With any generalization supported by specific examples, one counterexample can discredit, or "embarrass," the conclusion. Warranted conclusions must be consistent with the data used in their support, and where necessary, qualified appropriately—*most, some, usually, occasionally, in most cases.*

Garfield ®   by Jim Davis

Garfield doubts his conclusion when he finds three counterexamples.

Thinking Critically About Surveys and Statistics

Because surveys and statistics suggest an authority they may not warrant, we must read them critically rather than accept them without question. Statistics should contribute to reasoning, not serve as a substitute for it.

Time magazine ran a cover story on the high cost of a college degree titled "How Colleges Are Gouging You" by Erik Larson. In his article, Larson accused colleges of protecting their endowment funds while charging whatever the traffic will bear for tuition. The piece elicited this angry response:

> To generalize the situation at the University of Pennsylvania and other Ivy League schools and apply it to major universities across the board is like using the cost of a Lexus to discuss the price of an average family van. In the real world of most institutions, faculty members do not average earnings of $140,000 a year. And they are teaching larger classes with fewer resources and support staff and reduced budgets for essential expenses. Unfortunately, Larson's diatribe will probably be used by state legislatures as justification to cut budgets of many public institutions.
>
> —JOHN BRUNCH, ASSISTANT PROFESSOR, DEPARTMENT OF MANAGEMENT, KANSAS STATE UNIVERSITY, MANHATTAN, KANSAS

This professor from a public university is rightfully concerned that a generalization based on a study of private universities will be applied to public universities (which often do not have endowment funds), with the consequence of fewer resources for him and his students.

In 1948 Alfred C. Kinsey published *The Kinsey Report*, one of the first surveys on the sexual mores of Americans. Kinsey concluded among other things that 10 percent of the population was homosexual. James H. Jones, who wrote a biography of Kinsey, points out that the sample on which this conclusion was based was not representative of all Americans because "Kinsey did a great deal of interviewing in prisons, where the incidence of homosexuality was higher than in the general population."

Bad science is made worse by the media's often reporting of all surveys in abbreviated and often sensational ways, frequently giving subtle slants in emphasis to statistics. For example, in the same issue of a major daily newspaper, the summary caption on page one stated that "A new poll finds that 1 in 5 Californians still resent Japan for the attack on Pearl Harbor," while the inside story was headed, "50 years after attack on Pearl Harbor, only 1 in 5 is still resentful, poll shows." What are the different implications of these two captions?

Mistaking Correlation for Causation

Even when a study is carefully done by a reputable institution, the press will often reduce the results to the most attention-getting headline. The media reported that heavy coffee drinkers had two to three times the risk of heart disease on the basis of a study done at Johns Hopkins University using many subjects over several years. But a careful reading of the study from beginning to end revealed that its authors didn't ask participants about their diet, smoking habits, and exercise levels, mitigating factors in any study of heart disease. The report concluded that there was "a need for further investigation" into the dangers of caffeine, a conclusion the media failed to report. All that one could safely conclude from the Johns Hopkins study is a **correlation** between heavy caffeine use and heart disease, not **causation**. The distinction between correlation and causation is an important one. There is a correlation between home ownership and car accidents. If you are a home owner, you're more likely to own a car, so you're more likely to be in a car accident, but that doesn't mean that home ownership causes car accidents.

To determine causation, researchers must conduct randomized, controlled studies; such studies are difficult to design and complete. Large numbers of people are assigned by chance to different groups. In tests of medications, for example, neither the scientists in charge of the study nor its participants know whether the subjects being studied have been taking a particular drug or a placebo (an unmedicated substance) until the study is completed and the results analyzed.

Observational studies, on the other hand, begin with a hypothesis such as a belief that a low-fat diet protects against heart disease. Researchers then gather relevant patient data and plug this data into computers, which then identify correlations between diet and disease. But mathematical correlations do not necessarily mean causation, a point to remember whenever we see the results of a new study.

Epidemiology

Epidemiology is a branch of medical research devoted to determining the incidence, distribution, and possible control of disease. Since the 1950s it has focused on the causes of chronic diseases, in particular heart disease and cancer. When it comes to the relationship between diet, lifestyle factors, and chronic disease, epidemiologists face special challenges when conducting surveys.

One of these challenges, according to Michael Pollan, author of *In Defense of Food*, is the fact that people lie when answering questions about their diet. "How do we know this? Deduction. Consider: When the study began, the average participant weighed in at 170 pounds and claimed to be eating 1,800 calories a day. It would take an unusual metabolism to maintain that weight on so little food."

Another challenge: the mitigating factor of wealth. The Nurses' Health Study run by Harvard Medical School and Harvard School of Public Health attempted to eliminate this factor by having all the women in the study in the same profession; but what about the husbands of these nurses? What was their income? How many children did each woman have? Did a nurse's income support one person or five?

And the biggest challenge of all is the fact that participants in studies are often healthier than the general population. For example, it's difficult to determine the impact of vitamin supplements on the people who take them. They tend to be educated people who take an active interest in their health and therefore exercise, watch what they eat, and see their doctor on a regular basis. If they are healthier than most, is that because of the vitamin supplements?

AN INTERNET JOKE:

Here's the final word on nutrition.

> The Japanese eat very little fat and suffer fewer heart attacks than the British or Americans.

> The French eat a lot of fat and also suffer fewer heart attacks than the British or Americans.

> The Japanese drink very little red wine and suffer fewer heart attacks than the British or Americans.

> The Italians drink excessive amounts of red wine and also suffer fewer heart attacks than the British or Americans.

> **Conclusion:** Eat and drink what you like. Speaking English is apparently what kills you.

Considering the Source

When evaluating a survey and its conclusions, we must consider the source of the survey—who conducted the survey and who paid for it—to determine if there is a **conflict of interest** or a **hidden agenda**. A study of silicone breast implants concluded that there was no link between ruptured implants and connective tissue disease. Lawyer and consumer advocate Mary Alexander criticizes this study, not only for the limited size of its sample and its failure to allow for the 8.5 years of latency between implantation and silicone disease, but also because two of its authors "admitted on the threat of perjury that they were paid consultants of breast implant manufacturers." Furthermore, Dow Corning, the world's largest silicone breast implant manufacturer, had donated $5 million to one of the hospitals involved in the study. Such a study is riddled with conflict of interest. It is not in the best interest of those who benefit directly from Dow Corning to find fault with the company's product.

Class action lawyers filed an $800 million suit against Motorola, claiming cell phones cause brain cancer. This suit motivated cell phone manufacturers to fund studies of their own. These studies, none of which lasted more than three years, concluded that cell phone use did not cause brain cancer. Both the length of these studies and their sponsors cause us to question their conclusions.

The difficulty lies in the reality that sometimes even the most reliable journals and research organizations lead us astray. One of the most respected medical publications, the *New England Journal of Medicine*, has been found guilty of violating its conflict-of-interest policy. In 1996, the journal ran an editorial claiming that the benefits of diet drugs outweighed the risks but failed to note that the two authors had been paid consultants for firms that made or marketed one of the diet drugs under discussion. And in 1997, the journal featured a negative review of a book connecting environmental chemicals and various cancers, a review written by the medical director of a large chemical company.

Another respected medical journal, *JAMA* (*Journal of the American Medical Association*), has also been careless about determining conflict of interest. In 2005 *JAMA* published a study that concluded that fetuses younger than seven months probably did not feel pain. One of the two authors was a former abortion-rights attorney; the other ran an abortion clinic.

Studies may not be free of bias even when there isn't a conflict of interest or hidden agenda. *New York Times* columnist David Brooks comments on this phenomenon:

> The world is fluid. Bias and randomness can creep in from all directions. For example, between 1966 and 1995 there were 47 acupuncture studies conducted in Japan, Taiwan and China, and they all found it to be an effective therapy. There were 94 studies in the U.S., Sweden and Britain, and only 56 percent showed benefits. The lesson is not to throw out studies, but to never underestimate the complexity of the world.

CRITICAL READING OF SURVEYS

1. Is the sample representative of the target population? Is it large enough? How long did the study last? Was the study random and controlled or was it observational?

2. Does the media's report on the survey seem fair and reasonable?

3. Does the survey establish causation or correlation?

4. Who wrote or published or called your attention to the survey? Are they impartial or do they have a hidden agenda or conflict of interest? Is the survey cited in advertising or in another context in which the motive is to sell you something?

EXERCISE 71

Evaluating Inductive Reasoning

In the following studies, identify the **conclusion**, the **projected property**, the **target population**, and the **sample**. Then, drawing on the principles of reliable inductive generalizations, **evaluate their reliability**.

1. The quality control inspector at Sweet and Sour Yogurt removes and tests one container out of approximately every thousand (about one every 15 minutes) and finds it safe for consumption. She then guarantees as safe all the containers filled that day.

2. On November 1, to consolidate his frequent flier miles, businessman Eric Nichols decided to select one domestic airline from his two favorites. He planned to base his decision on each airline's reliability. From November through April he made 20 evenly spaced trips on United, experiencing two cancellations, nine delayed departures, and eight late arrivals. From May through October, he flew American Airlines 22 times, but improved his record with only one cancellation, seven delays, and five late arrivals. Without further consideration, he chose American as the more reliable of the two.

3. Setting out to document her theory on the prevalence of racism on television, a sociologist examines 40 episodes from the new fall prime-time situation comedies and finds that 36 of them contain racist stereotypes. She concludes that 90 percent of television drama is racist.

4. In her book *Women and Love*, Shere Hite claims that a large percentage of American women are unhappy in their marriages and feel that men don't listen to them. She felt confident in her conclusions after mailing out 100,000 questionnaires to women's political, professional, and religious organizations and having 4 percent of the questionnaires returned.

5. The French Ministry of Social Affairs reported that three well-known research physicians at the Laënnec Hospital in Paris had observed "dramatic biological improvements" in a group of patients with AIDS. The physicians reported a "dramatic" slowing of acquired immune deficiency syndrome in one of the six patients and a complete halt in the disease's progress in another after only five days of treatment with a compound called cyclosporine. (Hint: The conclusion is implicit.)

6. A study by the University of Medicine and Dentistry of New Jersey concluded that "women who were abused [physically, emotionally, or sexually] as children have more health problems and require more hospital care than women who were not abused." Seven hundred women from a private gynecological practice were interviewed. Mostly white, middle class with college degrees, they ranged in age from 16 to 76.

7. A study published in *Science* concluded that women did not talk more than men, a contradiction of the commonly held belief that women talk more than men. This study was based on audio clips taken from 200 university students, 100 men and 100 women, who agreed to be recorded for several days sometime between 1998 and 2004. The recording devices would turn on automatically for 30 seconds every 12.5 minutes without the subjects' knowledge. Researchers transcribed and counted these words to estimate how many words each person used in a day.

EXERCISE 7J

Distinguishing Between Correlation and Causation

Read the following essay by Dr. Susan Love, a professor of surgery at UCLA School of Medicine, and answer the questions that follow.

Preventive Medicine, Properly Practiced

There are at least 6 million women in this country who are asking themselves,   1
"What happened?" Over the last several years they have read books and magazine articles, listened to TV pundits and talked to doctors and friends—all of whom assured them that taking hormone replacement therapy for the rest of their lives would keep them healthy. Then one bright summer day, their world shifted. Their little daily pill carried not the promise of health but the risk of disease. How could this be?

    What happened is that medical practice, as it so often does, got ahead of med-   2
ical science. We made observations and developed hypotheses—and then forgot

to prove them. We start with observational studies, in which researchers look at groups of people to see if we can find any clues about disease. But all this observation can do is find associations: it can't prove cause and effect.

With hormone replacement therapy, we did many observational studies. We found that women who were on hormone therapy had a lower incidence of heart disease, stroke, colon cancer and bone fracture. And we accepted these findings before we did the definitive research, overlooking the fact that these women were also more likely to see a doctor (which is how they were put on hormone therapy in the first place), and probably more likely to exercise and to eat a healthful diet, than women who were not taking the drug. It wasn't clear whether hormones made women healthy or whether healthy women took hormones.   3

To answer this question we needed randomized, controlled research. The latest study, sponsored by the National Institutes of Health, enrolled 16,608 healthy women from ages 50 to 79 and randomly assigned them to take hormone replacement therapy or a placebo. Much to everyone's surprise, after 5.2 years the study showed that the risks of hormone treatment outweighed the benefits in preventing disease. . . .   4

There is a bigger issue than simply hormone therapy, however. There is a tendency, driven by wishful thinking combined with good marketing and media hype, to jump ahead of the medical evidence. In the 1950's, it was DES, a drug given to pregnant women to prevent miscarriages. It was many years later that a randomized, controlled study showed that it had no effect in preventing miscarriages. Finally, in 1971 it was learned that daughters of women who took DES were at increased risk of developing vaginal cancer.   5

In the 1990's, the bone marrow transplant—high-dose chemotherapy with stem-cell rescue—was proposed to treat aggressive breast cancers. It was widely used until four randomized, controlled studies showed it was no better than standard therapy, and had far more side effects. Arthroscopic surgery for osteoarthritis was commonly performed but just last week a controlled study showed it had no objective benefit. Hormone replacement therapy is just one more example of this phenomenon. . . .   6

1. What is the difference between an observational study and a "randomized, controlled" study?

2. Identify the projected property, the target population, the sample, and the conclusion of the National Institutes of Health study of hormone replacement therapy, and then evaluate the reliability of the conclusion.

3. According to Dr. Love, why does medical practice "jump ahead of the medical evidence"? What other examples of this phenomenon, in addition to hormone replacement, does she cite? Can you add to this list?

EXERCISE 7K

Collecting Generalizations

Humorist James Thurber had fun exploiting our tendency to overgeneralize in his essay "What a Lovely Generalization." Many of his examples are absurd, but some suggest the dangers that can spring from such patterns of thought. For those interested in collecting generalizations, he suggests listening "in particular to women, whose average generalization is from three to five times as broad as a man's." Was he sexist or making a joke? He listed many others from his collection, labeling some "true," some "untrue," others "debatable," "libelous," "ridiculous," and so on. Some examples from his collection: "Women don't sleep very well," "There are no pianos in Japan," "Doctors don't know what they're doing," "Gamblers hate women," "Cops off duty always shoot somebody," "Intellectual women dress funny." And so his collection ran, brimming with hasty generalizations.

Your task is to collect two "lovely generalizations" from the world around you, comment on the accuracy, absurdity, and dangers of each, and discuss the implications of your generalizations for those who seem to be the target.

WRITING ASSIGNMENT 12

Questioning Generalizations

Add the two generalizations you chose for Exercise 7K, Collecting Generalizations, to the following list of generalizations and choose one to write a one-page paper in support of, or in opposition to. This list could be even longer and more diverse if your instructor collects the entire class's generalizations and makes them available to you.

1. Women are better dancers than men.
2. Men are better athletes than women.
3. Everyone is capable of being creative.
4. Nice guys finish last.
5. Appearances can be deceiving.
6. The purpose of a college degree is to prepare an individual for a career.
7. A college graduate will get a higher-paying job than a high school graduate.
8. A woman will never be elected president of the United States.
9. All people are created equal.
10. War is a necessary evil.

Audience
A reader who is not strongly invested in the proposition one way or another but who is interested in hearing your point of view.

Purpose
To cast a critical eye on a generalization that people tend to accept without question.

WRITING ASSIGNMENT 13

Conducting a Survey: A Collaborative Project

Conduct a survey at your school to determine something of significance about the student body and then write a report in which you state either a question or a hypothesis, describe the survey, and speculate on the results.

The class as a whole can brainstorm possible questions to ask the student body, the target population. What do students think about the current administration on campus or in Washington? Our nation's war on terrorism? Or a host of other political issues. How many students take a full academic load and work part-time as well? How many students expect to graduate in four years? There are many possibilities.

Choose five or six topics from these many possibilities and divide into groups around them. These groups will then create a survey—a questionnaire appropriate to the topic they are researching—and a strategy for distributing it to a representative sample.

The next step is to collect, tabulate, and discuss the data. Either each student can then write her own report or the group can write a single report, assigning a section to each member of the group.

The report will contain the following:

1. A description of the survey:

   What questions did you ask?

   When and where did you ask them?

2. A description of the sample:

   Whom did you ask?

   How many did you ask?

3. Evaluation of the survey:

   Was the sample large enough?

   Was it representative?

   Were your questions unbiased?

   What could you do to make it better?

4. Analysis of the results:

   How does it compare with what you expected the results to be before you began gathering the data?

   What do you imagine are the causes that led to these results?

   What are the implications of the results?

Audience

Your campus community—students, faculty, and staff.

Purpose

To inform your campus community about its student members.

SUMMARY

Inductive and deductive reasoning are distinct from one another in two ways:
1. In a **deductive argument**, the conclusion follows by necessity from the premises if the method of reasoning is valid. In an **inductive argument**, the conclusion can follow with only some degree of probability.
2. In a **deductive argument**, the inference moves from a generalization to a particular instance or example that fits that generalization. In an **inductive argument**, the inference usually moves from a series of specific instances to a generalization.

Induction and deduction are interdependent; it takes an interplay of the two thinking methods to arrive at our conclusions.

There are three possible relationships between classes: **inclusion**, **exclusion**, and **overlap**.

Both inductive and deductive reasoning often depend on supporting a conclusion on the basis of relationships between classes.

For a **categorical argument** to be sound, the structure of the argument must be valid and the premises acceptable.

For a **hypothetical argument** to be valid, the second, or minor premise, must either affirm the antecedent or deny the consequent.

The **statistical generalization**, based as it is on an inductive leap from some to all, is never as certain as a conclusion drawn from sound deductive reasoning.

The direction of inductive reasoning can vary. We may note specific instances and from them make general inferences, or we may begin with a general idea and seek specific examples or data to support it.

For a statistical generalization to be reliable, the sample must be adequate in size and representative of the target population.

With any generalization supported by specific examples, one **counterexample** can discredit the conclusion.

A **correlation** between two characteristics, such as speaking English and having heart attacks, does not mean that speaking English causes heart attacks.

KEY TERMS

Antecedent   the part of a hypothetical argument that establishes a condition.

Categorical syllogism   a deductive argument composed of three classes; the argument has two premises and one conclusion derived from the two premises.

Causation   anything that directly produces an effect.

Class   in logic all of the individual things—persons, objects, events, ideas—that share a determinate property.

Consequent the part of a hypothetical argument that results from the antecedent.

Correlation a mutual relationship or connection between two or more things, but not necessarily a direct cause–effect relationship.

Deduction a pattern of reasoning in which the conclusion follows of necessity from the premises if the reasoning is valid.

Epidemiology a branch of medical research devoted to determining the incidence, distribution, and possible control of disease.

Exclusion a relationship between classes in which classes share no members.

Hypothesis a tentative generalization, an unproved theory or proposition we are interested in proving.

Hypothetical argument a common type of deductive argument concerned with conditions.

Inclusion a relationship between classes in which every member of one class is a member of another class.

Induction a pattern of reasoning in which the conclusion follows only with some degree of probability.

Necessary condition a condition without which the consequence cannot occur; for example, fire cannot occur without oxygen.

Overlap a relationship between classes in which classes share at least one member.

Particular proposition refers to some members of a designated class.

Predicate includes everything being asserted about the subject.

Projected property what is to be determined about the target population.

Sample the surveyed members of the target population.

Soundness describes a deductive argument whose premises are acceptable and whose structure is valid.

Statistical generalization a prediction about the distribution of a particular feature in a given group.

Subject that part of the sentence about which something is being asserted.

Sufficient condition one condition, among others, that leads to a particular consequence; for example, a match is one way to start a fire but not the only way.

Target population the group about which the conclusion will be drawn.

Universal proposition refers to all members of a designated class.

Validity the conclusion follows of necessity from the premises; the form of the argument is correct.

CHAPTER 8

The Language of Argument—Style

Style is the dress of thought.

—SAMUEL WESLEY

Good sentences promise nothing less than lessons and practice in the organization of the world.

—STANLEY FISH

Some may dismiss style as ornament, as the decorative frills of writing, or as something limited to matters of correct grammar and usage. But an effective style can capture your reader's attention and possibly win the day for your argument. Style certainly includes a carefully proofread, grammatically correct final draft, but it also means **well-crafted sentences** that carry meaning gracefully to your readers.

We address well-crafted sentences in Chapters 3 and 4, when we discuss the importance of **logical joining** in argument, and in Chapter 5, when we present **appositives** as a technique for defining and describing terms within a sentence. In this chapter we introduce **parallel structure** and stress the use of **concrete and consistent sentence subjects** and **active voice verbs**. With these strategies, we emphasize **the value of rhetorical repetition** and **the elimination of wordiness**.

In the age of Twitter, texting, and eBay, the ability to write a concise yet detailed and eloquent sentence has never been more useful.

PARALLELISM

Parallel structure, used to organize items in a sentence and ideas in a paragraph, is another strategy for promoting coherence. The emphasis you achieve by harnessing your points into balanced grammatical structures increases the force of your written arguments. Politicians in particular have long been aware of the power of parallel structure.

> "... government **of the people**, **by the people**, **for the people**, shall not perish from the earth."

> —ABRAHAM LINCOLN, GETTYSBURG ADDRESS

"Let every nation know, whether it wishes us well or ill, that we shall **pay any price**, **bear any burden**, **meet any hardship**, **support any friend**, **oppose any foe** to assure the survival and the success of liberty."

—JOHN F. KENNEDY, *INAUGURAL ADDRESS*

The Structure of Parallelism

Parallel structure is simply a repetition of like grammatical units—a list of items—often joined by the conjunctions *and*, *but*, *or*, and *yet*.

Look at the following two sentences:

I came, I saw, I conquered.
The president had three choices: war, diplomacy, or appeasement.

Parallelism is a useful rhetorical device, providing a powerful means of emphasizing relationships by organizing ideas into predictable patterns. We hear a **repetition** and expect the pattern to continue. When our expectations are thwarted, we may falter briefly in our reading or even lose the thread of the writer's thoughts. In most cases, our ear tells us when a series is wandering off track, but sometimes it can be helpful to check the grammatical structure. Here is a strategy for examining your own sentences.

Think of **parallel structures as lists**; in the preceding case, it is a list of the president's options. We can illustrate this list and the need for it to conform to the principles of parallelism by placing parallel lines at the beginning of the list:

The president had three choices // war, diplomacy, or appeasement.

The conjunction *or* joins three nouns.

We can do the same thing to a more complicated sentence taken from writer Joan Didion's essay on Alcatraz, "Rock of Ages."

It is not an unpleasant place to be, out there on Alcatraz with only // the *flowers* and the *wind* and a bell *buoy* moaning and the *tide* surging through the Golden Gate. . . . [a list of nouns as direct objects of the preposition *with*]

Now read the next sentence (aloud if possible) and hear how the loss of expected balance or harmony offends the ear.

When I should be studying, I will, instead, waste time by // *watching television or daydream.*

The two verbs are not in the same form and are therefore not parallel. They can be made parallel by simply changing *daydream* to *daydreaming* to match *watching*.

EXERCISE 8A

Supplying Parallel Elements

A. Complete these sentences with a parallel element.

1. Writing a good paper is a task that demands // hard work, patience, and . . .

2. She // rushed home, threw her assorted debris into a closet, and . . .

3. Fewer Americans are saving these days // not because they don't think it's wise to save, but . . .

4. The first lady is a woman who // has an open mind but . . .

5. The first lady is a woman who has // an open mind and . . .

B. In the following sentences, identify the misfits—the element of the sentence that is not parallel—and revise the sentence so that all the elements of the list are parallel. Putting slashes where each series starts will help you see where the sentence goes off track.

1. Many influences shape a child's development: family, church, peer groups, economic, social, and school.

2. Michelle lives in a neighborhood where knife wounds, killings, and people are raped are as common as the sun rising in the morning.

3. He helped to wash the car and with cleaning out the garage.

4. Free inquiry in the search for truth sometimes necessitates the abandonment of law and order but which always demands freedom of expression.

5. Pineapple juice is my favorite because it is a good source of energy, it isn't artificially sweetened, and because of its low cost.

6. The mayor launched a campaign against drunk driving and promoting the use of seat belts.

C. Read the following passage taken from *The Road from Coorain* by Jill Ker Conway and note her effective use of parallel structure. Use our system of notation to mark off the different series or lists. How many did you find?

Those night train journeys had their own mystery because of the clicking of the rails, the shafts of light pouring through the shutters of the sleeping compartment as we passed stations, and the slamming of doors when the train stopped to take on passengers. In the morning there was the odd sight of green landscape, trees, grass, banks of streams—an entirely different palette of colors, as though during the night we had journeyed to another country. Usually I slept soundly, registering the unaccustomed sounds and images only faintly. This time I lay awake and listened, opened the shutters and scanned unknown platforms, and wondered about the future.

Logic of the Parallel Series

The items in a list, however, must not only be **grammatically** similar but also relate **logically** to one another. Sometimes faulty parallelism offends not only our ear but also our reason.

> People who have "book smarts" usually work in places like // *libraries* or *assistants to attorneys.*

Though the writer has joined two nouns (grammatically compatible elements), an assistant of any kind cannot be a "place." The writer has lost control of the sentence by forgetting where the list begins. There is more than one way to fix this sentence, to make it logical and balanced. How would you correct it?

To understand further what we mean, look at the following sentence:

> We will have to look at the language used in the text for sexism, racism, and bias.

The list in this sentence is "sexism, racism, and bias." The list is *grammatically* parallel because all three words in the list are nouns, but not *logically* parallel since sexism, racism, and bias are presented as three separate and distinct categories when in fact sexism and racism are particular forms of bias. They are included in what we can call the class or group of *bias*, not separate from it. (Remember class logic in Chapter 7.) One way to correct this faulty logic would be to replace *bias* with *other forms of bias* and thus illustrate the logical and actual relationship that exists between the three terms.

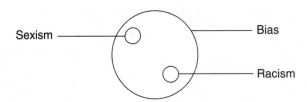

EXERCISE 8B

....

Editing the Illogical Series

Revise the following sentences for logical parallel structure.

1. In their attempt to excel, our employees often work extra hours and work through many lunch hours.
2. I have seen city ordinances that do not allow smoking popping up all over the place: in offices, in buildings.
3. I asked Linda if she had any materialistic aspirations such as living in a mansion, having a nice car, or being extremely wealthy.

4. The customers at the bank where I work are wealthy depositors, checking account holders, cooperative individuals, and those who are thoughtlessly rude to me.

5. For the most part, he is handsome, active, well dressed, and wears a suit and tie.

Emphasizing Ideas with Parallelism

Parallelism can be a powerful rhetorical device, especially in argument. Beyond the sentence, parallelism can provide emphasis and organize major ideas in a paragraph. Note how writer Joe Keohane illustrates this technique in the introductory paragraph to his essay, "How Facts Backfire," featured in Chapter 2.

> It's one of the great assumptions underlying modern democracy that an informed citizenry is preferable to an uninformed one. "Whenever the people are well-informed, they can be trusted with their own government," Thomas Jefferson wrote in 1789. This notion, carried down through the years, underlies everything from humble political pamphlets to presidential debates to the very notion of a free press. Mankind may be crooked timber, as [philosopher] Kant put it, uniquely susceptible to ignorance and misinformation, but it's an article of faith that knowledge is the best remedy. If people are furnished with the facts, they will be clearer thinkers and better citizens. If they are ignorant, facts will enlighten them. If they are mistaken, facts will set them straight.

The last three sentences sum up and emphasize the points made in the paragraph.

EXERCISE 8C

Creating Parallel Structure

In your next essay or in an assignment you are revising, construct a paragraph with a series of parallel sentences to emphasize a point you are making. The device may sound mechanical at first but may be useful in mounting your arguments, both written and spoken.

SHARPENING SENTENCES, ELIMINATING WORDINESS

> *He draweth out the thread of his verbosity finer than the staple of his argument.*
> —SHAKESPEARE, *LOVE'S LABOUR'S LOST*

We are all familiar with the confusion and obfuscation of much official prose—political, bureaucratic, academic. Some of this muddled language may be deliberate, to conceal meaning, to obfuscate. But often it is inadvertent, a result of writers surrendering to the abstractness of language. (See Chapter 5 on abstract language.) Such writing tends to be wordy and unclear.

Look at this example.

> Agreement on the overall objective of decision usefulness was a prerequisite to the establishment of a conceptual framework. Now, at least, we know where we are headed. (*The Week in Review*, newsletter of Deloitte Haskins & Sells)

Do we know where they are going?

Compare the following memo from the Internal Revenue Service and a possible revision.

Original

Advice has been requested concerning tax deductions for research expenses, including traveling expenses, incurred by college professors.

Revision

College professors have requested advice about tax deductions for their research expenses, including traveling expenses.

Which version is clearer, easier to read? We assume that the majority of readers will prefer the second. What are the differences? The revision is shorter by two words. This is one distinction. Are there others?

Calvin and Hobbes   by Bill Watterson

Concrete Subjects

Look at the grammatical subjects in the IRS examples above—*advice* in the first, *professors* in the second—and notice what kinds of nouns they are. One is an **abstract noun**, the other a **concrete noun**. Because the sentence subject tends to reflect what a passage is about, the subject is where the main point of emphasis usually sits. A concrete noun is capable of producing a visual picture and thus can also focus a reader's attention more closely. When that concrete noun is a person or people, readers can visualize an action and so more readily follow the precise progression of ideas in a sentence. Hence, *professors* as the subject of the revision is preferable to the *advice* of the original. The reader can see the *professor* but not the abstraction *advice*.

Active and Passive Verbs

Now look at the verbs. In the original sentence on tax deduction, the verb is *has been requested* while in the revision the verb is *has requested*. The first is **passive voice**, the second, **active voice**. The basic distinction is:

With a passive verb, the subject is acted upon; the subject is not doing anything in the sentence—it is passive.

Advice is being requested, not doing the requesting.

When the verb is active, its subject is performing the action of the sentence.

Thus the reader can see a subject **doing** something. The *professors* are doing the requesting.

We must wade through the original IRS memo to understand the point, whereas in the revision we see from the beginning that professors are requesting advice, people are doing something. Bureaucrats, often writing about vague or abstract subjects, can easily fall into the passive verb trap. They are rarely the ones actually *doing* anything they are writing about. Don't let your academic writing succumb to this danger.

Sentences written in the passive are easy to spot because they always follow a grammatical pattern:

subject + a form of the verb *to be* (*am, is, are, was, were, has been*)

+

the past participle of the verb (usually with an *-ed* ending) + a *by* phrase (sometimes implied), which contains the agent of the verb

(subject)	(to be)	(past participle)	(*by* phrase)
Advice	has been	requested	by college professors

The following two sentences say essentially the same thing, but catch how the change in the form of the verb shifts the emphasis from the concrete subject, *J. Robert Oppenheimer*, to the abstract, *elemental danger*.

Active: J. Robert Oppenheimer, one of the creators of the atom bomb, **felt** the elemental danger loosed on the earth.
Passive: The elemental danger loosed on the earth **was felt** by J. Robert Oppenheimer, one of the creators of the atom bomb.

Which version do you prefer? Why?

Passive Verbs and Evasion

When we want to avoid responsibility, we tend to rely on passive verbs to evade responsibility. Olympic swimming champion Michael Phelps turned to passive verbs when confronted with a photo of him smoking a marijuana pipe. Hoping to avoid attention, Phelps said, "You know, it happens. When stupid things **are done**, bad judgment **is made** and mistakes **are made**.

Phelps was trying to separate himself from his folly by leaving himself out of the sentence, thus avoiding the blame.

When the Passive Is Appropriate

Aiming for direct, assertive prose, careful writers usually prefer active verbs. But on occasion, when one wants to emphasize someone or something not performing the action in a sentence, the passive is useful. Scientists and social scientists, for example, must often focus on the content of their research rather than on themselves as researchers. Under such circumstances, the passive serves a useful purpose.

> This research *was undertaken* with a grant from the National Science Foundation.

> rather than

> I *undertook* this research with a grant from the National Science Foundation.

Consistent Sentence Subjects

Central to a good **paragraph** is the logical progression of ideas. Read the following paragraph closely to see how research physician and writer Lewis Thomas maintains consistent sentence subjects, emphasizing the topic of the paragraph—how **we** relate to the concept of **death**. Note how the grammatical subjects provide a coherent line of reasoning even though at the heart of the passage lies an abstract idea.

> **We** continue to share with our remotest ancestors the most tangled and evasive attitudes about death, despite the great distance **we** have come in understanding some of the profound aspects of biology. **We** have as much distaste for talking about personal death as for thinking about it; it is an indelicacy, like talking in mixed company about venereal disease or abortion in the old days. **Death** on a grand scale does not bother us in the same special way; **we** can sit around a dinner table and discuss war, involving 60 million volatilized human deaths, as though **we** were talking about bad weather; **we** can watch abrupt bloody death every day, in color, on films and television, without blinking back a tear. But when the numbers of dead are very small, and very close, **we** begin to think in scurrying circles. At the very center of the problem is the naked cold **deadness** of one's own self, the only reality in nature of which **we** can have absolute certainty, and **it** is unquestionable, unthinkable. **We** may be even less willing to face the issue at first hand than our predecessors because of a secret new hope that maybe **it** will go away. **We** like to think, hiding the thought, that with all the marvelous ways in which **we** seem now to lead nature around by the nose, perhaps **we** can avoid the central problem if **we** just become, next year, say, a bit smarter.

Revising for well-crafted sentences and coherent paragraphs helps to maintain the clear, direct expression you and your readers demand, no matter what your academic or professional discipline. Keep in mind, however, that revising is often most effective at a late stage in the writing process. We may expect a first draft to have several wordy and unclear sentences and paragraphs. Look back at Chapter 1 to refresh your memory on the writing process and at Chapter 5 on abstract language.

EXERCISE 8D

Sharpening Sentences and Pruning Deadwood

A. Revise the following sentences, combining where appropriate for a smooth, logical flow of ideas. Think in terms of assertive sentences, ones that use active verbs and concrete subjects and say directly who is doing what. All these strategies will create clarity and eliminate wordiness.

Example:

First Draft
Feeling in good spirits, it was concluded by the students that Accounting 400 was a good class.

Revision
Feeling in good spirits, the students concluded that Accounting 400 was a good class.

1. A strike is used when employees want things their employers are unwilling to provide.
2. When it is seen that a criminal act is being committed, a call should be placed to the police.
3. Fear of brutality from customers is a concern many prostitutes have.
4. The leaders have determined that the spiritual initiate has no need of worldly things, so only minimum wages are paid.
5. There is a much bigger emphasis placed on the role of the individual in this generation than in our parents' generation.
6. Teenagers are easily influenced by TV. Specific violent acts have been committed by teenagers after such acts have been shown on prime time.
7. The people of this tribe are literate, given that they have twenty terms for *book*. There also may be several kinds of artwork they create, since they have nine words for *artist*.
8. Having developed a complex social order, cultural patterns have been shown by the people of this tribe. These patterns are reflected in their arts and their theatre.

B. Now try your hand at revising this student paragraph with the same strategies in mind. Note how difficult it is to follow the writer's reasoning in this poorly focused paragraph.

There are many ways to be a bad teacher. There are mistakes made by bad teachers that come in a variety of forms. Assignments are given unclearly so that when papers are graded it isn't known what students are graded on or what the grade means. Grading by the ineffective teacher is according to arbitrary standards, so students think their grades are unfair. There are problems with explanations given by bad teachers and understanding is hard to arrive at. This disorganization can be seen by students when the poor teacher fails to bring all materials to class. There are many explanations given, but the dissatisfaction of students is clearly not done away with. In such cases it is not clear who is responsible for a bad grade—the student or the teacher.

EXERCISE 8E

Writing Concise Sentences

1. Write one sentence in which you describe and sell on eBay one article of clothing you're now wearing.
2. Write two sentences for an Amazon.com book review in which you summarize and evaluate a recent book you've read.

Refer to logical joining in Chapters 3 and 4 and appositives in Chapter 5 for structures that will allow you to pack your sentences with details. Parallel structure and sentence focus in this chapter will help you to streamline your detailed sentences.

WRAP-UP ON WRITING STYLE

1. Use parallel structure to increase coherence, organize lists, and emphasize ideas.

2. When possible, use concrete, consistent grammatical subjects that reflect the subject you are writing about.

3. Choose active verbs that allow for direct, vigorous expression of your ideas, unless you have compelling reasons for preferring the passive voice.

   Caution: Do not think about these writing strategies until you have completed a first draft. Content and organization come first.

Now that you are near the end of this book, it may be a good time to briefly review steps you can take to revise a paper, either one you are currently working on, or one you have completed but your teacher has asked you to rewrite.

REVISION: A CHECKLIST

1. Is the purpose of the essay clear? Does it contain the necessary information for the intended audience? (See Chapter 1.)

2. If your paper presents an argument, are your premises adequately supported? Do you include counterargument and refutation? Do you practice Rogerian Strategy? (See Chapter 4.)

3. Are you guilty of any fallacious reasoning? (See Chapter 6.)

4. Are your sentences clear and your paragraphs coherent? (See Chapter 8, in particular, "Wrap-up on Writing Style" above.)

5. Final step: Proofread for mechanical errors—typographical errors and omitted words—as well as for appropriate verb tenses, subject/verb agreement, and clear pronoun references.

6. Final, final step: Read your paper aloud, ideally to another person, but if no one is available, read it aloud to yourself. You may be surprised at what you hear that you failed to see.

SUMMARY

Style as well as correctness is an essential part of effective written argument.
  Parallelism is a useful rhetorical device, providing a powerful means of emphasizing relationships by organizing ideas into predictable patterns.
  For a vigorous and concise style, writers prefer **concrete, consistent subjects and active verbs**.

KEY TERMS

Active voice   a sentence construction in which the subject performs the action of the sentence. [Example: The Supreme Court ruled on the constitutionality of the 1991 civil rights legislation.]

Parallel structure   a repetition of like grammatical units, often joined by the conjunctions *and, but, or,* or *yet.*

Passive voice   a sentence construction in which the subject is acted upon, not doing anything in the sentence. [Example: The constitutionality of the 1991 civil rights legislation was ruled on by the Supreme Court.]

A QUICK GUIDE TO EVALUATING SOURCES AND INTEGRATING RESEARCH INTO YOUR OWN WRITING

Where to Begin

Your college library is a great place to begin your online research. Try General One File, Academic One File, Infotrac Custom Newspapers, or Newsbank for articles from around the world. Or, go to Google.com, Bing.com (Microsoft's search engine), or Wikipedia.org (Wikipedia's entries are anonymous and collaborative—accuracies checked by users). Avoid social media—Facebook, Twitter, and YouTube—as sources of information for your writing assignments as it is often impossible to identify the source of the information. Whatever search engine or website you use, you should ask the following questions in order to evaluate the accuracy and validity of the articles you find.

Evaluating Online Sources

Who?

Who is the author of the article? Is this author an appropriate authority on the subject you are researching? Does he or she have credentials relevant to the subject? If the article is written by a journalist, is the journalist affiliated with a reputable newspaper or magazine? Beware of self-proclaimed authorities. For example, Suzanne Somers, a former television actress, speaks and writes extensively on women's health but has no training or credentials in the field. On the other hand, Dr. Susan Love of UCLA is an authority on the subject as her title, her university affiliation, and her list of publications indicate. If there is no biographical information included in the document itself, you will have to conduct a search of the author's name.

What?

What is the purpose of the Website/article? The primary purpose should be to inform its readers, not to sell products. *New York Times Magazine* columnist Virginia Heffernan warns her readers about WebMD, a highly profitable ($504 million in 2010) medical website connected to large pharmaceutical companies. Prescription drugs are the answer to all queries posed by the website user. She recommends instead MayoClinic.com, a nonprofit medical practice and research group that does not rush its reader to prescription drugs but suggests alternative therapies and generic medications.

When?

When was the article published? Usually, the more current the article the better, especially in the sciences, but if a particular title, not recent, keeps turning up in the literature, it may be a pivotal or classic paper on the topic that you should be familiar with. For example, if you were writing a paper on political language, you would want to have read George Orwell's "Politics and the English Language" even though it was published in 1946.

Where?

Where is the article published? Depending on the assignment, you may want to rely on academic journals as opposed to publications written for the general public such as *huffingtonpost.com* or *politico.com.* If you are not familiar with the appropriate publications, ask your teacher for the names of the most respected journals in the discipline.

Checking for Bias

As a researcher, you must examine your sources for bias and its impact on the information you're seeking. For example, if you're writing a paper on global warming, it's important to know that magazines and Web information published by Greenpeace or the Sierra Club support environmental protections and thus emphasize the dangers of global warming. The American Enterprise Institute (www.aei.org) or the *National Review* (www.nationalreviewonline.com) are conservative organizations and are therefore more likely to downplay the dangers of climate change.

The point here is that when you select a controversial topic, particularly one that involves a political issue, you should compare varied sources on your subject and ask teachers and librarians about the bias of a particular source if it isn't immediately evident. For example, *politico.com* is generally considered neutral, *mediaresearch.org* has a primarily conservative slant, and *dailykos.com* is usually liberal.

EXERCISE

Scrutinizing the Media

Read these two excerpts from different papers, the *New York Times* and the *Los Angeles Times*, reporting on the same Supreme Court decision.

High Court Upholds Buffer Zone of 15 Feet at Abortion Clinics

LINDA GREENHOUSE
New York Times

Washington, Feb. 19—The Supreme Court today upheld a lower court's order keeping demonstrators at least 15 feet away from the doorways and driveways of clinics in upstate New York that were the targets of blockages and boisterous protests. The decision reaffirmed the Court's broadly protective approach toward maintaining access for patients entering abortion clinics. . . .

On the same date, the *Los Angeles Times* reported:

Abortion Foes Entitled to Confront Patients Supreme Court Says It's Free Speech

DAVID G. SAVAGE
Los Angeles Times

Washington, Feb. 19—Abortion protesters have a free-speech right to confront pregnant women on the sidewalks outside clinics and to urge them vehemently not to go ahead with the procedure, the Supreme Court ruled yesterday. The 8–1 decision calls into doubt a wave of new city ordinances and judges' orders that have barred persistent protesters from confronting and harassing doctors, nurses and patients outside clinics. . . .

1. How are the two excerpts different?
2. What inferences might you draw about the writers who presented the two differing slants on the abortion clinic ruling quoted above?
3. Look for a single news story that is reported in different ways. Compare two different print versions of a story from the same date, as we illustrate. Quote from these two stories and describe how different sources present the same facts.

Three Options for Including Research

Once you have completed your research, you have three choices for incorporating it into your paper:

Direct quotation: A word-for-word transcription of what an author says, requiring quotation marks and documentation. For the most part, keep quotations short. It is your paper, not the words of others that your instructor wants to read. Reserve direct quotations for those times when the author's precise language is important, either because it is colorful or exact or cannot be paraphrased without distorting the author's original intent.

Paraphrase: A restatement of an idea in language that retains the meaning but changes the exact wording. Such references require documentation but not quotation marks.

Summary: A short restatement in your own words of the main points in a passage, an article, or a book (see Chapter 3).

Blend Quotations and Paraphrases into Your Own Writing

If you want your paper to read smoothly, you must take care to integrate direct quotations and paraphrases into the flow of your sentences. Don't just "drop" them with a thud into a paragraph. Rely, rather, on a ready supply of introductory or signal phrases with which to slide them in gracefully; for example, "As Freud **discovered**," "Justice Scalia **notes**," and "**according to** *thedailybeast.com*." What follows is an incomplete list of verbs with which to ease the ideas of others smoothly into your sentences: believes, claims, comments, contends, describes, explains, illustrates, mentions, notes, observes, points out, reports, says, states, suggests.

Make the Purpose Clear

As well as introducing quotations and paraphrases smoothly into the syntax of your sentence, you must also pay attention to the meaning of your sentence. Don't assume that the relevance of the quotation is self-evident. Make its relationship to your reasoning explicit. Is it an example? An appeal to authority? Premise support? A counterargument? A concession? A refutation? Whatever the case, the purpose of the quotation—how it relates to the point you are making—should be made clear.

Punctuation and Format of Quotations

Periods and commas are placed *inside* quotation marks unless the quotation is followed by a parenthetical citation, in which case the period follows the citation.

> "Writing, like life itself, is a voyage of discovery," said Henry Miller, author of *Tropic of Cancer.*

> "Thinking is the activity I love best, and writing to me is simply thinking through my fingers."
>
> —ISAAC ASIMOV

> "The true relationship between a leader and his people is often revealed through small, spontaneous gestures" (Friedman 106).

Colons and semicolons go *outside* quotation marks.

> Read Tamar Lewin's essay, "Schools Challenge Students' Internet Talk"; we'll discuss it at our next class meeting.

Use single quotation marks [' '] for quotations within quotations.

"In coping with the violence of their city, Beirut also seemed to disprove Hobbes's prediction that life in the 'state of nature' would be 'solitary'" (Friedman 210).

If the prose quotation is more than four lines long, it should be indented, about 10 spaces for MLA (Modern Language Association) format, 5 spaces for APA (American Psychological Association) format, and double-spaced as in the rest of the text. Drop the quotation marks when you indent.

Omitting Words from a Direct Quotation—Ellipsis

Sometimes we don't want to include all of a quotation, but just certain sections of it that apply to the point we are making. In this case, we may eliminate a part or parts of the quotation by the use of *ellipsis* **dots: three spaced periods that indicate the intentional omission of words**. If the *ellipses* conclude a sentence, add a final period.

1. Something left out at the beginning:

   ". . . a diploma from Harvard or Emory nearly guarantees a financially rewarding career," says columnist Cynthia Tucker of the *Atlanta Constitution*.

2. Something left out in the middle:

   Explaining the desperation of a writer, William Faulkner once said, "Everything goes by the board: honor, pride, decency . . . to get the book written. If a writer has to rob his mother, he will not hesitate; the 'Ode on a Grecian Urn' is worth any number of old ladies."

3. Something left out at the end:

   As Henry Louis Gates says, "The features of the Black dialect of English have long been studied and found to be not an incorrect or slovenly form of Standard English but a completely grammatical and internally consistent version of the language...."

Plagiarism

In a summary, you paraphrase another writer's ideas, putting them into your own words. When writing a paper of your own, you must be circumspect in giving credit to the sources you consult and place quotation marks around the words of others. **To pass off someone else's ideas or words as your own is to plagiarize**. The word *plagiarism* is derived from the Latin *plagiarius*, meaning kidnapper. Now, there are ideas or facts that are part of the public domain—they belong to all of us, such as the Latin root of *plagiarism*. No one person "owns" that information; it's (almost) common knowledge. But if we went on to trace history's most famous cases of plagiarism, research would be required, and we would have to document all of our sources and place quotation marks around sentences taken from these sources.

The Internet, while it has been an enormous help to students and teachers alike in its ability to provide us with an abundance of information on any subject, also makes it easier for students, and others, to plagiarize. In response to the problem, colleges subscribe to websites that allow professors to submit students' papers, which are then analyzed for plagiarism.

Read the words of Gillian Silverman, an English professor at a public university, whose essay on plagiarism appeared in *Newsweek* magazine:

> The thing my students don't seem to realize, however, is that as easily as they can steal language from the Web, I can bust them for it. All it takes is an advanced [Web] search....Plug in any piece of questionable student writing and up pops the very paper from which the phrase originates.

Silverman goes on to say that she uncovered eight cases of plagiarism in one semester, "a new record," and failed each of the offenders.

The consequences of plagiarism can be much more severe than failing a class. In 2011, Germany's defense minister, Karl-Theodor zu Guttenberg, was forced to resign from his post and had his doctoral title revoked when it came to light that he had plagiarized two passages in his doctoral dissertation in 2007.

A Final Note

We don't have the space available here to cover completely the topics of research and documentation. For a complete and thorough guide to conducting your research, finding sources, and documenting these sources in MLA (Modern Language Association) or APA (American Psychological Association) style, go to *mycomplab.com*.

ADDITIONAL READINGS

Here are three essays, all of which present longer, more complex texts than we have included in Chapters 1 through 8.

"The Conservative Case for Gay Marriage," published in *Newsweek Magazine*, caused a stir because its author, lawyer Ted Olsen, is a lifelong conservative who served in the Ronald Reagan and the George W. Bush administrations. Olsen uses the rhetorical skills we emphasize in Chapter 4—counterargument and refutation.

Published in *The New York Times Magazine*, "You Are What You Speak" by Guy Deutscher focuses on the impact language has on its speakers' view of the world. We touch on this subject in Chapter 5 and ask you in Chapter 2 to write an essay about a Lost Tribe based on a found list of the tribe's vocabulary.

Malcolm Gladwell's "The Order of Things" in *The New Yorker* takes on the annual "Best Colleges" guide published by *U.S. News & World Report*, questioning its methodology and ideology. In his argument Gladwell often relies on analogies to make his point. We introduce analogy in Chapter 1 and return to it in Chapter 6; you may want to refer to these sections when evaluating the effectiveness of Gladwell's analogies.

We offer these essays not necessarily as models for your own written arguments, but as vehicles for thinking critically about issues and as springboards for your writing. We follow each essay with questions, some of which you may use as topics for a written argument.

The Conservative Case for Gay Marriage

TED OLSEN

Together with my good friend and occasional courtroom adversary David Boies, I am attempting to persuade a federal court to invalidate California's Proposition 8—the voter-approved measure that overturned California's constitutional right to marry a person of the same sex.   1

My involvement in this case has generated a certain degree of consternation among conservatives. How could a politically active, lifelong Republican, a veteran of the Ronald Reagan and George W. Bush administrations, challenge the "traditional" definition of marriage and press for an "activist" interpretation of the Constitution to create another "new" constitutional right?   2

My answer to this seeming conundrum rests on a lifetime of exposure to persons of different backgrounds, histories, viewpoints, and intrinsic characteristics, and   3 on my rejection of what I see as superficially appealing but ultimately false perceptions about our Constitution and its protection of equality and fundamental rights.

Many of my fellow conservatives have an almost knee-jerk hostility toward gay 4
marriage. This does not make sense, because same-sex unions promote the values conservatives prize. Marriage is one of the basic building blocks of our neighborhoods and our nation. At its best, it is a stable bond between two individuals who work to create a loving household and a social and economic partnership. We encourage couples to marry because the commitments they make to one another provide benefits not only to themselves but also to their families and communities. Marriage requires thinking beyond one's own needs. It transforms two individuals into a union based on shared aspirations, and in doing so establishes a formal investment in the well-being of society. The fact that individuals who happen to be gay want to share in this vital social institution is evidence that conservative ideals enjoy widespread acceptance. Conservatives should celebrate this, rather than lament it.

Legalizing same-sex marriage would also be a recognition of basic American 5
principles, and would represent the culmination of our nation's commitment to equal rights. It is, some have said, the last major civil-rights milestone yet to be surpassed in our two-century struggle to attain the goals we set for this nation at its formation.

This bedrock American principle of equality is central to the political and legal 6
convictions of Republicans, Democrats, liberals, and conservatives alike. The dream that became America began with the revolutionary concept expressed in the Declaration of Independence in words that are among the most noble and elegant ever written: "We hold these truths to be self-evident, that all men are created equal, that they are endowed by their Creator with certain unalienable Rights, that among these are Life, Liberty and the pursuit of Happiness."

Sadly, our nation has taken a long time to live up to the promise of equality. In 7
1857, the Supreme Court held that an African-American could not be a citizen. During the ensuing Civil War, Abraham Lincoln eloquently reminded the nation of its founding principle: "our fathers brought forth on this continent, a new nation, conceived in liberty and dedicated to the proposition that all men are created equal."

At the end of the Civil War, to make the elusive promise of equality a reality, 8
the 14th Amendment to the Constitution added the command that "no State shall deprive any person of life, liberty or property, without due process of law; nor deny to any person the equal protection of the laws."

Subsequent laws and court decisions have made clear that equality under the 9
law extends to persons of all races, religions, and places of origin. What better way to make this national aspiration complete than to apply the same protection to men and women who differ from others only on the basis of their sexual orientation? I cannot think of a single reason—and have not heard one since I undertook this venture—for continued discrimination against decent, hardworking members of our society on that basis.

Various federal and state laws have accorded certain rights and privileges to 10
gay and lesbian couples, but these protections vary dramatically at the state level, and nearly universally deny true equality to gays and lesbians who wish to marry. The very idea of marriage is basic to recognition as equals in our society; any status short of that is inferior, unjust, and unconstitutional.

The United States Supreme Court has repeatedly held that marriage is one of   11
the most fundamental rights that we have as Americans under our Constitution. It
is an expression of our desire to create a social partnership, to live and share life's
joys and burdens with the person we love, and to form a lasting bond and a social
identity. The Supreme Court has said that marriage is a part of the Constitution's
protections of liberty, privacy, freedom of association, and spiritual identification.
In short, the right to marry helps us to define ourselves and our place in a community. Without it, there can be no true equality under the law.

It is true that marriage in this nation traditionally has been regarded as a re-   12
lationship exclusively between a man and a woman, and many of our nation's
multiple religions define marriage in precisely those terms. But while the Supreme
Court has always previously considered marriage in that context, the underlying rights and liberties that marriage embodies are not in any way confined to
heterosexuals.

Marriage is a civil bond in this country as well as, in some (but hardly all) cases,   13
a religious sacrament. It is a relationship recognized by governments as providing
a privileged and respected status, entitled to the state's support and benefits. The
California Supreme Court described marriage as a "union unreservedly approved
and favored by the community." Where the state has accorded official sanction to
a relationship and provided special benefits to those who enter into that relationship, our courts have insisted that withholding that status requires powerful justifications and may not be arbitrarily denied.

What, then, are the justifications for California's decision in Proposition 8 to   14
withdraw access to the institution of marriage for some of its citizens on the basis of
their sexual orientation? The reasons I have heard are not very persuasive.

The explanation mentioned most often is tradition. But simply because some-   15
thing has always been done a certain way does not mean that it must always
remain that way. Otherwise we would still have segregated schools and debtors'
prisons. Gays and lesbians have always been among us, forming a part of our society, and they have lived as couples in our neighborhoods and communities. For
a long time, they have experienced discrimination and even persecution; but we,
as a society, are starting to become more tolerant, accepting, and understanding.
California and many other states have allowed gays and lesbians to form domestic
partnerships (or civil unions) with most of the rights of married heterosexuals. Thus,
gay and lesbian individuals are now permitted to live together in state-sanctioned
relationships. It therefore seems anomalous to cite "tradition" as a justification for
withholding the status of marriage and thus to continue to label those relationships
as less worthy, less sanctioned, or less legitimate.

The second argument I often hear is that traditional marriage furthers the   16
state's interest in procreation—and that opening marriage to same-sex couples
would dilute, diminish, and devalue this goal. But that is plainly not the case. Preventing lesbians and gays from marrying does not cause more heterosexuals to
marry and conceive more children. Likewise, allowing gays and lesbians to marry
someone of the same sex will not discourage heterosexuals from marrying a person
of the opposite sex. How, then, would allowing same-sex marriages reduce the
number of children that heterosexual couples conceive?

This procreation argument cannot be taken seriously. We do not inquire 17
whether heterosexual couples intend to bear children, or have the capacity to have
children, before we allow them to marry. We permit marriage by the elderly, by
prison inmates, and by persons who have no intention of having children. What's
more, it is pernicious to think marriage should be limited to heterosexuals because
of the state's desire to promote procreation. We would surely not accept as constitutional a ban on marriage if a state were to decide, as China has done, to discourage procreation.

Another argument, vaguer and even less persuasive, is that gay marriage some- 18
how does harm to heterosexual marriage. I have yet to meet anyone who can explain
to me what this means. In what way would allowing same-sex partners to marry diminish the marriages of heterosexual couples? Tellingly, when the judge in our case
asked our opponent to identify the ways in which same-sex marriage would harm
heterosexual marriage, to his credit he answered honestly: he could not think of any.

The simple fact is that there is no good reason why we should deny marriage 19
to same-sex partners. On the other hand, there are many reasons why we should
formally recognize these relationships and embrace the rights of gays and lesbians
to marry and become full and equal members of our society.

No matter what you think of homosexuality, it is a fact that gays and lesbi- 20
ans are members of our families, clubs, and workplaces. They are our doctors, our
teachers, our soldiers (whether we admit it or not), and our friends. They yearn for
acceptance, stable relationships, and success in their lives, just like the rest of us.

Conservatives and liberals alike need to come together on principles that surely 21
unite us. Certainly, we can agree on the value of strong families, lasting domestic
relationships, and communities populated by persons with recognized and sanctioned bonds to one another. Confining some of our neighbors and friends who
share these same values to an outlaw or second-class status undermines their sense
of belonging and weakens their ties with the rest of us and what should be our
common aspirations. Even those whose religious convictions preclude endorsement of what they may perceive as an unacceptable "lifestyle" should recognize
that disapproval should not warrant stigmatization and unequal treatment.

When we refuse to accord this status to gays and lesbians, we discourage them 22
from forming the same relationships we encourage for others. And we are also
telling them, those who love them, and society as a whole that their relationships
are less worthy, less legitimate, less permanent, and less valued. We demean their
relationships and we demean them as individuals. I cannot imagine how we benefit
as a society by doing so.

I understand, but reject, certain religious teachings that denounce homosexu- 23
ality as morally wrong, illegitimate, or unnatural; and I take strong exception to
those who argue that same-sex relationships should be discouraged by society
and law. Science has taught us, even if history has not, that gays and lesbians
do not choose to be homosexual any more than the rest of us choose to be heterosexual. To a very large extent, these characteristics are immutable, like being
left-handed. And, while our Constitution guarantees the freedom to exercise our
individual religious convictions, it equally prohibits us from forcing our beliefs on
others. I do not believe that our society can ever live up to the promise of equality,

and the fundamental rights to life, liberty, and the pursuit of happiness, until we stop invidious discrimination on the basis of sexual orientation.

If we are born heterosexual, it is not unusual for us to perceive those who are 24 born homosexual as aberrational and threatening. Many religions and much of our social culture have reinforced those impulses. Too often, that has led to prejudice, hostility, and discrimination. The antidote is understanding, and reason. We once tolerated laws throughout this nation that prohibited marriage between persons of different races. California's Supreme Court was the first to find that discrimination unconstitutional. The U.S. Supreme Court unanimously agreed 20 years later, in 1967, in a case called *Loving v. Virginia*. It seems inconceivable today that only 40 years ago there were places in this country where a black woman could not legally marry a white man. And it was only 50 years ago that 17 states mandated segregated public education—until the Supreme Court unanimously struck down that practice in *Brown v. Board of Education*. Most Americans are proud of these decisions and the fact that the discriminatory state laws that spawned them have been discredited. I am convinced that Americans will be equally proud when we no longer discriminate against gays and lesbians and welcome them into our society.

Reactions to our lawsuit have reinforced for me these essential truths. I have 25 certainly heard anger, resentment, and hostility, and words like "betrayal" and other pointedly graphic criticism. But mostly I have been overwhelmed by expressions of gratitude and good will from persons in all walks of life, including, I might add, from many conservatives and libertarians whose names might surprise. I have been particularly moved by many personal renditions of how lonely and personally destructive it is to be treated as an outcast and how meaningful it will be to be respected by our laws and civil institutions as an American, entitled to equality and dignity. I have no doubt that we are on the right side of this battle, the right side of the law, and the right side of history.

Some have suggested that we have brought this case too soon, and that nei- 26 ther the country nor the courts are "ready" to tackle this issue and remove this stigma. We disagree. We represent real clients—two wonderful couples in California who have longtime relationships. Our lesbian clients are raising four fine children who could not ask for better parents. Our clients wish to be married. They believe that they have that constitutional right. They wish to be represented in court to seek vindication of that right by mounting a challenge under the United States Constitution to the validity of Proposition 8 under the equal-protection and due-process clauses of the 14th Amendment. In fact, the California attorney general has conceded the unconstitutionality of Proposition 8, and the city of San Francisco has joined our case to defend the rights of gays and lesbians to be married. We do not tell persons who have a legitimate claim to wait until the time is "right" and the populace is "ready" to recognize their equality and equal dignity under the law.

Citizens who have been denied equality are invariably told to "wait their 27 turn" and to "be patient." Yet veterans of past civil-rights battles found that it was the act of insisting on equal rights that ultimately sped acceptance of those rights. As to whether the courts are "ready" for this case, just a few years ago, in *Romer v. Evans*, the United States Supreme Court struck down a popularly adopted Colorado constitutional amendment that withdrew the rights of gays and lesbians in that state to the protection of anti-discrimination laws. And seven years ago, in *Lawrence v. Texas*, the Supreme Court struck down, as lacking any rational basis, Texas laws prohibiting private, intimate sexual practices between persons of the same sex, overruling a contrary decision just 20 years earlier.

These decisions have generated controversy, of course, but they are decisions 28 of the nation's highest court on which our clients are entitled to rely. If all citizens have a constitutional right to marry, if state laws that withdraw legal protections of gays and lesbians as a class are unconstitutional, and if private, intimate sexual conduct between persons of the same sex is protected by the Constitution, there is very little left on which opponents of same-sex marriage can rely. As Justice Antonin Scalia, who dissented in the *Lawrence* case, pointed out, "[W]hat [remaining] justification could there possibly be for denying the benefits of marriage to homosexual couples exercising '[t]he liberty protected by the Constitution'?" He is right, of course. One might agree or not with these decisions, but even Justice Scalia has acknowledged that they lead in only one direction.

California's Proposition 8 is particularly vulnerable to constitutional challenge, 29 because that state has now enacted a crazy-quilt of marriage regulation that makes no sense to anyone. California recognizes marriage between men and women, including persons on death row, child abusers, and wife beaters. At the same time, California prohibits marriage by loving, caring, stable partners of the same sex, but tries to make up for it by giving them the alternative of "domestic partnerships" with virtually all of the rights of married persons except the official, state-approved status of marriage. Finally, California recognizes 18,000 same-sex marriages that took place in the months between the state Supreme Court's ruling that upheld gay-marriage rights and the decision of California's citizens to withdraw those rights by enacting Proposition 8.

So there are now three classes of Californians: heterosexual couples who can 30 get married, divorced, and remarried, if they wish; same-sex couples who cannot get married but can live together in domestic partnerships; and same-sex couples who are now married but who, if they divorce, cannot remarry. This is an irrational system, it is discriminatory, and it cannot stand.

Americans who believe in the words of the Declaration of Independence, in 31 Lincoln's Gettysburg Address, in the 14th Amendment, and in the Constitution's guarantees of equal protection and equal dignity before the law cannot sit by while this wrong continues. This is not a conservative or liberal issue; it is an American one, and it is time that we, as Americans, embraced it.

Questions for Discussion

1. Identify the counterarguments that Olsen includes in his argument and evaluate his refutations of them.

2. Determine your state's position on gay marriage and discuss your reaction to this position.

You Are What You Speak

GUY DEUTSCHER

Seventy years ago, in 1940, a popular science magazine published a short article   1
that set in motion one of the trendiest intellectual fads of the 20th century. At
first glance, there seemed little about the article to augur its subsequent celebrity.
Neither the title, "Science and Linguistics," nor the magazine, *M.I.T.'s Technology
Review*, was most people's idea of glamour. And the author, a chemical engineer
who worked for an insurance company and moonlighted as an anthropology lec-
turer at Yale University, was an unlikely candidate for international superstardom.
And yet Benjamin Lee Whorf let loose an alluring idea about language's power over
the mind, and his stirring prose seduced a whole generation into believing that our
mother tongue restricts what we are able to think.

In particular, Whorf announced, Native American languages impose on their   2
speakers a picture of reality that is totally different from ours, so their speakers
would simply not be able to understand some of our most basic concepts, like
the flow of time or the distinction between objects (like "stone") and actions (like
"fall"). For decades, Whorf's theory dazzled both academics and the general public
alike. In his shadow, others made a whole range of imaginative claims about the
supposed power of language, from the assertion that Native American languages
instill in their speakers an intuitive understanding of Einstein's concept of time as
a fourth dimension to the theory that the nature of the Jewish religion was determined by the tense system of ancient Hebrew.

Eventually, Whorf's theory crash-landed on hard facts and solid common   3
sense, when it transpired that there had never actually been any evidence to support his fantastic claims. The reaction was so severe that for decades, any attempts
to explore the influence of the mother tongue on our thoughts were relegated to
the loony fringes of disrepute. But 70 years on, it is surely time to put the trauma
of Whorf behind us. And in the last few years, new research has revealed that when
we learn our mother tongue, we do after all acquire certain habits of thought that
shape our experience in significant and often surprising ways.

Whorf, we now know, made many mistakes. The most serious one was to   4
assume that our mother tongue constrains our minds and prevents us from being
able to think certain thoughts. The general structure of his arguments was to claim
that if a language has no word for a certain concept, then its speakers would not
be able to understand this concept. If a language has no future tense, for instance,
its speakers would simply not be able to grasp our notion of future time. It seems
barely comprehensible that this line of argument could ever have achieved such success, given that so much contrary evidence confronts you wherever you look. When
you ask, in perfectly normal English, and in the present tense, "Are you coming tomorrow?" do you feel your grip on the notion of futurity slipping away? Do English
speakers who have never heard the German word *Schadenfreude* find it difficult to
understand the concept of relishing someone else's misfortune? Or think about it
this way: If the inventory of ready-made words in your language determined which
concepts you were able to understand, how would you ever learn anything new?

Since there is no evidence that any language forbids its speakers to think any-   5
thing, we must look in an entirely different direction to discover how our mother
tongue really does shape our experience of the world. Some 50 years ago, the
renowned linguist Roman Jakobson pointed out a crucial fact about differences between languages in a pithy maxim: "Languages differ essentially in what they *must*
convey and not in what they *may* convey." This maxim offers us the key to unlock-
ing the real force of the mother tongue: if different languages influence our minds
in different ways, this is not because of what our language *allows* us to think but
rather because of what it habitually *obliges* us to think *about*.

Consider this example. Suppose I say to you in English that "I spent yesterday   6
evening with a neighbor." You may well wonder whether my companion was male
or female, but I have the right to tell you politely that it's none of your business. But
if we were speaking French or German, I wouldn't have the privilege to equivocate
in this way, because I would be obliged by the grammar of language to choose
between *voisin* or *voisine; Nachbar* or *Nachbarin*. These languages compel me to
inform you about the sex of my companion whether or not I feel it is remotely your
concern. This does not mean, of course, that English speakers are unable to understand the differences between evenings spent with male or female neighbors, but it
does mean that they do not have to consider the sexes of neighbors, friends, teachers and a host of other persons each time they come up in a conversation, whereas
speakers of some languages are obliged to do so.

On the other hand, English does oblige you to specify certain types of infor-   7
mation that can be left to the context in other languages. If I want to tell you in
English about a dinner with my neighbor, I may not have to mention the neighbor's sex, but I do have to tell you something about the timing of the event: I have
to decide whether we *dined, have been dining, are dining, will be dining* and so on.
Chinese, on the other hand, does not oblige its speakers to specify the exact time
of the action in this way, because the same verb form can be used for past, present
or future actions. Again, this does not mean that the Chinese are unable to understand the concept of time. But it does mean they are not obliged to think about
timing whenever they describe an action.

When your language routinely obliges you to specify certain types of infor-   8
mation, it forces you to be attentive to certain details in the world and to certain
aspects of experience that speakers of other languages may not be required to
think about all the time. And since such habits of speech are cultivated from the
earliest age, it is only natural that they can settle into habits of *mind* that go beyond language itself, affecting your experiences, perceptions, associations, feelings,
memories and orientation in the world.

But is there any evidence for this happening in practice?   9

Let's take genders again. Languages like Spanish, French, German and Russian   10
not only oblige you to think about the sex of friends and neighbors, but they also assign a male or female gender to a whole range of inanimate objects quite at whim.
What, for instance, is particularly feminine about a Frenchman's beard (*la barbe*)?
Why is Russian water a she, and why does she become a he once you have dipped
a tea bag into her? Mark Twain famously lamented such erratic genders as female
turnips and neuter maidens in his rant "The Awful German Language." But whereas

he claimed that there was something particularly perverse about the German gender system, it is in fact English that is unusual, at least among European languages, in not treating turnips and tea cups as masculine or feminine. Languages that treat an inanimate object as a he or a she force their speakers to talk about such an object as if it were a man or a woman. And as anyone whose mother tongue has a gender system will tell you, once the habit has taken hold, it is all but impossible to shake off. When I speak English, I may say about a bed that "it" is too soft, but as a native Hebrew speaker, I actually feel "she" is too soft. "She" stays feminine all the way from the lungs up to the glottis and is neutered only when she reaches the tip of the tongue.

In recent years, various experiments have shown that grammatical genders can 11 shape the feelings and associations of speakers toward objects around them. In the 1990s, for example, psychologists compared associations between speakers of German and Spanish. There are many inanimate nouns whose genders in the two languages are reversed. A German bridge is feminine (*die Brücke*), for instance, but *el puente* is masculine in Spanish; and the same goes for clocks, apartments, forks, newspapers, pockets, shoulders, stamps, tickets, violins, the sun, the world and love. On the other hand, an apple is masculine for Germans but feminine in Spanish, and so are chairs, brooms, butterflies, keys, mountains, stars, tables, wars, rain and garbage. When speakers were asked to grade various objects on a range of characteristics, Spanish speakers deemed bridges, clocks and violins to have more "manly properties" like strength, but Germans tended to think of them as more slender or elegant. With objects like mountains or chairs, which are "he" in German but "she" in Spanish, the effect was reversed.

In a different experiment, French and Spanish speakers were asked to assign 12 human voices to various objects in a cartoon. When French speakers saw a picture of a fork (*la fourchette*), most of them wanted it to speak in a woman's voice, but Spanish speakers, for whom *el tenedor* is masculine, preferred a gravelly male voice for it. More recently, psychologists have even shown that "gendered languages" imprint gender traits for objects so strongly in the mind that these associations obstruct speakers' ability to commit information to memory.

Of course, all this does not mean that speakers of Spanish or French or 13 German fail to understand that inanimate objects do not really have biological sex—a German woman rarely mistakes her husband for a hat, and Spanish men are not known to confuse a bed with what might be lying in it. Nonetheless, once gender connotations have been imposed on impressionable young minds, they lead those with a gendered mother tongue to see the inanimate world through lenses tinted with associations and emotional responses that English speakers—stuck in their monochrome desert of "its"—are entirely oblivious to. Did the opposite genders of "bridge" in German and Spanish, for example, have an effect on the design of bridges in Spain and Germany? Do the emotional maps imposed by a gender system have higher-level behavioral consequences for our everyday life? Do they shape tastes, fashions, habits and preferences in the societies concerned? At the current state of our knowledge about the brain, this is not something that can be easily measured in a psychology lab. But it would be surprising if they didn't.

The area where the most striking evidence for the influence of language on 14
thought has come to light is the language of space—how we describe the orientation
of the world around us. Suppose you want to give someone directions for getting
to your house. You might say: "After the traffic lights, take the first left, then the
second right, and then you'll see a white house in front of you. Our door is on
the right." But in theory, you could also say: "After the traffic lights, drive north,
and then on the second crossing drive east, and you'll see a white house directly
to the east. Ours is the southern door." These two sets of directions may describe
the same route, but they rely on different systems of coordinates. The first uses
egocentric coordinates, which depend on our own bodies: a left-right axis and a
front-back axis orthogonal to it. The second system uses fixed *geographic* directions, which do not rotate with us wherever we turn.

We find it useful to use geographic directions when hiking in the open country- 15
side, for example, but the egocentric coordinates completely dominate our speech
when we describe small-scale spaces. We don't say: "When you get out of the eleva-
tor, walk south, and then take the second door to the east." The reason the egocentric system is so dominant in our language is that it feels so much easier and more
natural. After all, we always know where "behind" or "in front of" us is. We don't
need a map or a compass to work it out, we just feel it, because the egocentric coordinates are based directly on our own bodies and our immediate visual fields.

But then a remote Australian aboriginal tongue, Guugu Yimithirr, from north 16
Queensland, turned up, and with it came the astounding realization that not all
languages conform to what we have always taken as simply "natural." In fact,
Guugu Yimithirr doesn't make any use of egocentric coordinates at all. The anthropologist John Haviland and later the linguist Stephen Levinson have shown that
Guugu Yimithirr does not use words like "left" or "right," "in front of" or "behind,"
to describe the position of objects. Whenever we would use the egocentric system,
the Guugu Yimithirr rely on cardinal directions. If they want you to move over on
the car seat to make room, they'll say "move a bit to the east." To tell you where
exactly they left something in your house, they'll say, "I left it on the southern edge
of the western table." Or they would warn you to "look out for that big ant just
north of your foot." Even when shown a film on television, they gave descriptions
of it based on the orientation of the screen. If the television was facing north, and
a man on the screen was approaching, they said that he was "coming northward."

When these peculiarities of Guugu Yimithirr were uncovered, they inspired a 17
large-scale research project into the language of space. And as it happens, Guugu
Yimithirr is not a freak occurrence; languages that rely primarily on geographical coordinates are scattered around the world, from Polynesia to Mexico, from Namibia
to Bali. For us, it might seem the height of absurdity for a dance teacher to say,
"Now raise your north hand and move your south leg eastward." But the joke would
be lost on some: the Canadian-American musicologist Colin McPhee, who spent
several years on Bali in the 1930s, recalls a young boy who showed great talent for
dancing. As there was no instructor in the child's village, McPhee arranged for him
to stay with a teacher in a different village. But when he came to check on the boy's
progress after a few days, he found the boy dejected and the teacher exasperated.
It was impossible to teach the boy anything, because he simply did not understand

any of the instructions. When told to take "three steps east" or "bend southwest," he didn't know what to do. The boy would not have had the least trouble with these directions in his own village, but because the landscape in the new village was entirely unfamiliar, he became disoriented and confused. Why didn't the teacher use different instructions? He would probably have replied that saying "take three steps forward" or "bend backward" would be the height of absurdity.

So different languages certainly make us speak about space in very different ways. But does this necessarily mean that we have to *think* about space differently? By now red lights should be flashing, because even if a language doesn't have a word for "behind," this doesn't necessarily mean that its speakers wouldn't be able to understand this concept. Instead, we should look for the possible consequences of what geographic languages *oblige* their speakers to convey. In particular, we should be on the lookout for what habits of mind might develop because of the necessity of specifying geographic directions all the time. 18

In order to speak a language like Guugu Yimithirr, you need to know where the cardinal directions are at each and every moment of your waking life. You need to have a compass in your mind that operates all the time, day and night, without lunch breaks or weekends off, since otherwise you would not be able to impart the most basic information or understand what people around you are saying. Indeed, speakers of geographic languages seem to have an almost-superhuman sense of orientation. Regardless of visibility conditions, regardless of whether they are in thick forest or on an open plain, whether outside or indoors or even in caves, whether stationary or moving, they have a spot-on sense of direction. They don't look at the sun and pause for a moment of calculation before they say, "There's an ant just north of your foot." They simply feel where north, south, west and east are, just as people with perfect pitch feel what each note is without having to calculate intervals. There is a wealth of stories about what to us may seem like incredible feats of orientation but for speakers of geographic languages are just a matter of course. One report relates how a speaker of Tzeltal from southern Mexico was blindfolded and spun around more than 20 times in a darkened house. Still blindfolded and dizzy, he pointed without hesitation at the geographic directions. 19

How does this work? The convention of communicating with geographic coordinates compels speakers from the youngest age to pay attention to the clues from the physical environment (the position of the sun, wind and so on) every second of their lives, and to develop an accurate memory of their own changing orientations at any given moment. So everyday communication in a geographic language provides the most intense imaginable drilling in geographic orientation (it has been estimated that as much as 1 word in 10 in a normal Guugu Yimithirr conversation is "north," "south," "west" or "east," often accompanied by precise hand gestures). This habit of constant awareness to the geographic direction is inculcated almost from infancy: studies have shown that children in such societies start using geographic directions as early as age 2 and fully master the system by 7 or 8. With such an early and intense drilling, the habit soon becomes second nature, effortless and unconscious. When Guugu Yimithirr speakers were asked how they knew where north is, they couldn't explain it any more than you can explain how you know where "behind" is. 20

But there is more to the effects of a geographic language, for the sense of   21
orientation has to extend further in time than the immediate present. If you speak
a Guugu Yimithirr–style language, your memories of anything that you might ever
want to report will have to be stored with cardinal directions as part of the picture. One Guugu Yimithirr speaker was filmed telling his friends the story of how
in his youth, he capsized in shark-infested waters. He and an older person were
caught in a storm, and their boat tipped over. They both jumped into the water
and managed to swim nearly three miles to the shore, only to discover that the
missionary for whom they worked was far more concerned at the loss of the boat
than relieved at their miraculous escape. Apart from the dramatic content, the remarkable thing about the story was that it was remembered throughout in cardinal directions: the speaker jumped into the water on the western side of the boat,
his companion to the east of the boat, they saw a giant shark swimming north
and so on. Perhaps the cardinal directions were just made up for the occasion?
Well, quite by chance, the same person was filmed some years later telling the
same story. The cardinal directions matched exactly in the two tellings. Even more
remarkable were the spontaneous hand gestures that accompanied the story. For
instance, the direction in which the boat rolled over was gestured in the correct
geographic orientation, regardless of the direction the speaker was facing in the
two films.

Psychological experiments have also shown that under certain circumstances,   22
speakers of Guugu Yimithirr–style languages even remember "the same reality" differently from us. There has been heated debate about the interpretation of some of
these experiments, but one conclusion that seems compelling is that while we are
trained to ignore directional rotations when we commit information to memory,
speakers of geographic languages are trained not to do so. One way of understanding this is to imagine that you are traveling with a speaker of such a language and
staying in a large chain-style hotel, with corridor upon corridor of identical-looking
doors. Your friend is staying in the room opposite yours, and when you go into his
room, you'll see an exact replica of yours: the same bathroom door on the left, the
same mirrored wardrobe on the right, the same main room with the same bed on
the left, the same curtains drawn behind it, the same desk next to the wall on the
right, the same television set on the left corner of the desk and the same telephone
on the right. In short, you have seen the same room twice. But when your friend
comes into your room, he will see something quite different from this, because
everything is reversed north-side-south. In his room the bed was in the north, while
in yours it is in the south; the telephone that in his room was in the west is now in
the east, and so on. So while you will see and remember the same room twice, a
speaker of a geographic language will see and remember two different rooms.

It is not easy for us to conceive how Guugu Yimithirr speakers experience   23
the world, with a crisscrossing of cardinal directions imposed on any mental picture and any piece of graphic memory. Nor is it easy to speculate about how
geographic languages affect areas of experience other than spatial orientation—
whether they influence the speaker's sense of identity, for instance, or bring about
a less-egocentric outlook on life. But one piece of evidence is telling: if you saw a
Guugu Yimithirr speaker pointing at himself, you would naturally assume he meant

to draw attention to himself. In fact, he is pointing at a cardinal direction that happens to be behind his back. While we are always at the center of the world, and it would never occur to us that pointing in the direction of our chest could mean anything other than to draw attention to ourselves, a Guugu Yimithirr speaker points through himself, as if he were thin air and his own existence were irrelevant.

In what other ways might the language we speak influence our experience of   24 the world? Recently, it has been demonstrated in a series of ingenious experiments that we even perceive colors through the lens of our mother tongue. There are radical variations in the way languages carve up the spectrum of visible light; for example, green and blue are distinct colors in English but are considered shades of the same color in many languages. And it turns out that the colors that our language routinely obliges us to treat as distinct can refine our purely visual sensitivity to certain color differences in reality, so that our brains are trained to exaggerate the distance between shades of color if these have different names in our language. As strange as it may sound, our experience of a Chagall painting actually depends to some extent on whether our language has a word for blue.

In coming years, researchers may also be able to shed light on the impact of   25 language on more subtle areas of perception. For instance, some languages, like Matses in Peru, oblige their speakers, like the finickiest of lawyers, to specify exactly how they came to know about the facts they are reporting. You cannot simply say, as in English, "An animal passed here." You have to specify, using a different verbal form, whether this was directly experienced (you saw the animal passing), inferred (you saw footprints), conjectured (animals generally pass there that time of day), hearsay or such. If a statement is reported with the incorrect "evidentiality," it is considered a lie. So if, for instance, you ask a Matses man how many wives he has, unless he can actually see his wives at that very moment, he would have to answer in the past tense and would say something like "There were two last time I checked." After all, given that the wives are not present, he cannot be absolutely certain that one of them hasn't died or run off with another man since he last saw them, even if this was only five minutes ago. So he cannot report it as a certain fact in the present tense. Does the need to think constantly about epistemology in such a careful and sophisticated manner inform the speakers' outlook on life or their sense of truth and causation? When our experimental tools are less blunt, such questions will be amenable to empirical study.

For many years, our mother tongue was claimed to be a "prison house" that   26 constrained our capacity to reason. Once it turned out that there was no evidence for such claims, this was taken as proof that people of all cultures think in fundamentally the same way. But surely it is a mistake to overestimate the importance of abstract reasoning in our lives. After all, how many daily decisions do we make on the basis of deductive logic compared with those guided by gut feeling, intuition, emotions, impulse or practical skills? The habits of mind that our culture has instilled in us from infancy shape our orientation to the world and our emotional responses to the objects we encounter, and their consequences probably go far beyond what has been experimentally demonstrated so far; they may also have a marked impact on our beliefs, values and ideologies. We may not know as yet how to measure these consequences directly or how to assess their contribution to cultural or political misunderstandings. But as a first step toward understanding one another, we can do better than pretending we all think the same.

Questions for Discussion

1. What was Benjamin Lee Whorf's theory about language? What was linguist Roman Jakobsen's belief about language?

2. What do the French and German languages compel their speakers to communicate? What does English compel its speakers to communicate that Chinese doesn't?

3. If you are fortunate enough to speak another language in addition to English, can you supply more examples of information necessary to communicate in one language but not in the other?

4. Writing Assignment 2 in Chapter 2, Reconstructing the Lost Tribe, asks you to characterize a society based on a list of words from their language. If you have not done this assignment, your instructor may want to assign it now in light of what you have learned from Deutshcer's article. If you have written that assignment, you may want to revise it. In either case, feel free to refer to and quote from "You Are What You Speak."

The Order of Things

MALCOLM GLADWELL

Last summer, the editors of *Car and Driver* conducted a comparison test of three sports cars, the Lotus Evora, the Chevrolet Corvette Grand Sport, and the Porsche Cayman S. The cars were taken on an extended run through mountain passes in Southern California, and from there to a race track north of Los Angeles, for precise   1
measurements of performance and handling. The results of the road tests were then tabulated according to a twenty-one-variable, two-hundred-and-thirty-five-point rating system, based on four categories: vehicle (driver comfort, styling, fit and finish, etc.); power train (transmission, engine, and fuel economy); chassis (steering, brakes, ride, and handling); and "fun to drive." The magazine concluded, "The range of these three cars' driving personalities is as various as the pajama sizes of Papa Bear, Mama Bear, and Baby Bear, but a clear winner emerged nonetheless." This was the final tally:

1. Porsche Cayman 193
2. Chevrolet Corvette 186
3. Lotus Evora 182

Car and Driver is one of the most influential editorial voices in the automotive world. When it says that it likes one car better than another, consumers and

FROM *THE NEW YORKER*, 2/14/2011. © 2011 MALCOLM GLADWELL. REUSED BY PERMISSION OF THE AUTHOR.

2

carmakers take notice. Yet when you inspect the magazine's tabulations it is hard to figure out why Car and Driver was so sure that the Cayman is better than the Corvette and the Evora. The trouble starts with the fact that the ranking methodology Car and Driver used was essentially the same one it uses for all the vehicles it tests—from S.U.V.s to economy sedans. It's not set up for sports cars. Exterior styling, for example, counts for four per cent of the total score. Has anyone buying a sports car ever placed so little value on how it looks? Similarly, the categories of "fun to drive" and "chassis"—which cover the subjective experience of driving the car—count for only eighty-five points out of the total of two hundred and thirty-five. That may make sense for S.U.V. buyers. But, for people interested in Porsches and Corvettes and Lotuses, the subjective experience of driving is surely what matters most. In other words, in trying to come up with a ranking that is heterogeneous—a methodology that is broad enough to cover all vehicles—Car and Driver ended up with a system that is absurdly ill-suited to some vehicles.

Suppose that *Car and Driver* decided to tailor its grading system just to sports cars. Clearly, styling and the driving experience ought to count for much more. So let's make exterior styling worth twenty-five per cent, the driving experience worth fifty percent, and the balance of the criteria worth twenty-five per cent. The final tally now looks like this: 3

1. Lotus Evora 205
2. Porsche Cayman 198
3. Chevrolet Corvette 192

There's another thing funny about the Car and Driver system. Price counts only for twenty points, less than ten per cent of the total. There's no secret why: Car and Driver is edited by auto enthusiasts. To them, the choice of a car is as important as the choice of a home or a spouse, and only a philistine would let a few dollars stand between him and the car he wants. (They leave penny-pinching to their frumpy counterparts at Consumer Reports.) But for most of us price matters, especially in a case like this, where the Corvette, as tested, costs $67,565—thirteen thousand dollars less than the Porsche, and eighteen thousand dollars less than the Lotus. Even to a car nut, that's a lot of money. So let's imagine that Car and Driver revised its ranking system again, giving a third of the weight to price, a third to the driving experience, and a third split equally between exterior styling and vehicle characteristics. The tally would now be: 4

1. Chevrolet Corvette 205
2. Lotus Evora 195
3. Porsche Cayman 195
So which is the best car?

Car and Driver's ambition to grade every car in the world according to the same methodology would be fine if it limited itself to a single dimension. A heterogeneous ranking system works if it focuses just on, say, how much fun a car is to drive, or how good-looking it is, or how beautifully it handles. The magazine's ambition to create a comprehensive ranking system—one that considered cars along twenty-one variables, each weighted according to a secret sauce cooked up by the editors—would also be fine, as long as the cars being compared were truly   5 similar. It's only when one car is thirteen thousand dollars more than another that juggling twenty-one variables starts to break down, because you're faced with the impossible task of deciding how much a difference of that degree ought to matter. A ranking can be heterogeneous, in other words, as long as it doesn't try to be too comprehensive. And it can be comprehensive as long as it doesn't try to measure things that are heterogeneous. But it's an act of real audacity when a ranking system tries to be comprehensive *and* heterogeneous—which is the first thing to keep in mind in any consideration of *U.S. News & World Report*'s annual "Best Colleges" guide.

The *U.S. News* rankings are run by Robert Morse, whose six-person team   6
operates out of a small red brick office building in the Georgetown neighborhood of Washington, D.C. Morse is a middle-aged man with gray hair who looks like the prototypical Beltway wonk: rumpled, self-effacing, mildly preppy and sensibly shoed. His office is piled high with the statistical detritus of more than two decades of data collection. When he took on his current job, in the mid-nineteen-eighties, the college guide was little more than an item of service journalism tucked away inside *U.S. News* magazine. Now the weekly print magazine is defunct, but the rankings have taken on a life of their own. In the month that the 2011 rankings came out, the *U.S. News* Web site recorded more than ten million visitors. *U.S. News* has added rankings of graduate programs, law schools, business schools, medical schools, and hospitals—and Morse has become the dean of a burgeoning international rankings industry.

"In the early years, the thing that's happening now would not have been   7
imaginable," Morse says. "This idea of using the rankings as a benchmark, college presidents setting a goal of 'We're going to rise in the *U.S. News* ranking,' as proof of their management, or as proof that they're a better school, that they're a good president. That wasn't on anybody's radar. It was just for consumers."

Over the years, Morse's methodology has steadily evolved. In its current form,   8
it relies on seven weighted variables:

1. Undergraduate academic reputation, 22.5 per cent
2. Graduation and freshman retention rates, 20 per cent
3. Faculty resources, 20 per cent
4. Student selectivity, 15 per cent
5. Financial resources, 10 per cent
6. Graduation rate performance, 7.5 per cent
7. Alumni giving, 5 per cent

From these variables, *U.S. News* generates a score for each institution on a scale   9
of 1 to 100, where Harvard is a 100 and the University of North Carolina-Greensboro is a 22. Here is a list of the schools that finished in positions forty-one through fifty in the 2011 "National University" category:

41. Case Western Reserve, 60
41. Rensselaer Polytechnic Institute, 60
41. University of California-Irvine, 60
41. University of Washington, 60
45. University of Texas-Austin, 59

45. University of Wisconsin-Madison, 59
47. Penn State University-University
Park, 58
47. University of Illinois, Urbana-Champaign, 58
47. University of Miami, 58
50. Yeshiva University, 57

This ranking system looks a great deal like the *Car and Driver* methodol- 10
ogy. It is heterogeneous. It doesn't just compare U.C. Irvine, the University of
Washington, the University of Texas-Austin, the University of Wisconsin-Madison,
Penn State, and the University of Illinois, Urbana-Champaign—all public institutions of roughly the same size. It aims to compare Penn State—a very large,
public, land-grant university with a low tuition and an economically diverse student body, set in a rural valley in central Pennsylvania and famous for its football
team—with Yeshiva University, a small, expensive, private Jewish university whose
undergraduate program is set on two campuses in Manhattan (one in midtown,
for the women, and one far uptown, for the men) and is definitely *not* famous for
its football team.

The system is also comprehensive. It doesn't simply compare schools along 11
one dimension—the test scores of incoming freshmen, say, or academic reputation.
An algorithm takes a slate of statistics on each college and transforms them into a
single score: it tells us that Penn State is a better school than Yeshiva by one point.
It is easy to see why the *U.S. News* rankings are so popular. A single score allows
us to judge between entities (like Yeshiva and Penn State) that otherwise would be
impossible to compare. At no point, however, do the college guides acknowledge
the extraordinary difficulty of the task they have set themselves. A comprehensive,
heterogeneous ranking system was a stretch for *Car and Driver*—and all it did was
rank inanimate objects operated by a single person. The Penn State campus at
University Park is a complex institution with dozens of schools and departments,
four thousand faculty members, and forty-five thousand students. How on earth
does anyone propose to assign a number to something like that?

The first difficulty with rankings is that it can be surprisingly hard to measure 12
the variable you want to rank—even in cases where that variable seems perfectly
objective.

Consider an extreme example: suicide. Here is a ranking of suicides per hun- 13
dred thousand people, by country:

1. Belarus, 35.1
2. Lithuania, 31.5
3. South Korea, 31.0
4. Kazakhstan, 26.9
5. Russia, 26.5
6. Japan, 24.4
7. Guyana, 22.9
8. Ukraine, 22.6
9. Hungary, 21.8
10. Sri Lanka, 21.6

This list looks straightforward. Yet no self-respecting epidemiologist would look 14 at it and conclude that Belarus has the worst suicide rate in the world, and that Hungary belongs in the top ten. Measuring suicide is just too tricky. It requires someone to make a surmise about the intentions of the deceased at the time of death. In some cases, that's easy. Maybe the victim jumped off the Golden Gate Bridge, or left a note. In most cases, though, there's ambiguity, and different coroners and different cultures vary widely in the way they choose to interpret that ambiguity. In certain places, cause of death is determined by the police, who some believe are more likely to call an ambiguous suicide an accident. In other places, the decision is made by a physician, who may be less likely to do so. In some cultures, suicide is considered so shameful that coroners shy away from that determination, even when it's obvious. A suicide might be called a suicide, a homicide, an accident, or left undetermined. David Phillips, a sociologist at the University of California-San Diego, has argued persuasively that a significant percentage of single-car crashes are probably suicides, and criminologists suggest that a good percentage of civilians killed by police officers are actually cases of "suicide by cop"—instances where someone deliberately provoked deadly force. The reported suicide rate, then, is almost certainly less than the actual suicide rate. But no one knows whether the relationship between those two numbers is the same in every country. And no one knows whether the proxies that we use to estimate the real suicide rate are any good.

"Many, many people who commit suicide by poison have something else wrong 15 with them—let's say the person has cancer—and the death of this person might be listed as primarily associated with cancer, rather than with deliberate poisoning," Phillips says. "Any suicides in that category would be un-detectable. Or it is frequently noted that Orthodox Jews have a low recorded suicide rate, as do Catholics. Well, it could be because they have this very solid community and proscriptions against suicide, or because they are unusually embarrassed by suicide and more willing to hide it. The simple answer is nobody knows whether suicide rankings are real."

The *U.S. News* rankings suffer from a serious case of the suicide problem. 16 There's no direct way to measure the quality of an institution—how well a college manages to inform, inspire, and challenge its students. So the *U.S. News* algorithm relies instead on proxies for quality—and the proxies for educational quality turn out to be flimsy at best.

Take the category of "faculty resources," which counts for twenty per cent of 17 an institution's score. "Research shows that the more satisfied students are about their contact with professors," the College Guide's explanation of the category begins, "the more they will learn and the more likely it is they will graduate." That's true. According to educational researchers, arguably the most important variable in a successful college education is a vague but crucial concept called student "engagement"—that is, the extent to which students immerse themselves in the intellectual and social life of their college—and a major component of engagement is the quality of a student's contacts with faculty. As with suicide, the disagreement isn't about *what* we want to measure. So what proxies does *U.S. News* use to measure this elusive dimension of engagement? The explanation goes on:

> We use six factors from the 2009–10 academic year to assess a school's
> commitment to instruction. Class size has two components, the proportion
> of classes with fewer than 20 students (30 percent of the faculty resources

score) and the proportion with 50 or more students (10 percent of the score). Faculty salary (35 percent) is the average faculty pay, plus benefits, during the 2008–09 and 2009–10 academic years, adjusted for regional differences in the cost of living. ... We also weigh the proportion of professors with the highest degree in their fields (15 percent), the student-faculty ratio (5 percent), and the proportion of faculty who are full time (5 percent).

This is a puzzling list. Do professors who get paid more money really take their teaching roles more seriously? And why does it matter whether a professor has the highest degree in his or her field? Salaries and degree attainment are known to be predictors of research productivity. But studies show that being oriented toward research has very little to do with being good at teaching. Almost none of the *U.S. News* variables, in fact, seem to be particularly effective proxies for engagement. As the educational researchers Patrick Terenzini and Ernest Pascarella concluded after analyzing twenty-six hundred reports on the effects of college on students: 18

> After taking into account the characteristics, abilities, and backgrounds students bring with them to college, we found that how much students grow or change has only inconsistent and, perhaps in a practical sense, trivial relationships with such traditional measures of institutional "quality" as educational expenditures per student, student/faculty ratios, faculty salaries, percentage of faculty with the highest degree in their field, faculty research productivity, size of the library, [or] admissions selectivity.

The reputation score that serves as the most important variable in the *U.S. News* methodology—accounting for 22.5 per cent of a college's final score—isn't any better. Every year, the magazine sends a survey to the country's university and college presidents, provosts, and admissions deans (along with a sampling of high-school guidance counselors) asking them to grade all the schools in their category on a scale of one to five. Those at national universities, for example, are asked to rank all two hundred and sixty-one other national universities—and Morse says that the typical respondent grades about half of the schools in his or her category. But it's far from clear how any one individual could have insight into that many institutions. In an article published recently in the *Annals of Internal Medicine*, Ashwini Sehgal analyzed *U.S. News's* "Best Hospitals" rankings, which also rely heavily on reputation ratings generated by professional peers. Sehgal put together a list of objective criteria of performance—such as a hospital's mortality rates for various surgical procedures, patient-safety rates, nursing-staffing levels, and key technologies. Then he checked to see how well those measures of performance matched each hospital's reputation rating. The answer, he discovered, was that they didn't. Having good outcomes doesn't translate into being admired by other doctors. Why, after all, should a gastroenterologist at the Ochsner Medical Center, in New Orleans, have any specific insight into the performance of the gastroenterology department at Mass General, in Boston, or even, for that matter, have anything more than an anecdotal impression of the gastroenterology department down the road at some hospital in Baton Rouge? 19

Some years ago, similarly, a former chief justice of the Michigan supreme court, Thomas Brennan, sent a questionnaire to a hundred or so of his fellow-lawyers, asking them to rank a list of ten law schools in order of quality. "They included a good 20 sample of the big names. Harvard. Yale. University of Michigan. And some lesser-known schools. John Marshall. Thomas Cooley," Brennan wrote. "As I recall, they ranked Penn State's law school right about in the middle of the pack. Maybe fifth among the ten schools listed. Of course, Penn State doesn't have a law school."

Those lawyers put Penn State in the middle of the pack, even though every   21
fact they thought they knew about Penn State's law school was an illusion, because in their minds Penn State is a middle-of-the-pack brand. (Penn State does have a law school today, by the way.) Sound judgments of educational quality have to be based on specific, hard-to-observe features. But reputational ratings are simply inferences from broad, readily observable features of an institution's identity, such as its history, its prominence in the media, or the elegance of its architecture. They are prejudices.

And where do these kinds of reputational prejudices come from? According to   22
Michael Bastedo, an educational sociologist at the University of Michigan who has published widely on the *U.S. News* methodology, "rankings drive reputation." In other words, when *U.S. News* asks a university president to perform the impossible task of assessing the relative merits of dozens of institutions he knows nothing about, he relies on the only source of detailed information at his disposal that assesses the relative merits of dozens of institutions he knows nothing about: *U.S. News*. A school like Penn State, then, can do little to improve its position. To go higher than forty-seventh, it needs a better reputation score, and to get a better reputation score it needs to be higher than forty-seventh. The *U.S. News* ratings are a self-fulfilling prophecy.

Bastedo, incidentally, says that reputation ratings can sometimes work very   23
well. It makes sense, for example, to ask professors within a field to rate others in their field: they read one another's work, attend the same conferences, and hire one another's graduate students, so they have real knowledge on which to base an opinion. Reputation scores can work for one-dimensional rankings, created by people with specialized knowledge. For instance, the *Wall Street Journal* has ranked colleges according to the opinions of corporate recruiters. Those opinions are more than a proxy. To the extent that people chose one college over another to enhance their prospects in the corporate job markets, the reputation rankings of corporate recruiters are of direct relevance. The No. 1 school in the *Wall Street Journal's* corporate recruiter's ranking, by the way, is Penn State.

For several years, Jeffrey Stake, a professor at the Indiana University law school,   24
has run a Web site called the Ranking Game. It contains a spreadsheet loaded with statistics on every law school in the country, and allows users to pick their own criteria, assign their own weights, and construct any ranking system they want.

Stake's intention is to demonstrate just how subjective rankings are, to show   25
how determinations of "quality" turn on relatively arbitrary judgments about how much different variables should be weighted. For example, his site makes it easy to mimic the *U.S. News* rankings. All you have to do is give equal weight to "academic reputation," "LSAT scores at the 75th percentile," "student-faculty ratio," and "faculty law-review publishing," and you get a list of élite schools which looks similar to the *U.S News* law-school rankings:

1. University of Chicago
2. Yale University

3. Harvard University
4. Stanford University
5. Columbia University
6. Northwestern University
7. Cornell University
8. University of Pennsylvania
9. New York University
10. University of California, Berkeley

There's something missing from that list of variables, of course: it doesn't in- 26
clude price. That is one of the most distinctive features of the *U.S. News* methodology. Both its college rankings and its law-school rankings reward schools for
devoting lots of financial resources to educating their students, but not for being
affordable. Why? Morse admitted that there was no formal reason for that position. It was just a feeling. "We're not saying that we're measuring educational outcomes," he explained. "We're not saying we're social scientists, or we're subjecting
our rankings to some peer-review process. We're just saying we've made this judgment. We're saying we've interviewed a lot of experts, we've developed these academic indicators, and we think these measures measure quality schools."

As answers go, that's up there with the parental "Because I said so." But Morse 27
is simply being honest. If we don't understand what the right proxies for college
quality are, let alone how to represent those proxies in a comprehensive, heterogeneous grading system, then our rankings are inherently arbitrary. All Morse was
saying was that, on the question of price, he comes down on the *Car and Driver*
side of things, not on the *Consumer Reports* side. *U.S. News* thinks that schools
that spend a lot of money on their students are nicer than those that don't, and
that this niceness ought to be factored into the equation of desirability. Plenty of
Americans agree: the campus of Vanderbilt University or Williams College is filled
with students whose families are largely indifferent to the price their school charges
but keenly interested in the flower beds and the spacious suites and the architectur-
ally distinguished lecture halls those high prices make possible.

Of course, given that the rising cost of college has become a significant social 28
problem in the United States in recent years, you can make a strong case that
a school ought to be rewarded for being affordable. So suppose we go back to
Stake's ranking game, and re-rank law schools based on student-faculty ratio,
L.S.A.T. scores at the seventy-fifth percentile, faculty publishing, and price, all
weighted equally. The list now looks like this:

1. University of Chicago
2. Yale University
3. Harvard University
4. Stanford University
5. Northwestern University
6. Brigham Young University
7. Cornell University
8. University of Colorado
9. University of Pennsylvania
10. Columbia University

The revised ranking tells us that there are schools—like B.Y.U. and Colorado—   29
that provide a good legal education at a decent price, and that, by choosing not
to include tuition as a variable, *U.S. News* has effectively penalized those schools for
trying to provide value for the tuition dollar. But that's a very subtle tweak. Let's say
that value for the dollar is something we really care about. And so what we want is
a three-factor ranking, counting value for the dollar at forty per cent, L.S.A.T. scores
at forty per cent of the total, and faculty publishing at twenty per cent. Look at
how the top ten changes:

1. University of Chicago
2. Brigham Young University
3. Harvard University
4. Yale University
5. University of Texas
6. University of Virginia
7. University of Colorado
8. University of Alabama
9. Stanford University
10. University of Pennsylvania

Welcome to the big time, Alabama!   30

The *U.S. News* rankings turn out to be full of these kinds of implicit ideologi-   31
cal choices. One common statistic used to evaluate colleges, for example, is called
"graduation rate performance," which compares a school's actual graduation rate
with its predicted graduation rate given the socio-economic status and the test
scores of its in-coming freshman class. It is a measure of the school's efficacy: it
quantifies the impact of a school's culture and teachers and institutional support
mechanisms. Tulane, given the qualifications of the students that it admits, ought to
have a graduation rate of eighty-seven per cent; its actual 2009 graduation rate was
seventy-three per cent. That shortfall suggests that something is amiss at Tulane.

Another common statistic for measuring college quality is "student selectivity."   32
This reflects variables such as how many of a college's freshmen were in the top
ten per cent of their high-school class, how high their S.A.T. scores were, and what
percentage of applicants a college admits. Selectivity quantifies how accomplished
students are when they first arrive on campus.

Each of these statistics matters, but for very different reasons. As a society, we   33
probably care more about efficacy: America's future depends on colleges that make
sure the students they admit leave with an education and a degree. If you are a bright
high-school senior and you're thinking about your own future, though, you may well
care more about selectivity, because that relates to the prestige of your degree.

But no institution can excel at both. The national university that ranks No. 1   34
in selectivity is Yale. A crucial part of what it considers its educational function is
to assemble the most gifted group of freshmen it can. Because it maximizes selectivity, though, Yale will never do well on an efficacy scale. Its freshmen are so
accomplished that they have a predicted graduation rate of ninety-six per cent: the
highest Yale's efficacy score could be is plus four. (It's actually plus two.) Of the top
fifty national universities in the "Best Colleges" ranking, the least selective school
is Penn State. Penn State sees its educational function as serving a wide range of

students. That gives it the opportunity to excel at efficacy—and it does so brilliantly. Penn State's freshmen have an expected graduation rate of seventy-three per cent and an actual graduation rate of eighty-five per cent, for a score of plus twelve: no other school in the *U.S. News* top fifty comes close.

There is no *right* answer to how much weight a ranking system should give to 35 these two competing values. It's a matter of which educational model you value more—and here, once again, *U.S. News* makes its position clear. It gives twice as much weight to selectivity as it does to efficacy. It favors the Yale model over the Penn State model, which means that the Yales of the world will always succeed at the *U.S. News* rankings because the *U.S. News* system is designed to reward Yale-ness. By contrast, to the extent that Penn State succeeds at doing a better job of being Penn State—of attracting a diverse group of students and educating them capably—it will only do worse. Rankings are not benign. They enshrine very particular ideologies, and, at a time when American higher education is facing a crisis of accessibility and affordability, we have adopted a de-facto standard of college quality that is uninterested in both of those factors. And why? Because a group of magazine analysts in an office building in Washington, D.C., decided twenty years ago to value selectivity over efficacy, to use proxies that scarcely relate to what they're meant to be proxies for, and to pretend that they can compare a large, diverse, low-cost land-grant university in rural Pennsylvania with a small, expensive, private Jewish university on two campuses in Manhattan.

"If you look at the top twenty schools every year, forever, they are all wealthy 36 private universities," Graham Spanier, the president of Penn State, told me. "Do you mean that even the most prestigious public universities in the United States, and you can take your pick of what you think they are—Berkeley, U.C.L.A., University of Michigan, University of Wisconsin, Illinois, Penn State, U.N.C.—do you mean to say that not one of those is in the top tier of institutions? It doesn't really make sense, until you drill down into the rankings, and what do you find? What I find more than anything else is a measure of wealth: institutional wealth, how big is your endowment, what percentage of alumni are donating each year, what are your faculty salaries, how much are you spending per student. Penn State may very well be the most popular university in America—we get a hundred and fifteen thousand applications a year for admission. We serve a lot of people. Nearly a third of them are the first people in their entire family network to come to college. We have seventy-six per cent of our students receiving financial aid. There is no possibility that we could do anything here at this university to get ourselves into the top ten or twenty or thirty—except if some donor gave us billions of dollars."

In the fall of 1913, the prominent American geographer Ellsworth Huntington 37 sent a letter to two hundred and thirteen scholars from twenty-seven countries. "May I ask your cooperation in the preparation of a map showing the distribution of the higher elements of civilization throughout the world?" Huntington began, and he continued:

> My purpose is to prepare a map which shall show the distribution of those characteristics which are generally recognized as of the highest value. I mean by this the power of initiative, the capacity for formulating new ideas and for carrying them into effect, the power of self-control, high standards

of honesty and morality, the power to lead and to control other races, the capacity for disseminating ideas, and other similar qualities which will readily suggest themselves.

Each contributor was given a list of a hundred and eighty-five of the world's 38 regions—ranging from the Amur district of Siberia to the Kalahari Desert—with instructions to give each region a score of one to ten. The scores would then be summed and converted to a scale of one to a hundred. The rules were strict. The past could not be considered: Greece could not be given credit for its ancient glories. "If two races inhabit a given region," Huntington specified further, "both must be considered, and the rank of the region must depend upon the average of the two." The reputation of immigrants could be used toward the score of their country of origin, but only those of the first generation. And size and commercial significance should be held constant: the Scots should not suffer relative to, say, the English, just because they were less populous. Huntington's respondents took on the task with the utmost seriousness. "One appreciates what a big world this is and how little one knows about it when he attempts such a task as you have set," a respondent wrote back to Huntington. "It is a most excellent means of taking the conceit out of one." England and Wales and the North Atlantic states of America scored a perfect hundred, with central and northwestern Germany and New England coming in at ninety-nine.

Huntington then requested from the twenty-five of his correspondents who 39 were Americans an in-depth ranking of the constituent regions of the United States. This time, he proposed a six-point scale. Southern Alaska, in this second reckoning, was last, at 1.5, followed by Arizona and New Mexico, at 1.6. The winners: Massachusetts, at 6.0, followed by Connecticut, Rhode Island, and New York, at 5.8. The citadel of American civilization was New England and New York, Huntington concluded, in his magisterial 1915 work "Civilization and Climate."

In case you are wondering, Ellsworth Huntington was a professor of geogra- 40 phy at Yale, in New Haven, Connecticut. "Civilization and Climate" was published by Yale University Press, and the book's appendix contains a list of Huntington's American correspondents, of which the following bear special mention:

J. Barrell, geologist, New Haven, Conn.
P. Bigelow, traveler and author, Malden, N.Y.

I. Bowman, geographer, New York City
W. M. Brown, geographer, Providence, R.I.

A. C. Coolidge, historian, Cambridge, Mass.
S. W. Cushing, geographer, Salem, Mass.
L. Farrand, anthropologist, New York City

C. W. Furlong, traveler and author, Boston, Mass.
E. W. Griffis, traveler and author, Ithaca, N.Y.

A. G. Keller, anthropologist, New Haven,
Conn.

E. F. Merriam, editor, Boston, Mass.

J. R. Smith, economic geographer, Philadelphia, Pa.
Anonymous, New York City

"In spite of several attempts I was unable to obtain any contributor in the states   41
west of Minnesota or south of the Ohio River," Huntington explains, as if it were a
side issue. It isn't, of course—not then and not now. Who comes out on top, in any
ranking system, is really about who is doing the ranking.

Questions for Discussion

1. What is the extended analogy Malcolm Gladwell begins his argument with? Do you find it effective? Why or why not? What other analogies does he draw? (See Analogy in Chapter 1 and False Analogy in Chapter 6.)

2. Why is a comprehensive and heterogeneous ranking system of colleges problematic?

3. Why are the *U.S. News* rankings a self-fulfilling prophecy?

4. The *U.S. News* rankings do not factor in the cost of a college degree when comparing colleges. Do you think they should? Why or why not?

5. Individually or as a class, compose a list of qualities or categories by which to evaluate a college. Assign points to each category and be prepared to justify your categories and the weight you have given them.

TEXT CREDITS

INDEX